D1713249

THE FACTS ON FILE
GUIDE TO PHILOSOPHY

Knowledge, Logic, and Science

THE FACTS ON FILE
GUIDE TO PHILOSOPHY

Knowledge, Logic, and Science

David Boersema
Kari Middleton

Facts On File
An Infobase Learning Company

The Facts On File Guide to Philosophy: Knowledge, Logic, and Science

Copyright © 2012 by David Boersema and Kari Middleton

Facts On File, Inc.
An imprint of Infobase Learning
132 West 31st Street
New York NY 10001

Library of Congress Cataloging-in-Publication Data
Boersema, David.
    The Facts on File guide to philosophy. Knowledge, logic, and science / David Boersema, Kari Middleton.
        p. cm.
    Includes bibliographical references and index.
    ISBN 978-0-8160-8482-1 (alk. paper)
    1. Knowledge, Theory of. 2. Logic. 3. Science—Philosophy. I. Middleton, Kari. II. Title. III. Title: Knowledge, logic, and science.
    BD161.B54 2012
    121—dc23   2011029492

Text design by Erik Lindstrom
Illustrations by Pat Meschino
Composition by Julie Adams
Cover printed by Yurchak Printing, Inc., Landisville, Pa.
Book printed and bound by Yurchak Printing, Inc., Landisville, Pa.
Date printed: March 2012
Printed in the United States of America

This book is printed on acid-free paper.

Table of Contents

Introduction

There is an old saying: Do not believe everything you think. We think a lot of things. But, as we know, some of the things we think really do not make a lot of sense or have a very solid basis. To actually believe something involves more than simply thinking it. Just as actions can speak louder than words, really believing something carries with it a readiness to act as well as to believe other things that are related to it. I might think that I could flap my arms and fly, but if I really believed I could do that, it is much more likely that I would try it out. All of us (often!) give such notions a second thought and change our minds.

Just as we should not believe everything we think, also we should not claim to know everything we believe. We all have false beliefs at times. We have all had that experience of really believing that answer A on a multiple-choice test was the right answer, only to find out that we were wrong. Or we might really have believed that our favorite team would win the championship, only to have had them upset by a lucky underdog rival. Beliefs, then, are not the same thing as knowledge. Knowing something is more than simply believing it, even believing it firmly and unwaveringly. For centuries, people believed that the Earth was fixed in space and at the center of the universe, and they had a lot of everyday, commonsense evidence to support that belief. But they were wrong. They thought they knew something, but they did not.

A fundamental philosophical question is, what is knowledge? More specifically, what does it mean to know something (as opposed to simply thinking it or believing it)? The area of philosophy that focuses on the study of knowledge is called epistemology. Typical epistemological questions include the following: What is knowledge? How do we know what we know? What kinds of things can we know? For example, is knowing that two plus two equals four the same as knowing that water is a liquid or knowing how to ride a bicycle? What makes knowledge (or even a belief) true or false? Philosophers have asked these questions for centuries and have offered many answers and insights into them.

In addition to broad epistemological questions about the nature of knowledge, philosophers have also asked questions about the process of knowledge and even standards and criteria for what could be knowledge. One important field is the study of logic. Logic is the study of arguments (not arguments in the sense of heated shouting matches, but in the sense of claims backed up by evidence). But it is also more than that. The discipline of logic investigates the formal structures of reasoning and implication. Like mathematics, the emphasis in logic is on forms or structures or patterns as much as on specific content. Logic analyzes the very criteria for what constitutes a good argument. As such, it speaks to the basis of what generates genuine knowledge. For instance, if we know that Natalie is the mother of Jack, then we know that Natalie is older than Jack, and if we know that all dogs are mammals, then we know that at least some mammals are dogs. This knowledge comes from logical relationships.

Another area of philosophy that deals with questions of knowledge is the philosophy of science. The very term *science* is actually quite recent in human history; it was not used until the 1800s. Prior to that, the study of nature and the world was called natural philosophy. What we can know about the world and how we can know it—those things we associate with science today—were, in fact, for centuries considered a basic part of philosophy. Philosophy of science looks at fundamental issues within science and about science. For example, a basic issue within science is the notion of explanation. We assume that the various sciences do not merely describe things and events in the world but explain them. What is explanation is a conceptual, philosophical issue. In other words, what does it mean to explain something? Other basic issues about science are the relation between science and technology and the appropriate roles of science in society. How is our scientific understanding of the world—indeed, our scientific understanding of knowledge itself—related to a philosophical understanding of the world and of knowledge?

This book, then, is about the philosophical study of knowledge (examining epistemology broadly), logic, and science. It is one volume in the Facts On File Guide to Philosophy set, which is designed to provide an accessible and engaging introduction to philosophy for students.

Note that because major ideas can be important in different contexts, and because certain thinkers made important contributions in more than one area, material within the set is occasionally repeated, with the intention of providing full context for each discussion.

David Boersema
Kari Middleton

PART I

Epistemology

Introductory Discussion Questions

1. Can you ever prove that you know anything? If so, what do you know that you can prove, and how do you prove that you know it? If not, why can you not prove that you know anything?
2. A straight stick appears bent in the water; white snow appears pink under red light. Do these optical illusions suggest that you can never trust what your senses tell you? Why or why not?
3. Consider the different kinds of things you seem to know and how you came to know them. For example, say you know that two plus two equals four, you know your friends, you know how to ride a bicycle, you know that torture is wrong, you know what you are thinking right now, and you know that frogs are amphibians. Did you come to know these things in different ways? Do you think all these examples of knowledge have something in common?
4. Suppose that every time you strike a dry match against a rough surface a fire ignites. Does this show that striking the match causes fire? Why or why not? Suppose every time you wait for a school bus the school bus arrives. Does this show that waiting for the bus causes the bus to arrive? Why or why not? In general, what does it mean to say that one event causes another?
5. Sometimes it is not clear whether a claim is true; there are reasons for thinking it is true, but there are equally good reasons

for thinking the claim is false. For example, there might be reasons for thinking that a certain college is the best college for you but equally good reasons for thinking that that college is *not* the best college for you. Suppose every time you encountered such a claim you decided neither to believe the claim nor disbelieve it but, instead, to have no opinion about it. Would this bring you peace of mind? Could you live a good life in this way?

6. Suppose that for 20 consecutive years you have been able to successfully predict the winner of the World Series, even though you believe you are just guessing when you make your predictions and know little about the competing teams. When you make your prediction this year, is your belief justified? Do you actually *know* which team will win the World Series? Why or why not?

Introduction to Epistemology

Typically, we consider ourselves as knowing a great many things—that we are human, that the ocean is salty, that we are so many years old—and as not knowing a lot of other things. Sometimes we have beliefs yet hesitate to identify them as examples of knowledge. For example, we believe we will get a particular job or live in the same place for the next few years. It seems that there is something that distinguishes beliefs usually considered to be knowledge from beliefs that usually are not so considered. A philosophical question is exactly what that difference is: What makes knowledge knowledge? The philosophical study of knowledge is epistemology.

Other disciplines also study knowledge, of course: Psychologists might study how we acquire knowledge, for example. What makes the philosophical approach to knowledge distinctive is that epistemology is concerned with conceptual questions, that is, questions about the very concept of knowledge. Suppose science can tell us how a person acquires the belief that, say, she is a human being related to other human beings. It is a further question whether that belief counts as knowledge. For a belief to count as knowledge, it seems the belief needs to have good grounds: It needs to be justified, and what counts as justification is a philosophical question. So, epistemology is typically taken to be concerned with normative issues related to knowledge, that is, issues about appropriate standards related to knowledge. For example, one possible standard for establishing a belief as knowledge is that it must be true. Taken by itself, however, this does not seem to be a particularly good standard, because sometimes there are true beliefs that are not examples of knowledge. Maybe, for instance, a child believes that her parents will give her a puppy for Christmas because she really wants one. Even if her belief turns out to be true, it does not seem as if the child knew her parents were giving her a puppy; she just got lucky (wishful thinking does not normally provide good grounds for a belief). So, a belief being true does not seem to be a good standard for determining whether a belief counts as knowledge.

It might turn out that when we look closely at the nature of knowledge we do not have any knowledge at all; whether knowledge is possible is the issue of skepticism. Some philosophers deny that any knowledge is possible, and some philosophers deny only that some knowledge is possible, for example knowledge based on what we learn through the five senses (perceptual knowledge). Other philosophers claim that we can and do have knowledge. If we do have knowledge, then a further question is what kinds of things we can know. For instance, maybe we can know about things like ocean tides and geometry, but can we know things such as the nature of God and what is the right thing to do when faced with a moral dilemma?

Philosophers also discuss the sources of knowledge. Our beliefs come from somewhere—from what we saw or heard, perhaps, from our memories, or maybe just from our own reasoning process. Are all of these genuine sources of knowledge? Empiricism is the view that experience plays a more central role in how we acquire knowledge than reason; rationalism is the view that reason plays a more central role in how we acquire knowledge than experience. The nature of knowledge, the sources of knowledge, and what we can know (if anything) are all among the basic questions of epistemology. Related questions concern topics such as reason and perception, for these seem instrumental in acquiring knowledge; to know something about knowledge, then, seems to require knowing something about reason and perception too.

Although philosophers disagree about the nature of knowledge, they commonly accept certain distinctions between different kinds of knowledge. First, there is knowledge by acquaintance. This is knowledge acquired by directly perceiving or experiencing something. For instance, someone might say, "After 10 years of friendship, I really know my best friend" or remark of an expert chess player, "She sure knows chess." Another kind of knowledge is knowledge of how to do something, such as send a text message or drive a car. Third, there is propositional knowledge, or knowledge of propositions, or facts. A way of thinking about this is that propositional knowledge is knowledge that—knowledge that something is the case. For example, knowledge that rain is condensed moisture in the atmosphere, that J. K. Rowling wrote the Harry Potter series, and that one's birthday falls on such and such a date. The relation between these kinds of knowledge is controversial. Some philosophers, for example, argue that knowledge of how to do something is really just a kind of propositional knowledge (for example, maybe knowing how to drive a car is really just knowledge that turning the key in the ignition starts the car, that the steering wheel directs the movement of the car, and so on). Another distinction is between a posteriori and a priori knowledge, roughly understood as knowledge acquired through experience (such as knowledge that volcanoes sometimes erupt) and knowledge acquired independently of experience (such as knowledge of mathematics). However, leaving these issues aside, philosophers commonly focus on propositional knowledge, and they generally discuss knowledge in general (whether a posteriori or a priori) in discussions on the nature, possibility, and sources of knowledge.

In a traditional account, knowledge is justified true belief. So, in order for a person to know something, the following conditions must be met: She must believe it, her belief must be true, and she must be justified in having that belief. If someone believes, for instance, that her parents are space aliens just because her brother told her so, she can probably not be said to *know* that her parents are space aliens, even in the unlikely event that her belief turns out to be true: Taking her brother's word for it just does not seem to be good grounds for the belief, so she is not justified in holding it. These conditions for knowledge were thought to give a complete analysis of knowledge in the sense of giving conditions that were both necessary for knowledge (unless these conditions were met, a person could not be said to have knowledge) and sufficient for knowledge (no other conditions were required). So, according to this conception of knowledge, if you listed all the instances of true beliefs that were justified and all the instances of knowledge, you would end up with identical items on each list.

Not all philosophers accept this account of knowledge, however, and yet a further philosophical question is the nature of justification itself. So, even if knowledge is justified true belief, something needs to be said about what counts as justification. Contemporary accounts of justification are usually divided into internalist accounts and externalist accounts. According to internalism, what matters for justification are factors internal to the person who knows, such as what a person believes and has reason to consider true. According to externalism, justification is not just a matter of internal factors; factors external to a person (such as an external cause of a person's belief) are relevant to justification.

Foundationalist and coherentist views of justification are usually internalist. Each of these views notes that beliefs are usually justified by other beliefs. For example, one might believe it rained during the night because one believes that the streets are wet. However, according to foundationalism, there are some beliefs that do not depend for their justification on other beliefs. Metaphorically, according to the foundationalists, one's beliefs are like a building, or a pyramid. At the base are certain beliefs that are self-justifying. These beliefs provide the justification for all other beliefs, which rest on the foundational beliefs like bricks rest on a foundation for a building. Advocates of a coherentist view of justification deny that some beliefs are any more basic or foundational than other beliefs. For the coherentist, beliefs are not like a building but rather like a web, interconnected in various ways. Justification is a matter of how one's web of beliefs fits together or coheres: A person's belief is justified if it coheres with the other beliefs a person has. What it means to cohere varies according to different versions of coherentism. At least, however, beliefs must be generally consistent with each other. For example, suppose Sam believes that it will rain tomorrow and that the parade will be canceled; if Sam also believes that he will lead his marching band in the parade tomorrow, this belief is not justified because it is inconsistent with his other beliefs. This is a very simple example, of course, but the point applies to the set of all a person's beliefs in general.

In 1963, the traditional account of knowledge as justified true belief was challenged by the American philosopher Edmund Gettier (1927–   ), who argued that there could be cases in which a person had a belief that was both true and justified, yet fail to have knowledge. The idea behind the cases Gettier imagined is that sometimes it could be a matter of luck that a person's belief turned out to be true. Put another way, a person might have good grounds for a belief (and therefore be justified in that belief), yet the belief might turn out to be true for entirely different reasons. In response to Gettier, some philosophers have argued that there must be a fourth condition for knowledge: In order to know something, someone must have a belief, the belief must be true, the person must be justified in having the belief, and some fourth condition must be met. Figuring out what that condition is has proven difficult, however, and no proposal regarding exactly what it should be has been universally accepted. Other philosophers argue that Gettier's cases show that we must understand justification in one way rather than another.

Another approach to knowledge is contextualist. This approach does not try to establish necessary and sufficient conditions for knowledge. Roughly, according to contextualism, whether a person can be said to have knowledge (with respect to a given belief) depends on context. Different versions of contextualism give varying, detailed accounts of this basic idea. In one version, sometimes our standards for what counts as knowledge are stricter than in other cases. For instance, standards for whether a person knows that cigarettes cause cancer are stricter at a medical conference than in ordinary conversation. So, a nonmedical professional in the context of ordinary conversation might be said to know that cigarettes cause cancer but in the context of a medical conference might be said *not* to know, for the reason that a higher degree of expertise is expected at a medical conference.

In feminist epistemology, philosophers incorporate female experiences, values, and perspectives in epistemology and identify what they regard as male biases in epistemology and the practice of acquiring knowledge (or constructing knowledge). Feminist epistemologists tend to regard knowledge as social in nature, rather than simply the product of isolated, knowing individuals, and philosophers working in feminist epistemology often believe that gender makes a difference when it comes to what a person knows or how knowledge is constructed.

An additional school of thought in epistemology is naturalized epistemology. The idea of naturalized epistemology is to study knowledge and the acquisition of knowledge in the way scientists study phenomena in the natural world—that is, by using the methods of natural sciences. So, epistemology is said to be naturalized in the sense that it is studied as though knowledge is a natural phenomenon. ("Natural" here just means part of the empirical world.) Naturalized epistemology is sometimes thought to be a kind of psychology, for the reason that it conducts empirical investigations into how people think, learn, and know.

Plato and Aristotle
on Epistemology

Plato

The ancient Greek philosopher Plato (ca. 428–348 B.C.E.) believed that the good life comes from knowledge. That is, in order to live a good life, one must have knowledge, and in order to truly be a good person, one must have knowledge. So Plato's view of ethics (what is right) is closely connected to his view of the nature of knowledge. Plato's view of the nature of knowledge (his epistemology), in turn, is closely related to what he regarded as the nature of reality (his metaphysics). To understand his epistemology, then, it is worth saying something about how Plato viewed reality.

Plato thought that true knowledge, episteme, regards only what is permanent and unchanging—what he believed was most real. To see why one might think this, consider something you think you know, say, about the characteristics of an oak tree in your neighborhood. It might seem as if you know something about it—that its bark is rough and knobby to the touch, say, and that its leaves are green in the spring. But, of course, the tree is constantly changing: Some leaves die and fall, especially during the autumn; it grows a little bit each year; it might get attacked by bugs or struck by lightning; and windstorms might tear off small branches. The object of your supposed knowledge seems anything but permanent; it seems you cannot even be said to know, simply, that the tree has green leaves, because a lot of the time it does not. Given that the tree is constantly changing, could one be said to have genuine knowledge of the tree? Plato thought not. Knowledge applies to what is permanent and unchanging, to what (so far as Plato is concerned) is most real. And what was most real, for Plato, were not the ordinary objects of the physical world, such as oak trees and tea bags. Instead, what is most real—and the objects of true knowledge—are not physical objects at all. Rather, they are Ideas (also called Forms).

As this suggests, Plato believed that there are different levels of reality. To begin with a simple example, shadows are real, but they are not as real as the objects they are shadows of. For instance, a shadow of a dog is real (there really is a shadow of a dog, say, on a sunny day). However, if a cloud comes by and blocks the sun, causing the shadow to go away, the dog does not disappear! The dog's shadow is real, but the actual, physical dog is even more real; it exists even when the shadow does not. For Plato, however, while actual, physical, individual dogs are real, they are not as real as the concept of Dog, or the Idea of Dog. For example, if we had a concept of Dog, that concept could exist even if all the actual, physical dogs died off. (We have the concept of Dinosaur even though there are no actual dinosaurs.) Just as an actual, physical dog is more real than a shadow of a dog, so the concept, or Idea, of Dog is more real than actual, physical dogs. For Plato, what is most real are not the everyday objects of common experience. Ideas are the most real things.

Plato further claimed that Ideas are ideal, perfect objects, and actual, physical individuals are like imperfect copies of these ideal Ideas. For instance, we normally think of and experience many different breeds of dogs as well as individual dogs. All of these dogs have lots of features that are particular to them. That is, one dog might be black, while another is brown; one dog is large, while another is small. For them all to be dogs, there must be something they have in common (or some set of things they have in common). There must be some set of features, or conditions, that things have in order for them to be dogs rather than cats or trees. Those features are the essence of Dog and constitute the Idea of Dog.

With respect to knowledge, Plato argued that our senses give us knowledge only of those less real things such as shadows or physical individual objects. What is most real—Ideas—is not known by the senses but by reason. Whereas the senses give us information about the physical world and are connected to the body (bodily senses), reason gives us information about Ideas and is connected with the soul. For

Plato, the bodily senses could only know physical facts, not facts about Ideas. For example, we naturally come to know physical things and relationships between them (such as knowing different individual dogs and the fact that one is larger or darker than another). But there are also abstract objects, such as numbers and mathematical relationships. Our knowledge of these does not come from our senses; we never see or smell or taste numbers, much less objects like square roots. Of course, we can see two dogs and two other dogs and then claim that we know that we see four dogs. But the dogs are just instances; they are not the numbers themselves. (We could come to know that two plus two equals four even if we did not see those four dogs.) Knowledge of mathematics, for Plato, is not the result of bodily senses but the result of reason, and it is the soul, not the body, that reasons. So, as a means for acquiring knowledge, reason is superior to experience.

Corresponding to different levels of reality are different levels of knowledge, as Plato illustrated with his metaphor of the divided line. Plato imagined a line divided in half. One-half represents the sensible world, the world of things perceived via the senses; the other half represents the world of Ideas (or Forms). Each of these halves is itself subdivided. The sensible world is divided between physical objects and images and reflections of those objects. On one side of the subdivision are things like the shadow of a dog and a painting of a dog, and on the other side of the subdivision are dogs, trees, tea bags, and other sensible objects. The intelligible world (knowable through reason) is divided into lower Ideas and higher Ideas, such as the Idea of the Good. Knowledge of images, reflections, and shadows is the lowest form of knowledge of all; indeed, as far as Plato is concerned, it is not even properly called knowledge. Nor does knowledge of actual dogs, trees, tea bags, and so on count as true knowledge; knowledge of such actual objects is higher than knowledge of images and reflections, but such apparent knowledge is really just a matter of opinions and beliefs. In the intelligible world—the world of Ideas—however, it is another story. Knowledge of lower Ideas, such as Ideas concerning mathematics (e.g., the Idea of Circle) is knowledge, though incomplete. And knowledge of higher Ideas—in particular, the Idea of the Good—is true, complete knowledge: episteme. Opposite is a sketch of Plato's famous divided line.

As the divided line suggests, Plato thought there is more to knowledge than mere belief. And this seems right: Believing something, no matter

Higher Ideas (e.g., Idea of the Good)

Intelligible World (World of Ideas)—the object of knowledge

Lower Ideas

Actual sensible objects

Sensible World—the object of opinions and beliefs

Images, reflections, shadows—lowest form of knowledge

how firmly or confidently one believes it, is not the same thing as knowing it (we can have false beliefs). No matter how strongly someone believes that the Sun is only 50 miles in diameter, that person does not know that it is. So, for Plato, knowledge is not mere belief. In addition, it is not the same thing as true belief, because we might have a true belief but have it simply from a lucky guess. For example, on a multiple-choice question on an exam, someone might believe that the correct answer to the question is option B but not really know that is the correct answer. If it turns out that it is correct, then that person had a true belief, but not knowledge (just a good guess or a good hunch). For Plato, then, knowledge is true belief that has justification for it. This conception of knowledge as justified true belief shaped the study of epistemology for centuries.

Knowledge of the Ideas, Plato believed, requires the careful and rigorous use of reason and, in particular, the study of philosophy. It takes time and thought to acquire such knowledge. Moreover, it is difficult and even painful. Plato illustrated these ideas with his famous allegory of the cave, which appeared in Book 7 of his most famous work, *The Republic*. An allegory is like a moral fable or parable; it is a fictional story meant to express and illustrate some basic human experience and lesson. Plato's allegory captures in just a few pages the main themes of his philosophical views and is among the most renowned and cited statements in all of Western philosophy.

Plato has the reader imagine a cave in which people live their entire lives. Indeed, generations of people live there. They cannot see the entrance to the outside world and believe that the cave is all there is to the world. They are chained in such a way that they always face toward a wall in the back of the cave. (How they could live—move around, eat, have children, etc.—is not important; it is the moral message that matters in the allegory.) Behind the people, where they cannot see it, is a fire that illuminates the cave. Between the fire and the people is a sort of roadway where other people move along. As they do, the fire behind them casts shadows on the back wall of the cave. The people who are chained and looking at the wall see the shadows that are cast on the wall but do not know about the roadway or people moving along it. All of their experiences are always and only of the shadows that appear on the wall in front of them.

Imagine, Plato said, that one day one of these chained people manages to get free and gets up and starts to move around. When he looks behind him, he sees the roadway and the fire. He realizes that all of his experiences prior to that moment were only of shadows on the wall, not of real things. He then proceeds to see the things that cause the shadows (that is, the things moving along the roadway) and understands that the shadows are like those things, but only shadows of them. As he proceeds even farther up the cave, he finally starts to see the diffused light from the entrance of the cave, light that is caused by the sunlight outside. Eventually, he comes to the actual entrance of the cave and looks outside. He sees real things, like trees and natural sunlight. At first, the direct sunlight is too bright for him and it even hurts his eyes. Slowly, however, he gets used to the sunlight and sees the outside world.

Imagine further, Plato said, that having made this discovery, the man is excited and wants to go back to tell all the other people who are still chained inside the cave. Because his eyes have now become accustomed to natural sunlight, he has trouble seeing in the darkness when he goes back into the cave, trouble he never had before. Eventually, with some difficulty, he goes back to where the others are and tells them what he discovered—that what they think is real and have experienced all their lives as real is just shadows, at best mere imitations of real things. Their response is to think that he is crazy.

This allegory, said Plato, illustrates the experience of the philosopher. Having encountered and understood things that are often quite unfamiliar and even contrary to everyday experience, the philosopher seems to other people to be crazy or strange or, at the very best, impractical, perhaps even dangerous. But in fact, the philosopher is able to acquire true knowledge of what is most real, the Ideas, knowledge that ideally culminates in knowledge of the Idea of the Good (represented in the allegory by the Sun). Philosophical education is life's slow but steady emergence out of the cave of ignorance into the light of knowledge.

Aristotle

The Greek philosopher Aristotle (384–322 B.C.E.) was Plato's most famous student and equal in influence. Aristotle diverged from Plato in both how he regarded reality and in how he viewed knowledge. Whereas Plato regarded what is most real as Ideas, Aristotle regarded individual, concrete things as real—actual dogs, tea bags, and trees, etc., not the Ideas of those things. Aristotle denied that there is some entity, the Idea of Dog, that exists over and above individual dogs and that is more real than individual dogs. He agreed that there is something that dogs, for example, have in common, and that there is an essence of dogs (it is in this sense that Aristotle agreed that there are Ideas). Aristotle even agreed that one could have knowledge of such essences—and, as with Plato, Aristotle took this to be the object of true knowledge. However, unlike Plato, Aristotle believed sense perception played a crucial role in acquiring such knowledge. It is through sense perception of individual things that we can come to learn about essences. So, knowledge does require reason, but it also requires experience.

Plato thought there must be something all particular instances of knowledge have in common, some shared essence. He famously asked what is knowledge and answered this question by saying that there is a single kind of thing that knowledge is: It is justified true belief. In contrast, Aristotle, did not assume or look for some core essence to all cases of knowledge. Rather, Aristotle thought that what counts as knowledge depends in part on the goal of the inquiry. In other words, what we count as a case of knowledge depends in part, at least, on what we want to know and why we want to know it. Illustrating this view is Aristotle's distinction between three fundamental kinds of knowledge: *theoria,* praxis, and *techné. Theoria* is theoretical knowledge, with the goal of theoretical understanding. For Aristotle, this type of knowledge included mathematics and physics, but also theology (the study of God). Praxis is practical knowledge, with the goal of practical action and conduct. For Aristotle, this type of knowledge included ethics, economics, even social and political philosophy. *Techné* is technical knowledge, with the goal of making or producing something. For Aristotle, this type of knowledge included art and rhetoric. While we might think this focused on the sorts of things that today we would consider technology, it had to do even more with the notion of technique (in various fields, not just technology). Sometimes we want a basic theoretical understanding of how and why things are the way they are (such as a scientific theory); this is *theoria.* Other times we want more of a practical application of information in order to solve some problem or give us a way to get along in the world (such as building a bridge); this is praxis. Yet other times we want some technique for accomplishing some goal or creating something, but it is not necessarily a practical application of information (such as crafting a moving speech or song); this is *techné.* These different kinds of knowledge are similar to, though not exactly the same as, today's notions of knowledge that something is the case (like knowing that cats are mammals) and knowledge how to do something (like knowing how to ride a bike).

In addition, Aristotle thought that knowledge was acquired through syllogisms, a particular kind of argument in logic. Syllogisms are based on a subject/predicate view of language. This view holds that sentences contain a subject and something that is said about that subject (that is, a predicate). For instance, in the sentence "Whales are mammals," the word *whales* is the subject, and the phrase *are mammals* is the predicate. Some sentences do not have a subject/predicate form and therefore are not treated within the study of syllogisms. For instance, the command "Shut the door!" does not have a predicate that says something about a subject. Although there might be an implied subject in this case (namely, whoever is being commanded), there is still nothing being said about that subject.

Foundationalism and Skepticism

Foundationalism

Foundationalism is a view about the nature of justification of beliefs. Foundationalism takes its inspiration from the idea that our beliefs are justified by other beliefs. Suppose, for example, you believe your neighbors have a dog because you believe you heard a dog barking in their yard. This second belief is what justifies the first: It is the basis for and provides a good reason for the belief that your neighbors have a dog. According to foundationalism, what ultimately justifies one's beliefs are foundational beliefs, which are self-justifying. That is, unlike other beliefs, they are not justified by other beliefs; they are justified just because of the kind of beliefs they are. A main alternative to foundationalism is coherentism, according to which no belief or set of beliefs is foundational to any other. Rather, in this view, justification has to do with how beliefs fit together as a group (how they cohere).

To see why one might think there are foundational beliefs that justify all others, consider again the belief that your neighbors have a dog, based on the belief that you heard a dog barking in their yard. Now what justifies your belief that you heard a dog and not, say, a child pretending to be a dog? Well, perhaps you believe dogs sound one way rather than another and that what you heard sounded like a real dog barking. But what justifies your belief that genuine dog barks sound one way, rather than another? Well, perhaps you have heard other dogs bark, and you know what those dogs sound like. But what justifies your belief that the dog barks you heard are representative of most dog barks or are similar to the bark you think you just heard? To some foundationalists, it seems clear that this line of questioning cannot go on forever. Eventually, justification has to stop somewhere: Ultimately there must be a belief that is not justified by another belief but that is somehow justified. In general, for *all* one's beliefs, there must be such self-justifying beliefs that ultimately justify all other beliefs. Metaphorically, it is as if one's beliefs formed a pyramid, and at the base of this pyramid are certain beliefs at the foundation. Without these foundational beliefs, all beliefs resting upon them would have no justification (roughly, there would be no good reasons for holding them). This reasoning is called the regress argument, and it has been highly influential, although its conclusion has not been universally accepted.

There are at least three basic issues related to foundationalist views of justification. The first is whether, in addition to being self-justifying, foundational beliefs have certain features that all or most non-foundational beliefs do not. For example, foundational beliefs have sometimes been thought to be indubitable, meaning that it is impossible to doubt them. They have also been said to be infallible, meaning that it is impossible for them to be false. But even among foundationalists, this is controversial. A second issue is exactly what foundational beliefs are about. The French philosopher René Descartes (1596–1650) defended a version of foundationalism in which the belief that he existed was a foundation for all other beliefs. In other versions of foundationalism, foundational beliefs are beliefs about the external world, that is, the world outside of ourselves (the ordinary world of physical objects). In part because such beliefs are not infallible, however (they can be mistaken, as when a person mistakes a cardboard cutout of a horse for a real horse), some philosophers think that foundational beliefs are beliefs about the contents of sensory experiences. That is, foundational beliefs are beliefs about our experiences based on our five senses—what it *seems* to us we see, hear taste, touch, and smell. For example, perhaps a foundational belief is a belief that one sees an object that looks like a horse. (Perhaps one can be mistaken that one sees a real horse grazing in a field, for example, but it seems much less likely that one could be mistaken that one sees something that looks to oneself like a horse.)

A third basic issue regarding foundationalism is the relation between foundational beliefs and the rest of one's beliefs. It is thought that foundational beliefs are meant to justify other beliefs, but the question is *how* they do this. There are two possibilities: The first is that foundational beliefs provide deductive justification, and the second is that they provide inductive justification. In deductive justification, foundational beliefs logically entail non-foundational beliefs. As an example, consider the belief that all horses are mammals and the belief that Cleo is a horse. The contents of these beliefs logically entail the contents of a third belief, namely that Cleo is a mammal. Induction, however, does not similarly guarantee truth. For example, consider the belief that many horses are trained to be ridden. It does not logically follow that Cleo in particular must be trained to be ridden, for even if it is true that many horses are trained to be ridden, Cleo might be an exception to the general rule. To return to foundationalism, it seems unlikely that foundational beliefs provide justification for all true beliefs in a deductive way. For example, it seems unlikely that the contents of foundational beliefs logically *entail* that the Earth orbits the Sun. Rather, the belief that the Earth orbits the Sun seems to be justified, if at all, by beliefs about empirical observations that do not logically guarantee the truth of the belief that the Earth orbits the Sun. (Put another way, it would be logically possible for beliefs about what we have observed to be true, yet for it to be false that the Earth orbits the Sun.) So, if justification is a matter of deductive justification, it seems that our belief that the Earth orbits the Sun is not justified. This, however, seems unlikely. Many foundationalists now believe that foundational beliefs provide inductive justification rather than deductive justification. It is also controversial, however, whether inductive justification can truly provide adequate justification for non-foundational beliefs.

Ancient Skepticism

Against foundationalism (and other accounts of knowledge), skepticism casts broad doubts on claims to knowledge. In a broad sense, skepticism is the attitude of critical inquiry: It is a willingness to question beliefs and claims, even when they seem obvious and fundamental, and to examine them closely on their merits rather than simply accepting them at face value. In this sense, skepticism is at the heart of philosophy, perhaps best captured by the famous remark by the Greek philosopher Socrates (469–399 B.C.E.) that the unexamined life is not worth living.

Head of Socrates from the National Museum of Rome

To examine one's life requires examining what one does, which in turn requires the examination of one's beliefs, for how we act often depends on what we believe; and to examine one's beliefs is to subject them to critical inquiry. A skeptic in this spirit is an investigator, continually investigating the meaning and basis of claims to knowledge and truth, examining whether we know what we claim to know or whether we have adequate grounds for what we claim to know.

This kind of skepticism is closely associated with the skepticism of ancient Greece, and indeed the word *skeptic* derives from the Greek word *sképtesthai*, meaning "to investigate." Traditionally, ancient skepticism is divided between two schools of thought: Pyrrhonian skepticism and Academic skepticism. Pyrrhonian skepticism acknowledges Pyrrho of Elis (ca. 365–270 B.C.E.) as its founder. Pyrrho himself wrote nothing, and what we know of him and his views today comes mainly from the writings of Sextus Empiricus (ca. second century), who wrote several hundred years after Pyrrho's death. Academic skepticism is associated with the Academy, the school founded by Plato, when the Academy came to be led by skeptic philosophers such as Arcesilaus (ca. 315–240 B.C.E.) and Carneades (214–129 B.C.E.). It is often thought that Academic skeptics denied that knowledge was possible, whereas Pyrrhonian skeptics claimed neither that knowledge was possible nor that knowledge was not possible; they simply withheld judgment about the matter. However, the differences between Pyrrhonian skeptics and Academic skeptics are controversial.

Pyrrhonian skeptics clearly emphasized the suspension of judgment. To suspend judgment is neither to accept a claim nor to reject it; it is to refrain from making a judgment about the truth or falsity of the claim at all. To illustrate, consider a judgment in a criminal case. Suppose that someone, accused of stealing from her employer, says she had no motive to do so and that she and her employer were on good terms; suppose, further, that both claims seem plausible. But now suppose that property belonging to the employer was found in the employee's home. Pressed for an explanation, the defendant claims someone is trying to frame her. There is no clear evidence of framing, although at least one person had the means to do so and was on bad terms with the defendant. Faced with all these facts, a jury might choose to acquit the defendant. Jury members might regard the evidence as insufficient to show either that she is innocent or that she is guilty. In short, the jury might well suspend judgment on the question of whether the accused actually stole the property, believing neither that she did nor that she did not. The skeptics take this attitude of suspension of judgment beyond a few individual cases; for them, it is very often, perhaps always, reasonable to suspend judgment. Skeptics thought that one ought to suspend judgment about all manner of claims—about what is the right thing to do, for example, and claims about the nature of reality. They directed their skeptical attacks against the claims of Epicureanism and Stoicism, in particular, popular schools of thought during their time. For the skeptics, there was no reason for preferring an Epicurean or Stoic claim over an opposite claim; so one ought neither to believe nor disbelieve the claims in question.

In a somewhat similar way, Academic skeptics liked to argue for one claim and then for its opposite. Famously, Carneades is said to have argued in favor of justice one day and then argued against justice the very next day. The goal was to show that there were insufficient grounds for supposing that either claim was true or that one could be said to know that either was the case. Because Socrates himself carefully scrutinized claims to knowledge (sometimes claims that amounted to the received wisdom about a given topic) and said that the only thing he knew was that he knew nothing, the Academic skeptics regarded themselves as following in the tradition of Socrates.

The goal of Pyrrhonian skepticism was to attain peace of mind by suspending judgment. To see why suspending judgment might lead to inner tranquility, consider what might happen when someone does not suspend judgment. Suppose, for instance, someone believes that reconciliation with an estranged friend is necessary for a good life. If she fails to reconcile, she will feel distress and worry. If, however, she neither believes that reconciliation is necessary for a good life nor that it is not, these worries will not plague her. Similarly, if she has no beliefs about what future events would be good or bad, she will not fret about the future, fearful of some outcomes and desirous of others. Having made no judgment about what would be a good or bad outcome, she will be able to accept whatever happens with equanimity. As the Pyrrhonian skeptics saw it, then, the suspension of judgment is a way of achieving inner tranquility.

Apart from this goal, the skeptics offered specific reasons for the suspension of judgment. Some of these were specific to a claim at hand; for instance, if someone asserted that a tower looked round in the distance, a skeptic might point out that the tower appeared square when seen close up. (Thus, there is no more reason for thinking that the tower is actually round than for thinking that it is not actually round but square instead.)

Sextus Empiricus cited 10 reasons for skepticism. Called the Ten Modes, these are due to Aenesidemus (ca. first century). One of these modes is simply that different animals have different sensory organs than humans, so animals and humans perceive the world differently. For example, cats do not see the full spectrum of colors that humans do, and humans cannot see infrared light, though some insects can. This suggests that there is no more reason for thinking that the world itself really is one way rather than another (that, say, grass really is a rich green color rather than a gray color). Put another way, there is no reason for thinking that one kind of animal's perception is accurate in a way that the perception of others is not. How individual people perceive the world also depends on their individual circumstances, such as health and where a person is positioned when she perceives a given object.

An additional argument for the suspension of judgment regards what is called "the criterion of truth." The idea behind the argument is that, if a claim is true, there must be some way to evaluate that claim. That is, there must be some criterion for judging whether a claim is true or not. (If there is not, how could one ever tell that any given claim is true.) Yet there must also be some way of testing that criterion—otherwise, how could one know that the criterion is a good one? Suppose, for instance, the criterion of the truth for a claim is that the claim corresponds with reality. Now we want to know whether correspondence is a good criterion of truth. How can we judge whether it is? One way of doing this is to see if the correspondence criterion itself somehow corresponds with reality—say, by discerning whether the claim, "A claim is true if it corresponds with reality," corresponds with reality. The problem with this is that it is circular: If we want to know whether correspondence is a good criterion, it does little good to test it by seeing if correspondence itself somehow corresponds with reality, because that assumes the very thing we want to know (that the correspondence criterion is a good one). Now, if we cannot test the correspondence criterion by using correspondence, it seems that some other criterion for testing is needed. Suppose we had such a criterion. To know whether *that* criterion is a good one, there must be some way of testing it as well. But to know whether this third criterion is a good one, there must be some way of testing it too. Now the problem is evident: It looks as if there must be an infinite series of criteria, one criterion to test the first criterion, another to test the second criterion, another to test the criterion used for testing the second criterion, etc. The skeptics thought it was unlikely that there could be such an infinite regress. Since circular reasoning cannot demonstrate the soundness of a criterion of truth either, skeptics concluded that there was no way of establishing that a criterion of truth was definitely a good one. And if we lack a criterion of truth, then it seems we cannot judge the truth of claims—and, therefore, we must suspend judgment.

Critics resisted this skeptical conclusion. One common objection to the skeptical attitude of suspension of judgment was that it was impossible both to suspend judgment continually and live a normal life. There are stories told of Pyrrho's friends having to pull him out of the way of an oncoming wagon to prevent him from being injured or killed, because Pyrrho himself suspended judgment regarding whether the carriage really was approaching or endangering him. It is doubtful that this story, or others like it, are true, but they do suggest the problem posed by critics: If you continually suspend judgment, how is it possible to act? Living requires action, and action requires making decisions, and making decisions requires accepting some beliefs and not others— from daily matters such as the decision that a wagon's rapid approach is dangerous or that some foods and not others are safe to eat to life decisions such as the decision to pursue one career rather than another on the basis of the belief that doing so is a good thing. A skeptic's reply to this concern is that it is possible to act despite the suspension of judgment, by acting according to appearances. That is, if something appears a given way, then the skeptic acts as if that appearance reflects reality, even if the skeptic is not actually convinced that it does. For instance, upon seeing an approaching wagon, a skeptic might step out of the way, because the wagon appears to be headed in one's own direction; arguably, however, the skeptic does so without necessarily believing that there is a wagon or that it is actually doing so.

Cartesian Skepticism

Skepticism today tends to focus less on belief and the suspension of belief than on whether we have or could have knowledge. A strong version of skepticism denies that we have any knowledge; a stronger version claims not only that we have no knowledge but that we could not ever acquire knowledge. Some versions of skepticism focus on particular kinds of knowledge. Local skepticism is skepticism about one or more kinds of knowledge, but not all knowledge. For example, one form of local skepticism is skepticism about perceptual knowledge, knowledge based on perception (what we see, hear, taste, feel, or hear). Someone who denies that there is perceptual knowledge denies that we know anything that is based on perceptions. For instance, it might seem as if at night we see the Moon rise and set (and perhaps the Moon really does do those things). But, the skeptic about perceptual knowledge might say we do not really *know* that there really is a Moon in the sky and that it either rises or sets (perhaps it is an optical illusion that it does). Another kind of local skepticism is skepticism about a priori knowledge, knowledge that can be acquired independently of experience. Yet another kind is skepticism about knowledge about morality. Global skepticism is skepticism about all kinds of knowledge—perceptual, a priori, moral, and any other kind.

Arguments in favor of skepticism often proceed by pointing out some reason for doubting what is ordinarily considered to be knowledge. For example, Descartes, a modern philosopher associated with skepticism (although he was not a skeptic himself), argued that it was possible that a very powerful, evil demon deceived him about what he experienced and even his own reasoning process—for instance, perhaps whenever Descartes tried to perform simple arithmetic, the evil demon made it seem to Descartes that he was reasoning accurately even when he was not. Since this was possible, it appeared that Descartes could not know with certainty that any of his beliefs were true; it appeared, in short, that he had little, if any, knowledge. A modern version of this argument is the idea that one is just a brain in a vat, stimulated electronically into believing it has a body and is living a normal life, going places, meeting people, and interacting with the physical objects in a world outside one's own mind. (The movie *The Matrix* presents a similar idea.)

In general, with respect to perceptual knowledge, it is often pointed out that the senses are sometimes misleading. When an oar is immersed in water, for instance, it looks bent, even though it is not; when the Moon is on the horizon, it looks bigger than it does when it is higher in the sky, even though its size has not changed. Given that our senses can deceive us, a skeptical question is whether, or to what extent, they can be trusted at all. In Descartes's First Meditation in his book *Meditations on First Philosophy*, he gave what has become known as the dream argument. The argument is intended to show that we do not really *know* anything we believe on the basis of what we have experienced through the five senses (sight, hearing, taste, smell, and touch). Typically, we have all kinds of such beliefs, ranging from very particular beliefs (for example, that right now you are seeing real words on this page) to very general beliefs (such as that we live on the physical planet Earth). Typically, we also take such beliefs to be instances of knowledge; after all, who could doubt, say, that we meet real people and that these people exist outside our own minds? With the dream argument, Descartes tried to show that such beliefs *could* be doubted and therefore do not count as knowledge. Descartes's point was not that such beliefs are *false*; in fact, his overriding project in the *Meditations* is to establish a certain foundation for knowledge, and by the book's end he believed he had established that he knew all kinds of things, including things about what he experienced through his senses. However, Descartes began his project by examining what it was possible to doubt, including what we seem to know on the basis of sensory experience.

According to the dream argument, there is no way for a person to be able to tell with certainty when she is dreaming and when she is not. As evidence, Descartes noted that sometimes, when he was dreaming, he mistook his dreams for reality. While dreaming that he was seated near a fire in his study, for example, he believed he actually was seated near the fire, only to wake and find that he was lying in bed. Of course, sometimes dreams are scattered and incoherent, and perhaps it is possible to tell in *these* cases when one is dreaming. But it seems equally true that sometimes dreams are vivid and seem quite real, and according to Descartes in principle there is no sure way to distinguish these from the experiences a person has while awake. If there is no way for someone to distinguish with certainty when she is awake and when she is dreaming, then it is possible that she could be dreaming *all* of her sensory experiences—everything she sees, hears, touches, smells, and tastes. If it is possible that she could be dreaming all of her sensory experiences, then it is possible to doubt the reality of those experiences.

In other words, there is no certainty that anything she experiences with her five senses really exists outside her own mind. So, according to the argument, we do not *know* anything on the basis of our sensory experience. The dream argument thus establishes a local skepticism, specifically skepticism about perceptual knowledge.

Of course, most philosophers, even skeptical ones, do not really suspect an evil demon is deceiving them, believe they spend all their lives dreaming, or fear that they are no more than brains in vats. The point of these skeptical arguments is not necessarily that one should change how one lives one's life (though one might) or even that one should never believe anything. Rather, the point is to raise the philosophical question of under what circumstances we do or could have knowledge, such as knowledge of an external world (a world that exists outside our own minds) or knowledge of mathematical truths.

We seem to have such knowledge, but what skeptical arguments ask is how do I *know* I am not just a brain in the vat? How do I know I am not dreaming, and that what I experience is real? or on what basis do we know that there is a world outside ourselves? The issue here is not whether a world outside of ourselves really exists; almost everyone agrees that it does. Instead, the issue is what *justifies* that belief. It seems that what justifies the belief is not simply that we seem to experience a world external to us. After all, a brain in a vat would seem to experience a world external to it, and these experiences are vivid, detailed, and utterly convincing. A skeptical claim is simply that we *do not* have a justification for our belief in an external world: For all we know, we are brains in vats. What this in turn implies is that all of our beliefs that depend on a belief in an external world are not justified either. For example, if there is no justification for the belief in an external world, there is no justification for believing anything about the people we meet in that world—because, for all we know, there are no such people. They might exist only in our minds, the result of electricity stimulating our brains in exactly the right way. This reasoning leads to skepticism about many (perhaps all) of our claims to knowledge. That is, typically we believe we know a great many things about a world external to us, but arguments such as the brain in the vat thought experiment suggest we really do not know anything about an external world after all.

John Dewey at the University of Chicago in 1902 *(Photograph by Eva Watson-Scütze)*

There have been as many responses to skeptical arguments as there have been skeptical arguments. A key issue related to skepticism is the nature of justification. This is because, to count as knowledge, a belief requires justification. So, whether we have knowledge or not seems to depend on what is meant by justification: If justification is understood in one way rather than another, then perhaps we have knowledge after all (or, perhaps we do not). Related to justification is the issue of whether knowledge requires certainty. Critics argue that some skeptical arguments mistakenly rely on the idea that it does, that if, for instance, one cannot be absolutely certain that one is not dreaming, then one does not *know* that one is not dreaming. However, according to some philosophers, it is possible to know something even if one cannot be absolutely certain of it. Among the philosophers who deny that knowledge requires certainty are philosophers in the tradition of American pragmatism and some who are fallibilists, or both. The American philosopher John Dewey (1859–1952) in particular was explicitly critical of what he called the quest for certainty. Underlying this quest, Dewey claimed, was a desire for knowledge of a permanent, unchanging world that is independent of human practices, independent of what we actually do in the world. However, according to Dewey, the world is not like that, and inquiry—roughly, the search for answers to our questions—is closely related to our practices and goals.

Rationalism

Introduction to Rationalism

In philosophy, rationalism is the view that reason is more important in acquiring knowledge than experience. So rationalism is opposed to empiricism, according to which experience is more important in acquiring knowledge than reason. Experience is often understood as sensory experience in particular, that is, what one experiences through the five senses. Reason is often understood as including intuition, a kind of direct awareness of a truth, an awareness through the mind in particular rather than through sense experience.

There are varieties of rationalism. Rationalists differ, for example, in their metaphysics (their views about the nature of reality) and in their precise claims about what role reason plays (and does not play) in our acquisition of knowledge. Common to rationalist views is the idea that there is some significant knowledge that we can acquire more through reason than experience. One sort of knowledge that could be said to be acquired more through reason than experience is knowledge of analytic truths, sentences that are true either by definition or form. For instance, the sentence "Circles are round" is true by definition and seems to be knowable just by using one's reason. However, this is not very informative; rationalists believe that reason can deliver more significant knowledge than this, such as knowledge of the nature of reality. It has also often been thought that mathematical and logical knowledge are acquired through reason alone. (It has been controversial whether mathematical and logical truths are analytic; some empiricists have also agreed we learn such truths through reason, while disagreeing about how genuinely informative they really are.) One does not seem to need to investigate the world to know, say, that three is greater than two or that three times three equals nine.

In addition, in a rationalist view there seems to be some truths that cannot be known through experience alone. For instance, it seems that we cannot know through experience alone truths about the empirical world that are universal (that is, that apply in all circumstances). Consider, for example, the law of conservation of energy, which states that the amount of energy in the universe remains constant. This is a truth that seems to be universal, and scientists treat it as such. Yet it seems to be impossible to establish its truth through experience. This is because experience always involves the particular—particular events and particular objects at particular times. One always measures energy at a particular time; one never measures energy for *all* times, and indeed it would be impossible for us to do so. So we do not know the law of the conservation of energy through experience alone. Similarly, to know that smoking causes cancer seems to require more than sensory experience. After all, all that scientists encounter in experience itself are particular instances of smoking causing cancer, not every possible case of smoking causing cancer. If, then, universal truths such as scientific laws are true, we seem to grasp their truth through reason rather than through experience.

There have been philosophers defending rationalist views throughout the history of philosophy. For example, in ancient philosophy, Parmenides (fl. 580 B.C.E.) and his follower Zeno of Elea (fl. 465 B.C.E.) argued that even though experience seems to tell us that objects move (bats fly, people walk, plants lean toward the sun, and so on) and change occurs in the world, both motion and change are illusions. They arrived at these conclusions through reason, treating reason rather than experience as the true guide to the nature of reality. Plato famously argued that what is most real are a certain kind of Ideas rather than the ordinary, physical objects we encounter in sense experience. Knowledge of these Ideas, in turn, required using one's reason (in particular, by studying philosophy), rather than making observations of the empirical world. Moreover, according to Plato, all knowledge is recollection:

Everything we know, we know because we *remember* it, having known it once before prior to being born. So the mind itself, rather than experience, plays a crucial role in knowledge.

Rationalism is strongly associated with philosophers of the 16th and 17th centuries, especially René Descartes (1596–1650), Baruch Spinoza (1632–77), and Gottfried Leibniz (1646–1716); these philosophers are often contrasted with the empiricists of the same period, John Locke (1632–1704), George Berkeley (1685–1753), and David Hume (1711–76). One central disagreement between rationalists and empiricists was whether there are innate ideas. An innate idea is a concept that is somehow in a person's mind from birth. Philosophers differed over what it meant more specifically for an idea to be innate. It would not seem to mean, for example, that innate ideas must be ideas one is conscious of even at birth. For if that were so, then it would seem that even newborn babies are fully aware of any ideas that are innate, such as the idea of God. But it seems unlikely that a newborn is conscious of the idea of God. An innate idea, then, might instead be an idea that a person is inclined to have and that she can acquire consciously through experience. Leibniz's analogy was that such ideas might be in a person's mind in the way that a sculpture is in a block of marble: With enough work, the ideas (and the sculpture) will emerge.

A classic rationalist argument for innate ideas is that certain ideas could not be acquired through experience and therefore must be innate. Descartes argued that the ideas of God, mind, and matter are innate. As an illustration, he considered a piece of wax that undergoes various physical changes. Although it was once solid, if subjected to enough heat, the wax melts. As it melts, it changes its shape, color, and smell. Yet it is the *same* piece of wax despite the fact that it has undergone these changes. We do not know through the senses that it is the same piece of wax because, in Descartes's scenario, everything our senses tell us about the wax changes. So, it is through our reason that we know it is the same piece of wax. In particular, we know through our reason the substance of the wax, specifically that it is matter (for Descartes, this means it has extension; it takes up space). Leibniz thought that not only are there innate ideas but that *all* our ideas are innate, and that there are innate principles as well, such as logical principles (whereas *idea* here means concept, a principle is something that is true or false, such as the principle that the denial of a contradiction must be true).

If some of our ideas are innate, then some of the materials for knowledge are innate. Put another way, some of the ideas we use for constructing knowledge are acquired independent of experience. In addition, the classic rationalists believed that the *process* for acquiring knowledge was mainly a matter of using reason rather than learning through sensory experience. So, not only do we start with innate ideas out of which we can construct knowledge, but also such construction itself is a process of reason rather than sensory experience. Descartes thought that reason could establish the existence of God and the existence of a physical world independent of himself. Spinoza and Leibniz each constructed complex metaphysical systems, that is, views about the nature and structure of reality. Reality, in their views was rational, and to discover its fundamental nature it was necessary to use one's reason rather than sensory experience. In addition, ethical truths could be known through reason alone; Spinoza advocated an intellectual love of God. (None of this means that all rationalists ignored the empirical

This 1884 painting depicts René Descartes teaching Queen Christina of Sweden (at the table on the right). *(Painting by Pierre-Louis Dumesnil the Younger)*

methods of science or believed science was unimportant; both Descartes and Leibniz made scientific contributions.)

Today it is less common to frame disagreement about the nature of knowledge in terms of rationalism and empiricism. However, one contemporary view related to the classic rationalist view of innate ideas is the view of the American linguist Noam Chomsky (1928–   ) and others that the human mind has innate structures regarding language. Roughly, the idea is that human language follows certain universal rules that are innate in the mind.

Descartes's Method and Foundationalism

Central to Descartes's philosophical work was the desire for certainty. Much impressed by the certainty of mathematical truths and knowledge, Descartes sought the same level of certainty in all claims for knowledge—for example, knowledge that God exists and that there is a physical world—and he believed it was reason, not experience, that could establish the truth of knowledge claims. Descartes also formulated a specific method of inquiry: First, he resolved to be guided by reason and in particular to accept as true only ideas that are clear and distinct. Second, he believed he should divide up intellectual problems he faced into parts and, third, begin his inquiry with simpler matters before attempting to resolve more complex issues. Finally, he resolved to review the issue at hand and his reasoning for errors.

With these methods established, Descartes began his quest for certainty by doubting. What he could doubt, Descartes did not consider knowledge. (Later on, Descartes believed he had established that he knew quite a few things; his starting point, however, was to reject as knowledge anything it was possible to doubt.) On the other hand, he thought that if he could find something it was *not* possible to doubt, then he would have found something he did in fact know. Descartes believed he could doubt a great many things. He believed, for example, it was possible not only to doubt particular experiences (such as that he was sitting near a warm fire) but also that it was possible to doubt *all* of his experience of an external world. Put another way, he believed it was possible to doubt that a world outside his own mind existed. After all, Descartes thought, for all he knew he could merely be dreaming all his experiences of such a world—that he walked on the Earth, that he had family, and that he went to work every morning. Moreover, Descartes argued that it was possible to doubt knowledge that seems independent of such an external world, such as mathematical knowledge. This is because it was possible that an evil genius deceived him into thinking, falsely, that two plus two equals four; and an evil genius could deceive Descartes about *all* apparent mathematical and logical truths.

However, Descartes argued, what he could not doubt was that he was doubting. In general, he could not doubt that he was *thinking*. And if he was thinking, Descartes reasoned, then he must exist, because there must be *something* that is thinking. This famous phrase is: I think, therefore I am (in Latin, *cogito, ergo sum*). According to Descartes, he could be absolutely certain of his own existence. Descartes used this first item of knowledge to prove, at least to his own satisfaction, that he knew other things as well, including the existence of an external world, mathematical and logical truths, and God's existence (things he had begun by doubting). In this way, for Descartes, the knowledge of his own existence served as a foundation for all knowledge, just as the base of a pyramid provides a foundation for the rest of the structure.

Using the certain knowledge that he existed as a starting point, Descartes went on to argue that he knew mathematical truths and that material objects existed. For Descartes, the key was proving that God existed, for if he could prove that God existed, then he could also prove that he could trust his reason and therefore reject the possibility that an evil demon deceived him. Descartes's reasoning for God's existence is complex, but roughly it is this: The idea of God is of a perfect being. Now, Descartes's idea of God must have a cause; it could not have come from nothing. Further, there must be as much perfection in the cause of that idea as there is in the idea itself. If there must be as much perfection in the cause of the idea as the idea itself, then God itself must be the cause of that idea. This is because only God could have as much perfection as the idea of God. (Descartes himself could not be the cause of the idea of God because Descartes is imperfect.) Therefore, God exists.

According to Descartes, because God is good, God would not deceive Descartes. So God would not have given Descartes the capacity to reason unless reason, properly used, could lead to knowledge. So, Descartes thought, mathematical knowledge was certain after all: It is knowledge acquired through the proper use of reason. This is Descartes's answer to the evil demon argument. In answer to the dream argument, Descartes thought that he could not help believing that physical objects would exist, and that God would not have made Descartes that way unless physical objects actually exist.

However, there is a difficulty with this reasoning. Descartes proved the existence of God in order to prove that he can trust his own reasoning. This means he could not trust his own reasoning as he tried to prove the existence of God (after all, for all Descartes knew, an evil demon was deceiving him). But if this is the case, Descartes had no reason to believe that he could trust his own arguments for proving that God exists. The problem is that Descartes needed his reason to be trustworthy to prove that God exists, but he needed to prove that God exists in order to show that his reason is trustworthy. This circular reasoning has become known as the Cartesian circle, and it has been the subject of much discussion.

Empiricism

Empiricism is the view that knowledge depends on experience. It is opposed to rationalism, according to which reason is more important than experience in acquiring knowledge. Experience is usually understood as sensory experience—that is, what we experience through our five senses. So, according to empiricism, the source of knowledge is what we experience through our senses. Some versions of empiricism hold that *all* knowledge depends on experience; others hold that only some kinds of knowledge (such as knowledge of the empirical world) depend on experience. Historically, empiricism is associated with modern philosophy, especially with John Locke (1632–1704), George Berkeley (1685–1753), and David Hume (1711–76). Traditionally, these philosophers have been contrasted with the modern rationalists René Descartes (1596–1650), Gottfried Leibniz (1646–1716), and Baruch Spinoza (1632–77). However, other philosophers have given empiricist arguments, such as Epicurus (ca. 341–270 B.C.E.), Thomas Aquinas (1224–74), and Francis Bacon (1561–1626). Francis Bacon, for instance, argued that inquiry should proceed through a rigorous form of induction, in which inquirers (as a community) make many observations of the empirical world, formulate laws based on those observations, and go beyond the limitations of individual experience and personal prejudices.

There is an obvious sense in which experience seems to be necessary for knowledge, insofar as if a person never existed she would have no experience of any kind, and in that case no knowledge. What empiricists often emphasize, in contrast to rationalists, is that knowledge

Portrait of Francis Bacon

depends on experience (that is, sensory experience) in the sense that all of our concepts depend on experience. Put another way, all of our ideas have their origin in experience. This contrasts with the view that there are innate ideas, ideas that we are either born with or that we can acquire independently of experience.

John Locke

Whereas René Descartes and other rationalists emphasized mathematics as the model for acquiring knowledge, Locke was impressed by the empirical work of physicists such as Isaac Newton. At the same time, Locke believed reason was supremely important, remarking that it was "the last judge and guide" of all things. In one of his most influential works, *An Essay Concerning Human Understanding,* Locke sought to describe the capabilities of human understanding, such as what it is possible for humans to know and on what basis. Contrary to Descartes and others, Locke argued that there are no innate ideas. That is, humans are not born with any ideas already formed in their minds. If there were any innate ideas, Locke argued, then there would be ideas that all people would agree on. But, he claimed, there are no such ideas. In addition, Locke argued that if there were innate ideas, then children would consciously have such ideas; but they do not. (Young children would be consciously aware of innate logical principles, for instance, if there were any, but it seems clear that they have no such awareness.) For Locke, it is not a good defense of innate ideas to say that young children do have innate ideas but that they have not yet developed them (so that the ideas are innate in the sense that children have the capacity to develop them). This is because, if to be an innate idea is just to be an idea that a person is capable of developing at some point, then it looks as if any idea a person ever has can be considered innate. And it seems implausible to suppose that all the ideas one ever has are innate. For instance, a person might acquire the idea of electrons in middle school, and the idea of an iPod when iPods were first invented. But it would seem odd to suppose that these ideas were ever innate in one's mind.

Rather, Locke said, at birth the mind is like a white paper on which nothing is written; metaphorically, it is a blank tablet (in Latin, a tabula rasa). It begins empty and is metaphorically written on by experience; the mind receives information from the outside world passively, and it is only because the mind receives such information that people can acquire concepts and therefore knowledge based on these concepts. For example, a person might acquire the concepts of round and orange through experience, so knowledge that depends on these concepts (such as the knowledge that oranges are round) depends on experience. All materials for knowledge, according to Locke, are similarly dependent on experience. Yet this need not mean that every kind of knowledge requires experience. Locke believed that although we acquire all the materials for knowledge through experience alone, constructing knowledge out of those materials need not depend on experience. For instance, consider mathematical knowledge, such as the knowledge that two plus two equals four. Perhaps one needs experience to acquire the concepts two, four, and addition. But once having acquired those concepts, according to one empiricist view, a person does not need further experience to know that two plus two equals four. Rather, she can recognize that two plus two equals four just by thinking about it. No observation of the world is necessary. A minority of empiricists have disagreed with Locke on this point; notable among them was John Stuart Mill (1806–73), who argued that mathematical knowledge does require experience beyond simply acquiring mathematical concepts.

So, for Locke, the source of all our ideas is experience: The human mind cannot form any ideas that are not based on experience (either directly or indirectly). Locke understood experience broadly. First, experience includes sensations—what we experience through our five senses, such as what we feel. Second, experience includes reflection, which Locke understood as an observation of the operations of one's mind. For example, thinking and doubting are instances of reflection: They are operations of the mind that one can observe in oneself. From sensation and reflection, Locke argued, come all the materials for knowledge. Locke divided ideas themselves into simple ideas and complex ideas. Simple ideas are ideas that cannot be analyzed, meaning that they cannot be broken up into parts. An example of a simple idea is the idea of yellow. Complex ideas are made up of simple ideas, and Locke believed that we construct complex ideas from simple ideas in specific ways. We can, for example, use abstraction. This is the process of forming a general idea on the basis of simple ideas. For example, suppose a person sees many different sorts of dogs: Some are shaggy, some are shorthair, some have pointed ears, some have floppy ears, and so on. From the simple ideas acquired by seeing these different dogs, it is possible to abstract away from specific details of these individual dogs, focus on what all the dogs have in common, and accordingly form the general Idea of Dog. This general Idea of Dog does not entail that every dog has pointed ears or a shaggy coat—it is an idea of dog in general rather than an idea of any specific dog (or specific type of dog).

Locke used the term *idea* in a specific sense to mean whatever is the object of a person's understanding—that is, whatever it is that a person is thinking about or understanding. According to Locke, we experience directly only ideas, not things themselves. So, for instance, we do not perceive a banana directly; we perceive only our Idea of Banana. However, the banana *causes* a person to have an Idea of Banana. So, the banana does exist independently of human ideas (it does not just exist in our minds), although humans do not perceive it directly. In general, according to Locke, objects outside of ourselves cause us to experience ideas, and we experience those ideas rather than the objects themselves. In this way, we perceive only what is in our own minds, although there are real objects that exist independently of our minds.

Locke held that such objects have primary qualities and secondary qualities. A quality is just the power an object has to produce an idea in a person. For instance, to use Locke's example, a snowball has the power to produce in a person the Ideas of Cold and White. In other words, when someone picks up and looks at a snowball, the snowball causes her to have the Idea of Cold (it feels cold in her hands) and the Idea of White (the snowball looks white). Primary qualities are inseparable from objects; objects always have them, as long as they exist. The primary qualities are solidity, extension (occupying space), figure (shape), motion or lack of motion, and number (whether an object is one or more than one). The shape of the snowball, for instance, is a primary quality: As long as it exists, the snowball always has the power to produce the idea of a certain shape in the perceiver, and the shape of the snowball is in the snowball itself. Of course, the shape of the snowball might change (it might get bigger or smaller), but shape itself is inseparable from the snowball: The snowball always has a certain shape, whatever that shape is.

In contrast, secondary qualities are qualities that are not inseparable from objects and that are not really in objects. They include colors, tastes, and sounds. For instance, although the snowball has the power to produce the Idea of White in someone who sees it, the color white is not inseparable from the snowball. To see this, consider that the snowball need not always produce the Idea of White. In darkness, the snowball might appear gray, for example. So color is not actually in the snowball itself, although the snowball has the power to produce the ideas of particular colors in people looking at it. In Locke's terms, primary qualities more closely resemble objects than secondary qualities do. Locke also held that secondary qualities depend on primary qualities in the sense that an object's power to produce ideas such as taste, color, and sound depends on the object's primary qualities.

Primary and secondary qualities are qualities of an object, but Locke wrote that the qualities must belong to (or "subsist in") something. Put another way, it is not as if qualities are free-floating by themselves; *something* must support them. What supports them is substance. But, according to Locke, it is impossible to know the substance of an object, and indeed we have no clear idea of what substance is. We can know only that it is that which supports the qualities of an object. In addition, Locke thought, we cannot truly know the real essences of things, such as the real essence of gold (though we can acquire beliefs about it that are probably true).

One challenge to Locke's empiricism was that it seemed to open the door to skepticism. This is because, according to Locke, we do not directly experience objects that are external to us. For example, upon seeing a clock, the clock produces in us certain ideas, such as the idea of a certain color and the shapes of its two hands. What we experience are those ideas, not the clock directly. If we do not experience the clock directly, how do we know that our ideas accurately reflect the clock itself? In general, if we do not actually experience external physical objects, how do we know their true nature? Indeed, how do we know they exist at all? Such skeptical worries plagued empiricism. The challenge of skepticism was taken up by George Berkeley and, in a somewhat different way, David Hume, with very different results.

Empiricism:
Berkeley and Hume

George Berkeley

The Irish empiricist philosopher George Berkeley (1685–1753) agreed with John Locke that all our ideas are derived from experience—there are no ideas we are simply born with. Moreover, for Berkeley all knowledge is based on experience. Berkeley also agreed that we experience only ideas directly. (Like Locke, Berkeley used the term *ideas* in a broad sense to mean the content in a person's mind, including images, sensations, and concepts.) However, Locke claimed that there are material objects that exist independently of being perceived and that these material objects cause our ideas. For instance, a physical tree produces in us the Idea of Green, and a snowball produces in a person the Idea of Cold when she holds it in her bare hand. Berkeley, however, thought that the claim that there are material objects that exist independently of being perceived leads to skepticism: After all, if we never experience anything but our own ideas, how do we know that our ideas in any way match up with an independently existing reality? It appears that we *cannot* know. And that suggests that what we seem to know of ordinary, existing things—that apples are red, that pine needles smell a certain way, that mountains are tall, and so on—we do not actually know at all. Berkeley rejected this conclusion. His solution was simply to deny that matter exists at all: There are no material objects, Berkeley argued.

According to Berkeley, all that exists are minds and the ideas that they perceive. What we ordinarily take to be material objects are collections of ideas. A pine tree, for example, is a collection of ideas such as the color green, rough bark, and pine needles of a certain size and shape. That is *all* apparently material objects are—collections of ideas in the mind. This does not mean that sensible objects (objects perceived through the senses) are not real; it just means that their existence is mind-dependent. Now the question of how it is possible to know that our ideas match up with independently existing objects does not arise. That is because there are no such independently existing objects. Moreover, knowledge of what we experience can count as genuine knowledge because we experience all that there is to experience: our ideas. The view that what is real are ideas, not material objects, is idealism (not to be confused with having lofty ideals). Berkeley himself called his view immaterialism.

It might sound strange to believe that only ideas and minds exist and material objects do not. Berkeley believed, however, that his view was actually consistent with common sense in that what we ordinarily talk about and have beliefs in are objects of experience. Berkeley gave specific arguments for his idealism. As noted, we experience only our ideas; sensible objects are collections of ideas. But ideas can exist only in a mind; they cannot exist independently of a mind. If they exist, therefore, they exist because they are perceived by a mind. To be, Berkeley wrote, is to be perceived (in Latin, *esse est percipi*)—or, in the case of minds, to be is to perceive. Berkeley also rejected the primary/secondary qualities distinction formulated by Locke. Secondary qualities, thought Locke, are qualities that do not belong in an object itself but which objects can produce the ideas of in a person who perceives the object; for example, the scent of pine does not belong to a pine tree itself, although a pine tree has the power to produce in someone the idea of that scent. Primary qualities are the qualities that belong to objects themselves, such as shape and solidity. Now if secondary qualities are not in the objects themselves, then they depend on a perceiver. But, Berkeley argued, it was impossible to conceive of a sensible object without thinking of it as having secondary qualities. So, if secondary qualities depend for their existence on the perceiver, so, too, do primary qualities.

Our ideas do have a cause, Berkeley believed: The cause is God. To see why this is so, Berkeley noted that some of our ideas are involuntary; it is not up to us whether we have them. For instance, one cannot decide to see an apple just because one wants to. Yet they must have a cause, and for Berkeley that cause must be another mind, the mind of God. God's existence also explains why objects continue to exist even when an individual mind no longer sees them. They continue to exist because God perceives them. In general, sensible ideas are ideas in the mind of God.

Berkeley argued that we do have certain knowledge of the ordinary objects of experience precisely because these ordinary objects are just collections of ideas. For example, we can know that a clock really has a certain shape and a certain color and so on because its shape and color are just ideas; we cannot be mistaken about our own experience. Although Berkeley sought to put skepticism to rest, few philosophers have been willing to follow his version of idealism.

David Hume

The third of the classic British empiricists is David Hume, who is famous for his skepticism. Hume believed that the mental content of the human mind consists of ideas and impressions. Impressions are more lively than ideas—that is, they are more vivid. Impressions include sensations, passions, and emotions. Ideas are copies of impressions. For instance, a person might see a brilliantly orange sunset, and while she watches that sunset, she has an impression. Later, when she remembers the sunset, she has an idea of that sunset; her memory of the sunset is a faded copy of the original impression (seeing the sunset is more vivid than remembering the sunset). Ideas can be combinations of impressions, and in this way it is possible to have an idea of something one never actually encounters. For instance, a person might see mountains and the color gold, and she can combine her Idea of Mountain with her Idea of Gold to form the Idea of a Golden Mountain, despite having never seen a golden mountain. An idea that has no basis in an impression (or combination of impressions) has no sense, according to Hume—it is meaningless. For this reason, Hume rejected metaphysical concepts that could not be traced back to impressions (a view that later influenced the 20th-century school of thought called Logical Positivism).

Statue of David Hume *(Sculpture by Alexander Stoddart, photograph by David M. Jensen; used under a Creative Commons license)*

Hume's skeptical view about causation (the phenomenon of events causing other events) is especially notable. Very often people believe that one event in the world causes another. For instance, kicking a soccer ball seems to cause it to move; boiling an egg seems to cause it to cook; viruses are thought to cause illnesses. There seems to be a necessary connection between such events, so that kicking a soccer ball will always cause it to move and boiling an egg will always cause it to cook (under the appropriate conditions), and so on. So, nature seems to be uniform: Certain types of events that caused certain other types of events in the past will continue to cause those other certain types of events in the future. On the basis of this belief, scientists formulate general laws, stating for instance that the freezing point of water will remain in the future what it has been in the past. However, Hume denied that the belief that events necessarily cause other events (and the belief in the uniformity of nature) is based on reason. Consider when one billiard ball hits another. It looks as if the first ball's striking the other causes the second ball to move. But, Hume argued, we do not experience any necessary connection between these events (the first ball striking the second and the second ball moving). Moreover, it is not logically necessary that the second ball will move upon being struck by the first: It is not a logical contradiction to suppose that it will not. In addition, our past experience of billiard balls does not tell us that the ball will move in the future upon being struck. By Hume's lights, it is a mistake to argue that because the ball moved in the past when struck it will move again in the future when struck. It is a mistake because what is wanted is a justification for thinking that nature is uniform. To say that nature was uniform in the past and therefore will be uniform in the future is just to *assume* the very thing we want to prove (the uniformity of nature). All this suggests that we cannot know that in the future a billiard ball will move when struck by another. More important, it suggests that in general we cannot know that the future will be like the past. So, we cannot know that in the future viruses will cause illness or that water will freeze when the temperature drops to a certain point.

Hume's point was not that a billiard ball would not move when struck nor that the future will not be like the past in many important ways. Of course, he believed it would. His point was that the belief that there is a necessary connection between types of events (such as the event of one ball striking the other and the event of a ball moving) is not based on reason. Rather, according to Hume, our belief in the uniformity of nature is based on habit or custom. For example, to return to one billiard ball moving when struck by another, we have seen one ball move when struck by another so often that we have seen a constant conjunction of events. That is, we have seen one event (the ball moving) constantly following another (the ball being struck). This constant conjunction gives rise to our belief that there is a necessary connection between the events. But the belief is a matter of custom, not of reason. Hume did not think there was anything wrong with this custom; in fact, he thought a belief in causes—and in general, a belief in the uniformity of nature—was necessary. It was not a good idea, he noted, to throw oneself out a window (even if one's belief that doing so would cause pain is a matter of custom, not reason). Nonetheless, Hume's reasoning has far-reaching consequences. Insofar as science is based on scientific laws and the view that nature is uniform, Hume's reasoning implies that science is based on custom rather than reason. Hume believed that we should continue to act as if the future will be like the past; but as an empiricist, he argued that we do so only out of habit, not out of reasoned belief. For Hume, then, empiricism is linked to skepticism.

The problem of whether it is possible to know that the future will be like the past—put another way, whether nature is uniform—is known as the problem of induction. It has provoked much discussion in philosophy. One of the most famous attempts to give a philosophical account of cause came from the 19th-century British philosopher John Stuart Mill (1806–73), also an empiricist. Mill's account is usually referred to as Mill's methods. Mill argued that there are various ways or methods that we commonly use to identify a cause. Mill spoke of five methods: (1) the method of agreement, (2) the method of difference, (3) the method of agreement and difference, (4) the method of concomitant variation, and (5) the method of residue.

The method of agreement captures the notion that when we find a pattern in which every time that one thing happens (call it A), another thing follows (call it B). That is, there is an agreement between A happening and B happening. With such a pattern, said Mill, we identify A as the cause of B. For example, every time Bob eats hamburgers he gets indigestion; so he concludes that the hamburger is the cause of his indigestion.

The method of difference focuses on the notion that there is a pattern of one thing (call it B) following another (call it A) such that there is a case in which the first thing, A, is missing and that is followed by the second thing, B, being missing. In this case, there is an established pattern, which is followed by a difference (namely, A not occurring and then B not occurring). As an example, day after day Mary takes her dog, Fido, for a long walk, and when they get home Fido takes a nap; on the one day that she does not take Fido for a walk, he does not take a nap. So, she concludes that taking a walk is the (or a) cause of Fido taking a nap.

The method of agreement and difference is a combination of the previous two methods. It is the case of having a pattern in which whenever A is present, B follows, and also when A is absent, B is absent.

The method of concomitant variation simply means that two things vary relative to each other. For example, as a little boy, Bob discovers that whenever he turns the knob of his parents' old radio in one direction, the volume of the sound goes up, and when he turns the knob in the other direction, the sound goes down; that is, the knob-turning and the sound volume vary together (there is concomitant variation). So, he concludes that turning the knob causes the change in sound volume.

The method of residues is finding a pattern and, after ruling out other possible causes, having one factor left over—that is, having a residue among all the factors—that is identified as the cause. For example, Mary has two identical houseplants, but one of them is doing well, and the other is doing poorly. They both get the same amount of water and are planted in the same kind of soil, etc. The only factor that seems relevant and is different is the amount of sunlight they get. So, she concludes that the amount of sunlight is the cause of the plant's doing well or poorly.

While Mill claimed that these methods describe how, in fact, we often identify causes, others argued that, at best, these methods show correlations between things, not necessarily causes.

Kant

Immanuel Kant (1724–1804) is one of a handful of towering figures in philosophy, and his work influenced many philosophers after him. In epistemology, one way of understanding Kant is that he provided a bridge between the rationalist view of knowledge (roughly, the idea that knowledge is acquired through reason rather than experience) and empiricism (roughly, the view that knowledge is acquired through experience). Among Kant's most important works is *Critique of Pure Reason*. In that book, Kant attempted to answer the question of whether synthetic a priori judgments are possible. A synthetic a priori judgment is a judgment that is knowable independent of experience (so, one can know it just by using one's reason) but whose content goes beyond the information contained in the subject of the judgment. To understand this, consider that an analytic judgment is a judgment whose content is contained in the subject of the judgment. For instance, the statement "triangles have three sides" is analytic because what it says is contained in the subject of the sentence, triangles (triangles have three sides by definition). By contrast, a synthetic a priori judgment says something more than what is contained in the subject of the judgment. For instance, "rivers are cold" is synthetic, as it is not part of the definition of the term *rivers* that they are cold. If the judgment that rivers were cold were knowable a priori, "rivers are cold" would express a synthetic a priori judgment. (In fact, it does not seem to be knowable a priori; we have to do something such as put our toes in the river to gauge whether rivers are cold.)

Whether synthetic a priori judgments are possible is controversial. Kant believed that they were. (In particular, he thought that mathematical judgments and general statements in physics are synthetic a priori.) To arrive at this conclusion, Kant considered what makes experience possible in the first place. Plainly we experience; that is, we have sensations, see physical objects, and do things with them. But what makes this possible? Put another way, what are the conditions for the possibility of experience? In describing the nature and limits of knowledge, Kant called his arguments transcendental in the sense that they transcend—go beyond—discussion of the objects of experience by focusing on what makes experience possible in the first place.

The key insight in Kant's reasoning is the idea that rather than our knowledge conforming to objects, objects conform to our knowledge. To see what this means, consider that ordinarily we say that we experience what we do because objects in the world produce in us certain experiences. For example, one sees a red cup because the red cup produces in us the sensation of a red cup. But suppose, Kant thought, we see the red cup in part because the cup conforms to *how* we know: Rather than passively perceiving the cup, the mind actively structures how we experience the cup. It is in this sense that objects conform to our knowledge. What we know depends on how the mind structures experience. According to Kant, that the mind structures experience is what makes experience possible in the first place. For example, we experience what we experience in time and space. But, for Kant, space and time do not absolutely exist out there, independent of the mind. Rather, the mind orders experience such that we always experience what we experience in space and time. Empiricists had argued that we acquire the idea of space through experience, by encountering objects outside of ourselves. In contrast, Kant argued, that we encounter objects outside of ourselves presupposes the notion of space: If we did not have the notion of space already, we would not experience objects as outside ourselves in the first place. So the idea of space is something the mind brings to experience, rather than something we encounter in experience. Similarly, the idea of time is something the mind brings to experience, rather than encounters in experience.

That the mind structures experience in terms of space and time explains how it is possible to experience sensible objects (that is, objects perceived through the senses). In addition, Kant thought, what explains understanding and knowledge of such objects is that the mind structures experience using certain a priori concepts. These concepts are concepts the mind actively brings to experience; it is only because the mind organizes experience by using these concepts that we can make sense of what we experience. So, without them, knowledge is not possible. Kant called these concepts categories. To show that we experience objects only through the categories, Kant again considered what is necessary for experience in the first place. It seems that we cannot experience objects as objects unless we have the concept of object. But, according to Kant, one cannot have the concept of object unless one also has the categories. In other words, the very concept of object involves certain a priori concepts. For example, the concept of object requires the concept of substance, the concept of something permanent (a cup, say, is a permanent object in the sense that it does not flicker in and out of existence even when it undergoes change; even painted blue, for instance, a once-red cup is the *same* cup, just colored differently). When we make judgments about the objects we experience, Kant argued, we do so according to certain logical forms of the mind, and we always use the categories to do so.

Knowledge of the objects of experience, then, is possible only by applying these categories. For instance, it is possible to know that the wind causes leaves to fall only because the mind uses the concept of cause to organize experience. However, according to Kant, the categories apply *only* to the objects of experience. That is, they apply only to phenomena, the objects of perception (what we perceive through the senses). As Kant put the point, the categories apply only to appearances. (Kant uses *appearances* broadly, to include all perceptions, not just what one sees.) They do not apply to what is beyond sense experience, the things themselves, what are called the noumena. Noumena are the objects of thought, as opposed to objects one experiences through the five senses. So, noumena are entities beyond the five senses: One can think about them, but one can never see, feel, hear, smell, or taste them. For Kant, noumena are things as they actually are, independently of how they are perceived. If knowledge of the objects of experience requires the categories but the categories apply to appearances, this implies that it is impossible to have knowledge of the things themselves, the noumena.

For instance, a person might perceive an orange as round, orange-colored, and tart. That is how the orange appears to one; the perceived shape, color, and taste of the orange are phenomena. We can have knowledge of the appearance of the orange. Now consider the orange independently of how it is perceived, what the orange is in itself regardless of how it looks, feels, or tastes to anyone. That is the noumenon of the orange (noumenon is the singular of noumena). And, for Kant, although we can have the concept of the noumenon of the orange, it is impossible for us to have knowledge of it. Put another way, it is impossible for us to have knowledge of the orange independently of how we perceive it. For Kant, our knowledge is confined to phenomena—the appearances of things.

Now we are in a position to see why synthetic a priori judgments are possible, according to Kant. Consider, for example, the judgments in geometry. By its nature, geometry is about space. Now the possibility of experience presupposes the concept of space; so, we have the concept of space prior to experience. Geometrical claims about space, then, are a priori. But they are also synthetic, Kant believed (roughly, they are not just a matter of definitions).

An important point in all this is that Kant sides neither with rationalism nor empiricism. According to Kant, it is a mistake to suppose that all knowledge is based strictly on experience. This is because knowledge requires the application of categories, and the mind itself applies the categories. But it is also a mistake to suppose that knowledge is based on reason alone. This is because knowledge requires that judgments (which involve categories) be applied to something: specifically, the objects of experience. In addition, Kant argued (contrary to David Hume) that claims that one event is the cause of another are valid. After all, it is not possible not to understand what we experience without the concept of cause; our minds always structure experience using this concept (among others).

Moore, Russell, and Wittgenstein

In the 20th century, G. E. Moore (1873–1958) and Bertrand Russell (1872–1970) were among the most prominent figures in what has become known as analytic philosophy. As the name suggests, analytic philosophy is concerned with analysis. There is no single accepted account of what analysis is in the philosophical sense. At a fundamental level, however, analysis is often thought to be the examination of a thing's parts, and analytic philosophers such as Moore and Russell analyzed concepts as well as linguistic items such as sentences. That is, they considered the components of things in order to better understand them. The primary goal of conceptual analysis is clarity. By examining the parts of a concept, for instance, we can become clearer on what that concept is. For example, consider the concept of knowledge. Suppose someone claims to know that the New York Yankees won the World Series in some particular year. If the Yankees did not win the World Series that year, then the person did not *know* that the New York Yankees won (even though she might have believed it). What this suggests is that a component of knowledge is truth: Knowing something involves knowing something that is *true*. If we know that knowledge involves truth, then we know that to understand what knowledge is, we should investigate truth.

G. E. Moore

Moore defended a commonsense view of the world. For example, he wrote that there were certain propositions that everyone knew to be true, such as that the Earth has existed for some time before oneself was born and that there are people other than oneself. These propositions, he believed, people knew with certainty; it was not merely that they felt pretty sure about them. So, against the claims of skeptics, Moore defended such claims of common sense. Famously, Moore gave what he called a "proof of the external world," that is, a proof of a world that exists independently of our experience. The proof consists of holding up one's hand, with the remark, "Here is a hand," and then, holding up another hand, remarking, "Here is another one." A hand is an object external to one's own mind; so, if a person has two hands, there must be an external world. It is in this way that holding up one's two hands and pointing out that they are in fact hands is a "proof" of the external world.

Now, it seems clear that a skeptical philosopher is unlikely to accept this conclusion. A skeptic influenced by René Descartes (1596–1650), for example, might ask, "But how do you know that those are really hands? How do you know you are not just dreaming that you have hands?" Moore's argument does not seem to reply explicitly to such skeptical worries, and indeed Moore did not regard his "proof" as a proof against skepticism. It is a proof that there is an external world, not a proof directed against skeptical arguments claiming that we have no knowledge of such a world. Indeed, Moore seemed to regard skeptical arguments as not to be taken very seriously. For Moore, it made more sense to stick to the claims of common sense than to believe skeptical claims made in a philosophical theory. We can know things with certainty, he thought, even if we do not know how we know them. By Moore's account, it is as if the philosopher's starting point is common sense. It is common sense that there are human beings in addition to oneself and that the Earth has existed for some time before oneself. What was of philosophical interest, then, according to Moore, was not a debate about whether such propositions are true but how to understand such propositions correctly. The way to do this was through analysis of those propositions. For although Moore claimed that everyone knew the meaning of claims such as "The Earth has existed for many years past" and, further, that everyone knew such claims were true, Moore did not claim that everyone knew the proper *analysis* of such claims. People know what such claims mean in their ordinary sense; this does not mean that they know what such claims mean in a deeper, analytic sense, when each component of such claims is carefully considered in turn. To provide such analysis is a task of the philosopher.

Given Moore's defense of common sense, it is not surprising that Moore also defended for a time a view now known as direct realism (sometimes called naive realism). According to this view, what we perceive when we perceive the ordinary objects of experience (cats, trees, bowls, and so on) are ordinary, physical objects, and we perceive them directly. For example, what is it one really sees when looking at an orange? One answer, given by modern philosophers such as John Locke, is that one sees content ("ideas," Locke would have said) produced in oneself by the orange, such as the Idea of Orange and Round. But one does not see the orange itself. Moore gave a different account: When one looks at an orange, one sees the orange itself, and one sees it directly.

Bertrand Russell

As many philosophers have noted, the term *knowledge* is used in various ways. One can be said to know how to play chess; know one's best friend; know that rain is condensed moisture in the atmosphere. These examples point to differences between kinds of knowledge. Bertrand Russell also famously distinguished between knowledge by acquaintance and knowledge by description. Knowledge by acquaintance is knowledge acquired via direct awareness of something. For example, consider again someone looking at an orange. What she is directly aware of is a patch of color, specifically a patch of orange, so she is acquainted with this patch of color. Other examples of knowledge by acquaintance include the direct awareness of the sound of bells, the smell of strawberries, and one's own memories. In each case, one has knowledge of something or another (a sound, a scent, a memory), and one has a direct awareness of that something. A person does not need to figure out that she is aware of a particular scent, sound, color, or memory; she is aware of such things directly. Knowledge by description, by contrast, is knowledge acquired by learning descriptions associated with other things; it does not regard direct awareness of something. For instance, no one alive today ever encountered directly the ancient Greek philosopher Socrates, so no one alive today was ever acquainted (in Russell's sense) with Socrates. Yet we know at least some things about Socrates, such that he was Greek and that he was a philosopher. We

Photograph of Bertrand Russell

have certain descriptions associated with Socrates—so, our knowledge of truths about Socrates is knowledge by description.

What we are acquainted with, in the examples above, Russell called sense data—data provided by the senses, of which one is immediately aware, such as patches of color and sounds. Like Moore, Russell believed there is an external world, but he understood this world differently than an ordinary commonsense view. In a commonsense view (defended at one time by Moore) we directly perceive ordinary external objects, such as oranges and cats and spoons. Russell thought, on the contrary, that what we have direct awareness of are sense data. So, one has direct awareness of the patch of orange color and the scent of an orange, but not of the orange itself. Rather, for Russell, the orange itself is a logical construction; it is intellectually built out of sense data such as the patch of orange color and the scent of the orange.

As an empiricist (believing that knowledge is derived from experience), Russell argued that knowledge by description is ultimately based on knowledge by acquaintance. So, what we know of the empirical world is ultimately based on knowledge by acquaintance.

Ludwig Wittgenstein

Ludwig Wittgenstein's early work was similar to Russell's, especially in its description of the relation between the world and language. However, Wittgenstein's later work, notably his book *Philosophical Investigations,* led in new directions. Like other philosophers of his time, Wittgenstein studied language as a means of clarifying philosophical issues. In some cases, he thought, a study of language revealed that what appeared to be philosophical problems were not really problems at all but instead the result of a misunderstanding or misuse of language.

Wittgenstein coined the term *language game* to emphasize that the speaking (or writing) of language is part of an activity. That is to say, when we use language, we are not only uttering words or sentences, but we are engaging in some activity. This focus on the use of language and not merely on the structure or content of language is often referred to as pragmatics. The focus of the pragmatics of language is on how we use language and on how the meaning of words and sentences is connected with their use. For instance, if someone says, "That is a nice hat," and he means it sincerely, that means something different than if he says it sarcastically. The meaning of the words themselves—the semantics—do not change, but what is meant by the use of those words differs when they are said sincerely or sarcastically.

Wittgenstein stressed this pragmatic nature of meaning and argued that we use language in a great many ways: giving orders and obeying them, describing things, reporting an event, making up a story, play-acting, guessing riddles, making a joke, translating, asking, thanking, cursing, greeting, praying, and many more. Because language is used in so many ways, Wittgenstein urged that we not assume that the structure and content of language has some essence or is always the same. For example, when someone says, "I have a headache," that appears on the surface to have the same structure as when someone says, "I have a car."

However, having a car implies that there is some object, separate from the person that is possessed by that person. This is not the case with a headache; there is not necessarily some object that a person possesses when he reports having a headache. Or, in a given situation, if someone says, "It is cold in here," that person is not reporting the weather but perhaps asking someone else to close a window. The point is not that language means whatever someone wants it to mean, but that there is no single structure to it, even in cases where the structure appears to be like the structure of other uses of language.

The reason Wittgenstein called the various uses of language and the contexts within which those uses take place language games is not that they are trivial or just for fun and amusement. Rather, the point is that, like games, language is rule-governed and social. By saying it is rule-governed, Wittgenstein meant that language is not subjective but communal. We use language to communicate, and in order to do this, there must be rules that are followed, just as for games to be possible, there must be rules about how to play the game, and those rules must be capable of being known and understood by anyone.

All of this is related to epistemology in at least the following way. Just as there are rules in soccer, say, regarding how the ball can be controlled, there are rules governing uses of words like *knowledge* and *know*. Put another way, there are language games involving these terms. Wittgenstein claimed that it makes sense to claim one knows something only when what one is claiming is in doubt. Put yet another way, to make a claim to knowledge when no one genuinely questions the claim in question is to break one of the rules governing the use of the word *know*. To illustrate, suppose three people are sitting around a campfire when someone announces, "I know there is a campfire here." The oddity of this is that the campfire is obvious to all; there is no question that there is campfire, so to claim that one knows that there is seems strange. It would seem equally strange for one of our three campers to assert, "I do not know there is a campfire here." This is again because the question of there being a campfire, in ordinary circumstances, simply does not arise. Since everyone implicitly assumes that there is a campfire, both the claim to know that there is one and the claim that one does not know that there is one are odd; these claims break the rules. A way to put this point is that the ways we use the word *know* typically make sense only when there is something genuinely in question. In this scenario, that there is a campfire is not genuinely in question. Of course, there might be circumstances in which it is in question, say, if all three people believe they are possibly under the influence of some sort of hallucinatory drug; in such circumstances it might make sense to say either that one knows or does not know that there is a campfire. But in circumstances where there is no such question, it does not. These remarks apply generally to other claims to knowledge. To return to G. E. Moore, for instance, the announcements that one knows one has a hand, or that there is an external world, are misuses of *know*, insofar as no one genuinely doubts such claims.

Also important for our purposes is Wittgenstein's idea of family resemblance. The notion of family resemblance points to the similarities, while at the same time the differences, between family members. That is, in some respects, individuals share certain features with their family members, but only certain features. For example, an individual might look like his mother in some ways (having a nose a certain shape, say) and like his sister in various ways (say, having similarly colored eyes and similar basic face shape). At the same time, that individual might not share other features with those family members. For instance, he might have different-colored hair than his sister or different face shape than his mother. The fact is that people look like their fellow family members in some respects, but not necessarily all. They resemble their family members but are not carbon copies of them.

Traditionally, philosophers analyzed basic concepts by asking what is X, where X might be truth or beauty or knowledge or friendship. The typical process was to look for the essence of some concept by seeking a set of necessary and sufficient conditions that would characterize that concept. So, if we wanted to know what is knowledge, we might look for the features or characteristics that something would have to possess in order for it to be a case of knowledge and also what features or characteristics something would have to lack for it not to be a case of knowledge. Only those things that had all and only those particular features would then be cases of knowledge. One might suggest, as many philosophers have, that there are defining, essential, features of knowledge even if we do not yet know what they are. In addition, there are reasons why we rule out certain things from being cases of knowledge—for example, mere guesses—and that points to saying that guesses do not have the necessary or sufficient features of knowledge, whatever those features might be.

However, Wittgenstein claimed that for many concepts, there are no essences and, hence, no set of necessary and sufficient conditions that they satisfy. And it might turn out that knowledge is one such concept, and in that case, it would be a mistake for epistemologists to try to formulate a set of features that characterize all and only instances of knowledge. To see how a concept might fail to have an essence (and, hence, a set of necessary and sufficient conditions it satisfies), consider all of the things that we call games. Some games, such as Monopoly or Scrabble, involve a game board and various game pieces, but that is not true of all games (for instance, playing tag). Some games involve scoring points, but not all games do (for instance, tag, again). Some games involve multiple, competing players, but not all games do (for instance, playing solitaire). It might be the case that all games involve some set of rules in order to play (although that might not be true); but many things besides games also involve sets of rules, so having rules does not necessarily characterize or specify the unique essence of games. There simply does not seem to be a feature that is common to *everything* that counts as a game. An analogy to help illustrate this point is to consider the nature of a rope. A rope is composed of many overlapping threads, but no single strand of thread runs through the entire length of the rope. So, there might be no single feature that runs through all cases of games, but, instead, a collection of overlapping features. That is to say, some—but not all—games involve multiple players, while others—but not all—involve scoring points and the like.

Wittgenstein's point, then, was that it is philosophically a mistake to insist that concepts (or words) must have essences. Rather than having an essence, many basic concepts might just have a family resemblance. So, knowledge might not have an essence; there might very well be many kinds of things that we would appropriately call knowledge, even though they differ in some basic ways with other things we call knowledge. There might not be any single feature (or condition) in common among various cases of knowledge: knowing you have a headache, knowing your name, knowing how to ride a bike, knowing the square root of 25, knowing that George Washington was once the U.S. president, knowing that there are electrons, etc. Perhaps there is an essence to knowledge, but Wittgenstein claimed that we should not assume that there is and that philosophers should not assume that there must be.

Coherentism and Knowledge as Justified True Belief

Coherentism

Coherentism is a view about the nature of epistemic justification, specifically how it is structured. It is contrasted with foundationalism and often thought to take its inspiration from the difficulties of providing a foundationalist account of justification. So, it is worth saying something about foundationalism first. According to foundationalism, the justification of beliefs ultimately rests on a foundation of basic beliefs that are themselves not justified by other beliefs. To see why one might think this is so, consider the following. It seems evident that many beliefs are justified by other beliefs. For instance, the belief that Oslo is the capital of Norway is justified by the belief that Oslo is identified as such in authoritative maps. But something must justify that belief as well—presumably some other belief. Then, however, it seems that yet another belief must justify that belief also. It seems that there is no end in sight to this series of justifying beliefs. However, that such a series of justifying beliefs goes on for infinity seems untenable. This reasoning is called the regress argument. The foundationalist's response to the regress argument is that there must be some beliefs that are foundational: These beliefs are basic in the sense that they are not justified by other beliefs. Other beliefs ultimately rest on these basic beliefs. Put another way, nonbasic beliefs ultimately are justified by basic beliefs. Yet it has proven difficult to give an account of the nature of basic beliefs and precisely how they justify nonbasic beliefs.

At least in part for this reason, coherentists give a different answer to the regress argument. Coherentists agree that there is no infinitely long series of justifying beliefs, but they deny that there are basic beliefs. Rather, according to coherentism, justification is simply not structured in a linear way. Instead, coherentists claim, beliefs provide *mutual* support for each other. Whereas foundationalists often describe justification by using the metaphor of a pyramid or a building (basic beliefs provide a foundation for nonbasic beliefs, like the foundation of a building), coherentists often use the metaphor of a *web* of belief. This metaphor is associated with the American philosopher W. V. O. Quine (1908–2000) in particular. In a web, strands are connected to each other in various ways, but there is no thread that occupies a basic, privileged position; the web hangs together because of the way each of its parts fit together as a whole. For the coherentist, justification is rather like that: No beliefs are more basic than any other belief, and justification is a matter of how all the beliefs as a whole fit together—that is, justification is a matter of how they *cohere*. An individual belief is justified if it coheres with a system of beliefs as a whole. Some coherentists emphasize a holistic nature of justification, regarding justification as a matter of the justification of a system of beliefs as a whole. To see how a belief might depend on other beliefs for its justification, suppose someone glances out the window and comes to believe it is snowing. Now it might seem as if this belief is justified by no more than the experience of seeing what appears to be falling snow. Yet it seems more likely that one accepts this belief at least in part because it coheres with other beliefs one has, such as the belief that one is awake, that one is not hallucinating, that one's vision is functioning normally, and that it is unlikely that what one is seeing is falling bits of ash or paper. What this suggests is that even a simple belief such as that it is snowing is justified by its relation to other beliefs one has. One is not likely to believe it is snowing, and the belief that it is snowing would be much less justified, if one believed, say, that one's vision is not functioning normally.

It is one thing to say that for beliefs to be justified they must cohere. It is another thing to say what it means to cohere. Coherentists address the issue in different ways, and there is no single accepted account of coherence itself. One possible requirement is that most of the beliefs in a web of beliefs should be consistent with each other. For example, if a person believed that the people she called her parents in fact were her biological parents, had human physiology, and were themselves the offspring of other humans (her grandparents), then the belief that her parents are space aliens would be inconsistent with her overall set of beliefs. So, the belief that her parents are space aliens does not cohere with her other beliefs, and it is not justified. Also commonly thought to be important in coherence are the inferential relations between beliefs—that is, what beliefs logically or otherwise reasonably imply and what one can reasonably infer from beliefs. That Shakespeare wrote many plays, for example, implies that Shakespeare was an author. So, if one believed that Shakespeare wrote many plays but believed that Shakespeare was *not* an author, these beliefs do not cohere and are not justified relative to each other. Some coherence theorists also stress the explanatory relations between beliefs, meaning whether and to what degree beliefs explain other beliefs. The belief that it is close to zero degrees outside, for example, helps explain the belief that one should bundle up before going outside. For a more complex example, Newton's laws of motion help to explain many phenomena, from the orbits of planets to the motions of a roller coaster. So, the belief in Newton's laws of motion helps explain beliefs about various phenomena, such as the belief that the planets in our solar system will continue to orbit the Sun instead of flying off in some other direction. So, beliefs can cohere with each other in the sense that they help explain each other. Some coherence theorists also include probability as an important element in coherence, meaning that one component of coherence among a set of beliefs is the degree to which individual beliefs are probably true, given the other beliefs in a belief system. The belief that two people are one's biological parents, for example, if true, makes it very probable that it is also true that those two people are human beings.

One objection to coherentism is that there could be more than one, even many, systems of beliefs that are equally coherent. The problem is that if justification is just a matter of coherence, then it is not obvious on what reasonable basis one should choose to accept one such belief system over the others. Of course, one could choose to accept one belief system arbitrarily, but the idea behind the objection is that there should be good reasons for accepting one belief system over another. But, according to

Portrait of Sir Isaac Newton *(Engraving by William Thomas from a painting by Godfrey Kneller)*

the objection, coherentism fails to give any such reason. Another objection to coherentism is called the isolation objection. The idea is that by explaining justification in terms of coherence between beliefs, coherentists leave something important out: namely, the world itself. Put another way, coherentism *isolates* belief from the world. Take, for instance, the belief that it is snowing outside. For a critic, crucial to the justification of this belief is what is actually happening in the world: Are snowflakes actually falling? If justification is just a matter of coherence, however, arguably the world itself and our experience of it play little (if any) role in the justification of this belief: What matters, instead, is how the belief that it is snowing coheres with other beliefs. Coherentists have formulated various replies to these objections and others.

Knowledge as Justified True Belief

Foundationalism and coherentism are views about epistemic justification, specifically how it is structured. Justification is important in epistemology in part because of its relation to knowledge. According to the traditional conception of knowledge, knowledge is justified true belief. Put another way, for any particular belief to count as knowledge, the belief must both be true and justified. Consider the belief that someday one will visit the Moon. Call this belief *M* for short. Now suppose (1) Lewis has the belief *M*, (2) *M* is true, and (3) Lewis is justified in believing *M* (say, because Lewis can afford to pay for a private trip to the Moon, such trips are available, and Lewis plans to take one). If this is so, then according to the traditional account of knowledge, Lewis knows *M*. And if any of these conditions are *not* fulfilled, then Lewis does not know *M*. In general, for anyone to count as knowing a belief, a person must have that belief, the belief must be true, and the person must be justified in having that belief. Traditionally, these three conditions were considered both necessary for knowledge (unless they were fulfilled, a person could not be said to have knowledge regarding that belief) and sufficient for knowledge (no other conditions were needed for a person to count as having knowledge regarding that belief).

To understand better this traditional conception of knowledge, it is worth considering each of its three components (justification, truth, and belief) in turn. Let us begin with justification. Justification is used in various ways. A person who believes she will pass a test with flying colors because believing this will give her some much-needed confidence is prudentially justified in having that belief. That is, she is justified in this belief because it is to her own advantage to have that belief, and that is why she adopts it (it is prudent to do so). Someone who rushes a sick friend to a hospital might be morally justified in breaking speed limit laws in the sense that he has good moral grounds for speeding (if he fails to speed, he may put his friend at serious risk). It is a third kind of justification, epistemic justification, that is relevant here. Epistemic justification is illustrated by the following example: Frieda believes her car is out of gas because the gas gauge points to empty, because she cannot siphon gas from the tank, and because the car will not start. Frieda's belief is epistemically justified. Epistemic just means having to do with knowledge. So, roughly, epistemic justification is justification that has to do with knowledge—it is justification related to whether a belief counts as knowledge, as opposed to justification regarding what is in one's best interest, or justification regarding moral or immoral behavior. Someone who believes she will ace a test because it is in her best interests to believe that does not seem to have, on that basis alone, knowledge that she will pass the test. Plausibly, however, Frieda's belief that her car is out of gas does count as knowledge.

If knowledge is justified true belief, to study the nature of knowledge, one must study the nature of justification. But the nature of justification is much disputed. One way of characterizing justification is that it regards having good reasons for a belief, or good evidence for a belief. Another way of characterizing justification is to link it with truth, so that justified beliefs at least must be beliefs that are true or at least likely to be true. It is often said that justification is a *normative* concept. This just means that it has to do with norms in the sense of standards, such as standards of rationality or standards by which people ought to accept or reject beliefs. Believing that one's car is out of gas just because one dreamed that it was, for instance, does not seem to conform to a particularly good standard of rationality; believing it for the reasons Frieda believes her car is out of gas arguably does.

In contemporary epistemology, there are two broad approaches to justification, an internalist approach and an externalist approach. According to an internalist approach, justification has to do with factors that are internal to the person, such as a person's beliefs and memories. According to an externalist approach, factors outside a person are relevant in justification. Some versions of externalism agree that some internal factors matter too; these externalists just deny that internal factors are the *only* ones that matter. Internalism tends to focus on beliefs from a believer's own perspective. For example, Frieda is justified in believing her car is out of gas because she herself has good reasons for believing it and knows what those reasons are. On the other hand, if someone admitted she had no idea why she believed her car was out of gas, an internalist is not likely to consider her belief justified.

Externalist approaches to justification focus less on the reasons for a belief a person has from her own perspective and more on how a person acquired that belief, asking questions such as, what was the cause of that belief? or by what process did a person arrive at that belief? The most prominent externalist view of justification is reliabilism, according to which a belief is justified when it is the product of a reliable process. Suppose, for example, that following particular rules when performing mathematical calculations is likely to produce true beliefs about the results of those mathematical calculations—say, when a person follows simple rules for adding numbers, she gets certain results and arrives at true beliefs about those rules (that three added to two equals five, for instance). Then those beliefs, as the result of a reliable process, are justified, even if a person cannot explain or even clearly identify the rules she followed.

The second component of justified true belief is truth. It is probably not surprising that philosophers offer diverse accounts of the nature of truth. Here we will briefly consider three such accounts. According to the correspondence view of truth, truth is a matter of correspondence with the facts. So, if a belief is true, the belief corresponds with some fact. For instance, to use an example by Bertrand Russell (1872–1970), if the belief that Othello loves Desdemona is true, then that belief corresponds with the fact that Othello loves Desdemona. Sometimes correspondence theorists take it that there is a structural relation between facts and what is true. For example, the fact that Othello loves Desdemona consists of Othello, Desdemona, and a certain relation of loving—these are the components of that fact. The belief that Othello loves Desdemona shares a structural similarity, since the objects of the belief are Othello, Desdemona, and a certain relation of loving. Other correspondence theorists deny that there must be a structural similarity between a true belief and the fact; in this view, true beliefs must correspond with facts, but beliefs might be structured differently than facts. The correspondence view of truth is typically associated with the view that there is a real world that exists independently of a person's belief, and it is facts in that real world in virtue of which beliefs are true. Supposing that Othello and Desdemona are real people, for instance, whether one's belief that Othello loves Desdemona is true has nothing to do with the attitude one takes toward the belief (whether one wants it to be true, for instance, or not); it just matters that it corresponds to a fact in the real world, a world that exists independently of one's beliefs.

The correspondence view of truth has the advantage that it seems consistent with common sense; probably most people believe that a belief is true, if it is, because it somehow corresponds with reality. However, a criticism of the correspondence view is that the nature of correspondence is not always clear. Another issue is the nature of facts themselves and in what sense they are real. A fact does not seem to be real in the way that a cookie is real or a soccer ball is real (one can not ever trip over a fact, it seems); in what sense are facts real, and in what sense do they exist? Philosophers give various answers to these questions.

An alternative to the correspondence view of truth is the coherence view. According to this view, truth is not a matter of correspondence between true beliefs and facts. Rather, truth regards how beliefs fit together—that is, how they cohere. For defenders of the coherence view of truth, a belief is true if it coheres with other beliefs in a system of beliefs. (This sounds similar to the coherence view of justification; however, many philosophers distinguish coherentism as a view about justification from coherentism as a view about truth; most coherentists about justification are not coherentists about truth.) As with the coherence view of justification, philosophers offer different accounts of what it means to cohere. One view is that, for beliefs to cohere with each other, they must not only be consistent with each other, they must also mutually entail each other. That is, rather roughly, they must be consistent with each other, as well as imply each other. One consideration in favor of the coherence view of truth is that we often do reject a belief as false at least in part if it fails to cohere with other beliefs we consider true. For example, suppose one believed that the gas tank in one's car was empty yet found oneself able to drive 20 miles without adding gas to the tank. One would likely reject as false one's initial belief that the gas tank was empty. Why? Because it conflicts with other beliefs one holds to be true: that a gasoline-powered car cannot run without gasoline, for instance, that one did not hallucinate driving the additional 20 miles, and that gasoline cannot magically replenish itself in the tank.

Perhaps the most common criticism of the coherence view of truth is that it seems to separate truth from the world; if truth is just a matter of coherence between beliefs, then actual states of affairs in the world seem to have little to do with truth. It is also often argued that there could be more than one coherent set of beliefs. If this is the case, however, then it is not clear which set of beliefs should be taken as the best set of beliefs; yet, according to the concern, it seems odd to suppose that, insofar as the sets of beliefs have different contents (say different things), all such systems should be equally good.

A third view of truth is the pragmatic view of truth, associated in particular with the American school of thought, pragmatism, and especially with the American philosopher William James (1842–1910). A very rough statement of James's pragmatic view of truth is that truth

Self-portrait of William James from the James family papers at Harvard University

is what is useful; put another way, true beliefs are beliefs that are useful or expedient. To see what James meant by this requires some additional commentary. James and other defenders of the pragmatic view of truth consider truth as it relates to experience and in particular how a belief can makes a positive difference in one's life. James wrote that true ideas are those that we can verify. But a way of verifying a belief is to experience how that belief can make a positive difference in one's life. For example, suppose a person believes that a friend is trustworthy. This belief shapes how she behaves toward her friend; she shares intimate details of her life with her friend and feels wholly relaxed in her friend's company and quite enjoys her friend's company. Her belief that her friend is trustworthy helps bring about these happy circumstances; if she did not believe her friend was trustworthy, she would behave differently, and the friendship would be less fulfilling. The experience of this friendship, including the shared pleasure in each other's company, seems to verify the belief that the friend is trustworthy and makes a positive difference in the believer's life. For these reasons, by James's lights, the belief would count as true. Because true beliefs are verified through such processes, rather than simply starting out as true, James wrote that beliefs *become* true.

A common criticism of the pragmatic view of truth is that it wrongly suggests that whatever belief is useful must be true. Yet usefulness does not seem to guarantee truth. For instance, it might be useful to believe that everyone who disagrees with one's own political party is irrational or unpatriotic, because it spares one from having to do any uncomfortable questioning of one's own political beliefs. But that does not make it *true* that everyone who disagrees with one's own political party is irrational or unpatriotic. An equally common pragmatist response to this criticism is to argue that *mere* usefulness, of any sort, does not make a belief true; a belief must be expedient in many ways, and it must be expedient in the long run, not for the short term. Arguably, the belief that people who disagree with one's own political party are irrational or unpatriotic is not likely to be expedient in these ways (for instance, it would have the effect of limiting genuine conversation with other people, which would detract from a community's ability to find solutions to common problems).

We now turn to the third component of justified true belief: belief. Belief is usually understood as an attitude about certain content. One way this is often put is that belief is a mental state (a state of mind) concerning propositions. A proposition is what is expressed by a sentence that says something is the case. For instance, the sentence "Paris is in France" expresses the proposition that Paris is in France; the sentence "Smokey wants a treat" expresses the proposition that Smokey wants a treat. So, if Kay believes that Smokey wants a treat, the object of her belief is the proposition that Smokey wants a treat. That is, she believes what is expressed by the sentence "Smokey wants a treat;" that is the content of her belief. It is possible to take different attitudes about propositions. For instance, Kay might fear that Smokey wants a treat, hope that Smokey wants a treat, or desire that Smokey wants a treat. So, belief is one attitude about propositions different from other possible attitudes. When a person believes a proposition, she accepts the proposition. However, accepting a proposition does not necessarily mean accepting a proposition consciously, in the sense of explicitly thinking about it and agreeing with it at this moment. You probably have many beliefs that you have consciously thought about and accepted but rarely think about now, such as the belief that Saturn has rings and that arsenic is poisonous; yet even when you are not actively and consciously accepting those beliefs, you still have them. In addition, it is plausible that you have beliefs you have never consciously thought about. You likely believe, for instance, that it would be dangerous to play soccer on a busy highway, although you have probably never considered the matter before now. Beliefs that a person is consciously thinking about are called occurrent (if you are consciously believing right now that you are reading this entry, the belief that you are doing so is occurrent). Beliefs that a person is not thinking about consciously are called non-occurrent.

Although beliefs are typically defined as mental states, they are closely tied to behavior. People act in ways in large part because of what they believe. They eat the food they eat in part because they believe the food is safe; they take certain paths to go places because they believe those paths will lead them to where they want to go; they show up at parties at certain times because they believe that is when other people will be there. It would be very odd for someone to claim that she believes something if her behavior is consistently at odds with that belief. Someone who claims to believe that playing Scrabble is a lot of fun but consistently takes pains to avoid playing, even when she has the time, say, is not very credible; it seems unlikely that she really does believe that playing Scrabble is a lot of fun.

An important question regarding belief is whether it is possible to choose what one believes. As noted, one view of justification is that one ought to believe only what one has good reason to believe. This view seems to make sense, however, only if it is possible to choose what one believes. This is because it would be odd to say that one ought to do what is outside of one's control (as if one were to say you ought to make yourself invisible). Whether one can choose what to believe, however, is controversial. Sometimes it seems as if one can, as when a person carefully weighs evidence for and against a proposition before accepting or rejecting it. Other times it looks as if one cannot: No matter how hard they try, for instance, it is unlikely that most people can choose to believe that the Earth is not real.

The Gettier Problem

In 1963, the American philosopher Edmund Gettier (1927–   ) published a short essay that challenged the view in epistemology that knowledge is justified true belief. The Gettier problem is the problem of giving an adequate analysis of knowledge that escapes the objections Gettier made (or similar objections).

To counter the view that knowledge is justified true belief, Gettier described two different scenarios in which it appeared that a person had a justified, true belief yet did not have knowledge. In one scenario, Gettier imagines that two people, Smith and Jones, are each applying for a job. Smith believes that Jones will get the job. He also believes that Jones has 10 coins in his pocket. Now Smith has good reasons both for thinking that Jones will get the job and that Jones has 10 coins in his pocket; so he is justified in having these beliefs. Now if Jones will get the job and Jones has 10 coins in his pocket, it logically follows that the man who will get the job has 10 coins in his pocket. This suggests that if Smith believes that the man who will get the job has 10 coins in his pocket, then Smith is justified in having this belief also. And in Gettier's scenario, Smith does believe that the man who will get the job has 10 coins in his pocket. However, although Smith does not know it, it is Smith himself who will get the job (not Jones), and Smith also has 10 coins in his pocket. Because this is the case, Smith's belief that the person who will get the job has 10 coins in his pocket is true. The problem here is that, as Smith's belief is both true and justified, on the traditional view of knowledge, it looks as if Smith should *know* that the man who will get the job has 10 coins in his pocket; yet it seems he does not know it. Smith seems *not* to know it because the reasons for his belief have little to do with the reasons why his belief is actually true. In other words, that Smith's belief turns out to be true is matter of luck. To see this, consider that in Gettier's scenario Smith does not actually know how many coins are in his pocket—he just knows that Jones has 10 coins in *his* pocket. Similarly, Smith believes that Jones will get the job because someone in authority told him so; *that* is one reason he thinks the man who will get the job has 10 coins in his pocket. But that is not a reason why it turns out to be true that the man who will get the job has 10 coins in his pocket.

What Gettier's cases seem to suggest is that something other than justified true belief is needed to give a complete analysis of knowledge— or, perhaps, that what is needed is some other way of understanding what it means for a belief to be justified.

Internalism and Externalism

In epistemology, it is often thought that for a belief to count as knowledge, it must be justified. Put another way, not just any belief is a case of knowledge; there must be a good basis for beliefs that do. So, a basic issue in the study of knowledge is the nature of justification: In virtue of what is a belief justified? Internalism and externalism answer this question in different ways. According to internalism, what makes a belief justified are states that are internal to the person who holds that belief, such as a person's beliefs, memories, and perceptual states (states in which she sees, hears, touches, smells, or tastes). Two main forms of internalism are foundationalism and coherentism. According to externalism, justification is not just a matter of internal states: Factors that are external to the person holding a belief are relevant. A main form of externalism is reliabilism.

As an illustration of internalism, suppose that Natalie believes that polar bears hunt seals, and she believes this because she has read books by polar bear experts and seen professionally produced documentaries about polar bears, and these sources indicate that polar bears hunt seals. What justifies Natalie's belief that polar bears hunt seals are certain internal states, such as her memories of having read those books and watched those documentaries and her beliefs that they are trustworthy sources of knowledge (that the people who wrote the books and made the documentaries know what they are talking about when they talk about polar bears). Suppose, on the other hand, that Natalie could not offer any reason for her belief (maybe, although she does not know it, the belief was somehow planted in her head by scientists). Asked why she believes that polar bears hunt seals, she says she does not know; she just does. In this case, according to internalism, Natalie is not justified in believing that polar bears hunt seals, even if it turns out that her belief is true: After all, she seems to have no *reason* for believing that polar bears hunt seals. These scenarios illustrate two features common in internalist accounts of justification. The first is the view that justifying reasons for a belief must be accessible in some way to the person who has the belief in question. That is, upon reflection, a person must be able to think of the reasons she has for her belief. This suggests why, in the first scenario, Natalie's belief is justified, but in the second scenario, it is not. A second common component in internalist theories of justification is the view that people ought to think about what they believe and choose their beliefs on the basis of good reasons, rather than choosing beliefs willy-nilly, regardless of the evidence. So, in the first scenario, Natalie is behaving responsibly; in the second scenario, when Natalie finds herself believing that polar bears hunt seals but can offer no good reason for this belief, she ought to refrain from continuing to have this belief until or if she can acquire good reasons for it.

Externalism claims that justification involves factors external to the person who holds the belief in question (different versions of externalism disagree on whether internal states matter at all). One reason for having an externalist view of justification is the idea that an important aspect of justification is whether a belief is likely to be true. It would seem odd to call Natalie's belief justified, for instance, if it is not at all likely to be true. However, what makes a belief likely to be true are factors that are external to the person who holds that belief. For example, perhaps what makes Natalie's belief likely to be true is that the people from whom she acquired the belief (the authors and documentary makers) are experts in polar bear behavior. Since polar bear experts would know about polar bear behavior if anyone does, to acquire beliefs about polar bear behavior on the basis of what polar bear experts say seems to be a way of acquiring beliefs that are likely to be true. In this sense, such a process is reliable, and according to one version of externalism, a belief is justified when it is produced by a process that is reliable in this sense. So, if Natalie acquired her belief by adopting beliefs of polar bear experts, it looks as Natalie's belief is justified. Note that, for the externalist, this is the case even if Natalie herself cannot give reasons for her belief—even if, say, she has no idea that the books she read were written by polar bear experts or even if she does not remember reading them. For an externalist, this need not matter: What matters for justification are external factors—such as whether or not the books Natalie read were by polar bear experts—not Natalie's internal states.

The example above offers a rough illustration of what is perhaps the most influential form of externalism, process reliabilism, according to which a belief is justified when it is the product of a reliable process. To be a reliable process is to be a process that tends to produce more true beliefs than not; in addition, process reliabilism focuses on cognitive processes in particular (processes that involve cognition), such as perception and reasoning. For example, plausibly perception is a reliable process. Of course, sometimes what we seem to perceive is not actually the case; sometimes our senses deceive us. But very often what we perceive does seem to be the case: Chances are that if you see traffic on the street, there really is traffic, and when you feel sunlight on your skin, there really is sunlight on your skin. Beliefs based on such perceptions are likely to be true. In general, perception is a reliable process in the sense that beliefs that are formed as a result of perception tend to be true. So, according to a simple form of process reliabilism, beliefs that are formed as result of perception are justified. More complex forms of process reliabilism add other conditions to what counts for a belief to be justified in order to rule out cases where it appears that a believer has arrived at a true belief through a reliable process and yet the belief seems unjustified—for instance, where a belief seems to be true just by luck.

There are many arguments for and against internalism and externalism, broadly speaking. To cite just one objection to internalism, some critics argue that it is a mistake to suppose that a believer must have access to reasons that justify a belief. For instance, animals and young children seem to have justified beliefs yet do not have access to justifying reasons for those beliefs. A cat, say, might know that there are birds out the window but would not have access to the reasons for that belief (it would seem to lack the ability to identify and spell out its reasons for its belief). To cite just one objection to externalism, critics of forms of externalism such as reliabilism argue that just because a process that produces a belief is reliable does not mean that that belief is justified. For instance, a person with extrasensory powers might be able to accurately predict the number of a winning lottery ticket every single time; however, if she is not able to give reasons for why she believes that any given number is the winning number, it is not clear that her belief is justified. Mindful of objections to internalism and externalism, some philosophers have given accounts of justification that blend features of each.

Feminist Epistemology

Broadly speaking, feminist approaches in philosophy value the experiences and perspectives of women. Feminist philosophers not only point out what they see as male biases in philosophical views but also often seek to promote the empowerment and well-being of women. Feminist epistemology brings these concerns to the study of knowledge and other epistemic issues, such as justification and standards for what counts as rational. There is no single version of feminism; nor is there a single version of feminist epistemology. Philosophers working in feminist epistemology offer sometimes quite different perspectives on the nature of epistemology and how knowledge is or ought to be acquired (or, perhaps, constructed); different philosophers also emphasize different issues. Some feminist epistemologists focus on the practice of science, as among the practices usually thought to produce knowledge. The following is a description of common themes in feminist epistemology (not all themes are found in every view considered an instance of feminist epistemology, however).

As in many areas of inquiry, both philosophy and science have traditionally long been dominated by men in the sense that it is men who have mainly been the practitioners of those disciplines. So, it has been mainly men who have formulated explicit standards for what counts as rational and what counts as knowledge, and it has been mainly men who, in science, have been said to acquire knowledge about the natural world, and men who have been regarded as authorities on subjects within science. A feminist critique is that both these activities have been biased in favor of men. An obvious example is that sometimes the content of scientific and philosophical theories has been sexist. The classical Greek philosopher Aristotle (384–322 B.C.E.) and many others have explicitly claimed, for instance, that women's ability to reason is inferior to men's ability to reason. Some scientific theories have affirmed this same bias, for example, on the grounds that because women tend to have smaller brains than men, they must also be less intelligent. In addition, some feminists have claimed that male-dominated epistemology has served to maintain the privileged position of men in society and keep women in an inferior position. After all, if women are inherently less intelligent than men, it makes more sense to entrust to men high-level professions or positions of great responsibility (e.g., professions or positions in law, medicine, and political leadership). In addition, some philosophers claim that females have received less access to knowledge than males (for example, they have been less free than men to attend school or learn certain professions). According to a view called standpoint theory, however, there is a sense in which keeping women in an inferior position has benefited women, by allowing them to better understand the social structures according to which they live, as well as views outside those social structures; they have a perspective that those privileged in society often lack.

Further, some feminists have charged that the very standards of what counts as rational have traditionally been biased in favor of a male perspective. For instance, some (but not all) claim that epistemology has traditionally valued epistemic traits usually associated with men, such as objectivity, while devaluing epistemic traits more commonly associated with women, such as emotion and intuition. But, some philosophers say emotion and intuition have a role to play in the acquisition (or construction) of knowledge as well. A separate but related point is that, in traditional epistemology, it is common to assume that *who* a knower is is irrelevant when it comes to what counts as knowledge, what counts as rational, or what counts as a justified belief. Traditionally, philosophers seek to identify a set of necessary and sufficient conditions for knowledge—a set of conditions that would tell us what is necessary for knowledge and what is sufficient for knowledge. From this perspective, a case of a belief that met those conditions must count as knowledge, no matter who has that belief. Epistemologists have often treated justification in the same way.

Against this perspective, a common feminist criticism is that it does matter who is the knower in question; it is a mistake to try to understand epistemic concepts such as knowledge by focusing on a knower in abstraction, separate from the actual situations in which people might live. The way this point is often put is to say that knowers are "situated." That is, people who know (who have knowledge) are not abstractions but rather actual people who are of one sex or another, living in one time and place or another, and living in some set of economic circumstances or another (say, they are rich, poor, or somewhere in between), among other factors. Any adequate account of knowledge must take this fact into account, according to this criticism.

An example might make this idea clearer. Suppose a woman drives a man home from a party. When she stops to let him out, he grabs her car keys and tells her that if she wants the keys back, she must come inside his home to get them. It is late at night, the neighborhood is a bad one, and the woman knows no one in the vicinity (nor does she have a cell phone to call someone for help). Suppose she goes inside the man's home, and he assaults her. When a similar case actually occurred and went before a judge, the man was not convicted of assault on the grounds that the sex must have been consensual. Otherwise, went the reasoning, the woman would not have gone inside the man's home in the first place. The point here is this: From the woman's perspective, arguably it was rational for her to go inside the man's home to retrieve her keys. Putting the point another way, arguably her belief that this was the best option available to her was justified. This is because walking alone at night in the bad neighborhood and knocking on doors asking strangers for help would have seemed to put her at greater risk than going inside the man's home to get her car keys. To suppose it was irrational for the woman to have gone inside the man's home (or that her belief that doing so was the best option available to her was unjustified) is arguably a supposition from a specifically male perspective, for the reason that men are less likely to be vulnerable to attack than most women, when walking around a bad neighborhood late at night.

Another common theme in feminist epistemology is the view that knowledge is social in nature. Knowledge is made, or constructed. So, no adequate account of knowledge treats knowledge as something held or acquired by an individual person, considered in isolation from social factors. Consider, for example, the practice of science. Science is practiced by human beings, working in a community, and scientists all have particular background beliefs, biases, values, and perspectives, some of which are bound to affect their work. Moreover, a scientific result that cannot be replicated is not likely to be considered valid. What counts as knowledge depends on social factors such as what a community considers reasonable, what a community considers verified, and like factors. Different standards might yield different knowledge claims. It is in ways such as this that knowledge can be said to be socially constructed. Some thinkers in feminist epistemology specifically argue that the practice of science has built-in male biases and should be informed by female perspectives.

Other defenders of versions of feminist epistemology emphasize that not all knowledge is strictly propositional knowledge. That is, not all knowledge is knowledge *that* something is the case. Philosophers outside feminist epistemology, of course, have distinguished between different senses of knowledge, acknowledging for instance cases of knowing *how* to do something (rather than just knowing that something). Despite this, epistemology traditionally focuses on propositional knowledge. However, in addition to knowledge such as knowing how to do something, there is a sense of knowledge in the sense that a person knows an activity, a place, or a person through long familiarity or experience. This is the kind of knowledge captured by claims such as "I know my best friend really well" or "after 20 years' experience, she really knows horse training."

Perception

Much, perhaps all, of the information we have about the world is based on what we learn through the five senses (sight, hearing, touch, smell, and taste). The acquisition of such information is sense perception, called simply perception in the rest of this chapter. On one hand, it might seem obvious that we do have knowledge of the external world (the world outside of our individual selves) and that this knowledge is based on perceptions. For instance, one knows that coffee is bitter because one can taste it or that someone is at the door because one hears the doorbell ringing. On the other hand, sometimes our perceptions do not match reality: If someone flooded a snowy field with green light, for example, the snow would appear green, although it is really white. So perceptions cannot always be trusted. This raises the questions of how (or whether) perceptions provide a basis for knowledge and how (or whether) perceptions justify beliefs about the external world. A metaphysical question related to perception concerns the objects of perception, that is, *what* one perceives when one perceives. These two questions are related. If the objects of perceptions do *not* include ordinary, physical objects, for instance, then on the assumption that we do have knowledge of such objects, it needs to be explained how perception provides a basis for that knowledge. Put another way, this view raises the question: How do we have knowledge of things we do not perceive?

According to the direct realist view of perception, the objects of perception are objects that we see directly and immediately, such as fence posts, trees, and birds. It is not as if we have to reason it out that there are such objects on the basis of seeing properties of those objects—for instance, it is not as if one first sees a tall green and brown shape and then figures out that one is seeing a tree. Rather, one just sees the tree itself: The perception of objects is immediate and direct in this sense. In addition, the objects of perception are public in the sense that anyone can see them (or at least anyone with normal vision). When you and a friend are watching a deer, for example, you are both seeing the same deer, and if someone else came along, she could see the deer as well. Moreover, these objects exist independently of who perceives them. When you and your friend walk away and no longer see the deer, say, the deer continues to exist. So, this view is a *realist* view in the sense that it regards ordinary, physical objects as existing independently of perceivers.

Although this account of perception might sound plausible, there are serious reasons for doubting it. Many philosophers have pointed out that perceptions often vary depending on the perceiver. For example, George Berkeley (1685–1753) pointed out that the same pool of water can feel hot or cold depending on the temperature of your hands when you touch the water; if you have just been handling ice cubes, a pool of water might feel quite warm. But if you have just been warming your hands by a fire for 20 minutes, the same pool of water might feel cold. Similarly, objects look different depending on one's perspective: Up close, a tree might look enormous; viewed from far away, it might appear tiny. And we have seen already how objects might appear as different colors when they are viewed in differently colored lights. What all this suggests is that one does not perceive ordinary physical objects directly. After all, if one perceived such objects directly, then it would seem as if the same pool of water should feel the same temperature regardless of how cold or warm your hands are, objects should appear the same size and shape regardless of your perspective, and objects should appear the same color regardless of the light in which they are viewed.

In addition, there are two arguments against the naive realist view, based on the phenomena of illusions and hallucinations. First, consider an optical illusion—say, that an oar looks bent where it enters the water. Now insofar as you perceive something when you perceive the oar in the water, it looks as if what you perceive is something bent. But the oar is not really bent. So, contrary to the naive realist view, what you perceive must not be the oar itself. Second, consider a hallucination, the perception of something that is not really there. Someone under the influence of drugs might hallucinate that there are green lizards on her bed, although there are no such lizards. Now the perception of seeing green lizards when there are such lizards seems indistinguishable from the perception of green lizards when there are *not* such lizards. That is, as far as the perceptual experience is concerned, one cannot tell the difference between the hallucination and the perception of actual lizards. Of course, one might know intellectually that she is hallucinating (someone might know she is under the influence of a hallucinogenic drug). But the point is that, even if you know you are hallucinating, the perception is just the same as if you were not hallucinating. This is a problem for the naive realist view because, given that the two perceptions are indistinguishable, it appears that they are of the same nature. That is, it appears that they have the same basic characteristics. Among those basic characteristics *cannot* be that they are perceptions of the ordinary, physical objects—there *are* no such objects (lizards) in the hallucination case. So, contrary to the naive realist view, perception is not essentially the perception of ordinary, physical objects.

One possible response to these arguments is to abandon the naive realist view in favor of the sense data theory of perception. To return to the example of the oar that appears bent, if one perceives something bent and the oar is not bent, then it seems to follow that what one perceives is not in fact the oar itself. So, it must be something else, and according to the sense data theory, that something else is *mental* in character. In this instance the sense data consists of an oblong shape that is brown in color and bent at a certain point. *That* is the object perceived. One common understanding of sense data is that they are mental objects in the sense that they depend for their existence on the mind. This does not mean that the physical oar does not exist (or that the physical oar's existence depends on the mind). In a common sense data view, ordinary physical objects do exist. However, they are not perceived *directly*. To perceive a physical object such as an oar, one must first perceive sense data.

There are various alternatives to the sense data view. One is the adverbial theory of perception, according to which it is a mistake to suppose that in cases of illusion and hallucination, there is an object of perception. Of course, people have perceptions, but in this view this does not necessarily mean that there are objects they perceive. Perhaps it is natural to think that there are; after all, describing an illusion, one might say, "I see an oar." However, sometimes language is misleading. For instance, one might say of a funny person, "She has a real wit." This seems to suggest that there is some object, wit, which the person in question has. But this is mistaken. There is no such object. To say someone has wit is to say something along the lines of that she intentionally says clever, funny things. In somewhat the same way, "I see an oar" need not be understood as saying that there is something (whether physical or nonphysical) that the speaker sees. Instead, reports about perceptions can be understood as saying something about *how* the perceiver perceives, rather than saying *what* the perceiver says. For instance, we can understand the report "I see an oar" as meaning something along the lines "I see oarly." This view treats *oar* as an adverb (this is the kind of move that gives this view the name the adverbial theory). Although this might sound odd, the idea is just that reports of perceptual experience can be understood in a way that does not depend on there being objects of perception for all perceptions (such as illusions and hallucinations).

According to the intentional view of representation, perceptions are analogous to beliefs in the sense that both perceptions and beliefs have intentionality. That is, both perceptions and beliefs are *about* something. The belief that rain is wet is about rain; the perception that it is snowing is about snow. Whereas beliefs can be true or false, a perception can accurately represent the way things really are or fail to do so. The perception that an oar is straight when the oar is straight, say, represents things as they are; the perception that an oar is bent where it enters the water does not. Phenomenalism is another view about perception. According to phenomenalism, ordinary objects (trees and pencils and so on) should be understood as collections of perceptions. Berkeley's idealism expresses this view. Each of these views of perception (along with others) has been extensively discussed and debated. Currently there is no universal consensus either about the objects of perception or the nature of perceptual knowledge.

Concluding Discussion Questions

1. What is Plato's metaphor of the divided line? According to the metaphor, what are the objects of true knowledge? What are the objects of mere opinion and beliefs?
2. What is the problem of induction, as posed in the work of David Hume? How does this problem relate to scientific knowledge?
3. In what ways is Kant's view about knowledge like an empiricist view about knowledge? In what way is his view like a rationalist view about knowledge?
4. What is the regress argument? How do foundationalists respond to the argument? How do coherentists (about justification) respond? Which response do you think is the better one? Why?
5. How does the phenomenon of optical illusions pose a problem for the direct realist view about perception? Do you think the phenomenon shows that direct realism must be wrong? Why or why not?
6. What are some common themes in feminist epistemology? Do you think any of these themes raise good points? If yes, which ones and why? If no, why not?

Further Reading

BonJour, Laurence, and Ernest Sosa. *Epistemic Justification: Internalism vs. Externalism, Foundations vs. Virtues.* Hoboken, N.J.: Wiley-Blackwell, 2003.

Crumley, Jack S., II. *An Introduction to Epistemology.* 2nd ed. Orchard Park, N.Y.: Broadview, 2009.

Huenemann, Charlie. *Understanding Rationalism.* Durham, England: Acumen, 2008.

Landesman, Charles, and Roblin Meeks, eds. *Philosophical Skepticism: An Anthology.* New York: Wiley-Blackwell, 2002.

Lehrer, Keith. *Theory of Knowledge.* 2nd ed. Boulder, Colo.: Westview, 2000.

Lemos, Noah. *An Introduction to the Theory of Knowledge.* Cambridge: Cambridge University Press, 2007.

Luce, J. V. *An Introduction to Greek Philosophy.* New York: Thames and Hudson, 1992.

Priest, Stephen. *The British Empiricists.* London: Routledge, 2007.

Pritchard, Duncan. *What Is This Thing Called Knowledge?* Abingdon, Oxon, England: Routledge, 2006.

Smith, A. D. *The Problem of Perception.* Cambridge, Mass.: Harvard University Press, 2002.

Stroud, Barry. *The Philosophical Significance of Scepticism.* Oxford: Oxford University Press, 1984.

Tanesini, Alessandra. *An Introduction to Feminist Epistemologies.* Hoboken, N.J.: Wiley-Blackwell, 1999.

Thomson, Garrett. *Bacon to Kant: An Introduction to Modern Philosophy.* Prospect Heights, Ill.: Waveland, 2001.

Glossary

coherence (theory of truth)   the view that truth is a matter of coherence between beliefs in a system of beliefs; philosophers offer different accounts of what it is to cohere.

coherentism (theory of justification)   the view that there are no foundational or basic beliefs and that justification is a matter of how beliefs in a belief system cohere together; contrasted with foundationalism.

correspondence (theory of truth)   the view that truth is a matter of correspondence with reality; for instance, true beliefs are those that correspond with the facts.

direct realism   the view that in perception we directly perceive ordinary objects, such as tables, rocks, and trees, in a world that exists outside ourselves.

empiricism   the view that experience plays a more important role in acquiring knowledge than reason; experience via the five senses is often emphasized, although experience can also include experience of one's own mind.

externalism   the view that justification is not merely a matter of states internal to a knower, such as memories and perceptual states, but involves factors that are external to a knower, such as the external cause of a person's belief; some externalists hold that only external factors are relevant to justification, while others hold that a knower's internal states are also relevant.

feminist epistemology   broadly, views in epistemology according to which gender is important and which seek to identify and correct male biases related to theories of knowledge and other epistemic concepts.

foundationalism   the view that beliefs are justified by foundational beliefs, which are themselves not justified by other beliefs; foundational beliefs are often thought to be somehow self-justifying.

Gettier problem   the problem of giving an analysis of knowledge that avoids the kind of objections identified by Edmund Gettier in his critique of knowledge as justified, true belief; in particular, such an analysis should avoid having any instances of belief count as knowledge when those beliefs are knowledge only as a matter of luck.

idealism   the view that reality is mind-dependent; for instance, George Berkeley defended the idealist view that all that exists are minds and ideas.

induction, problem of   the problem of knowing whether the future will be like the past—for instance, that kinds of events that have caused other kinds of events in the past will continue to do so in the future; associated with David Hume in particular.

innate ideas   ideas people are somehow born with (e.g., the idea of self).

internalism   a view about justification, according to which what makes a belief justified are states that are internal to the person who holds that belief, such as a person's beliefs, memories, and perceptual states (states in which she sees, hears, touches, smells, or tastes).

justification, epistemic   justification related to knowledge; a person can be said to be epistemically justified, very roughly, if there are good reasons that warrant his belief; the nature of justification is controversial.

knowledge, propositional   knowledge that something is the case, such as knowledge that green is one's favorite color or that donkeys are equines; propositional knowledge is distinguished from knowledge of how to do something and knowledge by acquaintance.

pragmatic (theory of truth)   the view that truth is a matter of what makes a positive difference in a person's life, in various ways and in the long run; that is, true beliefs are those beliefs that have such features.

rationalism   the view that reason plays a more important role in acquiring knowledge than experience.

skepticism   broadly, a questioning, doubting attitude about claims to knowledge; local skepticism is skepticism regarding particular kinds of knowledge, such as perceptual knowledge; global skepticism is skepticism regarding all kinds of knowledge.

skepticism, ancient   a movement in ancient Greek philosophy focusing on the suspension of belief in order to achieve inner tranquility.

tabula rasa   Latin for "blank tablet"; according to John Locke, at birth the mind is like a blank tablet in the sense that it has no innate ideas but instead acquires all ideas from experience.

Key People

Aristotle (384–322 B.C.E.) *Ancient Greek philosopher who disagreed with Plato about the nature of Ideas and distinguished between four different kinds of knowledge. In the following paragraphs, Aristotle claims that knowledge is acquired through syllogisms, a particular kind of argument.*

We suppose ourselves to know anything absolutely and not accidentally after the manner of the sophists, when we consider ourselves to know that the ground from which the thing arises *is* the ground of it, and that the fact cannot be otherwise. Science must clearly consist in this, for those who suppose themselves to have scientific *knowledge* of anything without really having it imagine that they are in the position described above, while those who do possess such *knowledge* are actually in that position in relation to the object.

Hence it follows that everything which admits of absolute *knowledge* is necessary. We will discuss later the question as to whether there is any other manner of knowing a thing, but at any rate we hold that that "*knowledge* comes through demonstration." By "demonstration" I mean a scientific syllogism, and by "scientific" a syllogism the mere possession of which makes us know.

If then the definition of *knowledge* be such as we have stated, the premises of demonstrative *knowledge* must needs be true, primary, immediate, better known than, anterior to, and the cause of, the conclusion, for under these conditions the principles will also be appropriate to the conclusion. One may, indeed, have a syllogism without these conditions, but not demonstration, for it will not produce scientific *knowledge*. The premises must be true, because it is impossible to know that which is not, e.g., that the diagonal of a square is commensurate with the side. The conclusion must proceed from primary premises that are indemonstrable premises, for one cannot know things of which one can give no demonstration, since to know demonstrable things in any real sense is just to have a demonstration of them.

[Aristotle. *Aristotle's Posterior Analytics*. Translated by E. S. Bouchier, B. A. Oxford: Blackwell, 1901. Available online. Online Library of Liberty. URL: http://oll.libertyfund.org/title/902. Accessed June 28, 2011.]

Bacon, Francis (1561–1626)   *An empiricist who argued in favor of a rigorous form of induction (the drawing of general conclusions on the basis of many individual observations) and the social nature of science. In the following passage, Bacon stresses a new kind of induction as a method in science.*

. . . [The] induction which is to be available for the discovery and demonstration of sciences and arts, must analyse nature by proper rejections and exclusions; and then, after a sufficient number of negatives, come to a conclusion on the affirmative instances . . . But in order to furnish this induction or demonstration well and duly for its work, very many things are to be provided which no mortal has yet thought of . . . and this induction must be used not only to discover axioms, but also in the formation of notions. And it is in this induction that our chief hope lies.

[Bacon, Francis. *Novum Organum*. In *The Major Achievements of Science*, edited by A. E. E. McKenzie, 402. Ames: Iowa State University Press, 1960.]

Berkeley, George (1685–1753)   *Irish empiricist philosopher who argued that all that exists are minds and ideas. In the passage below, Berkeley argued that ordinary objects (such as tables) exist; however they are nothing but ideas and therefore dependent for their existence on a perceiving mind. We experience only ideas, according to Berkeley, but ideas are mind-dependent.*

The table I write on I say exists that is, I see and feel it; and if I were out of my study I should say it existed—meaning thereby that if I was in my study I might perceive it, or that some other spirit actually does perceive it. There was an odor, that is, it was smelled; there was a sound, that is to say, it was heard; a color or figure, and it was perceived by sight or touch. This is all that I can understand by these and the like expressions. For as to what is said of the absolute existence of unthinking things without any relation to their being perceived, that seems perfectly unintelligible. Their *esse* is *percipi,* nor is it possible they should have any existence out of the minds or thinking things which perceive them.

. . . It is indeed an opinion strangely prevailing amongst men that houses, mountains, rivers, and, in a word, all sensible objects have an existence, natural or real, distinct from their being perceived by the understanding. But with how great an assurance and acquiescence soever this principle may be entertained in the world, yet whoever shall find in his heart to call it in question may, if I mistake not, perceive it to involve a manifest contradiction. For what are the forementioned objects but the things we perceive by sense? And what do we perceive besides our own ideas or sensations? And is it not plainly repugnant that any one of these, or any combination of should exist unperceived?

[Berkeley, George. *A Treatise Concerning the Principles of Human Knowledge.* In *Works.* Vol. 2. Edinburgh: Thomas Nelson, 1710.]

Descartes, René (1596–1650) *French philosopher often called the father of modern philosophy, Descartes reoriented the focus of philosophy to epistemology and defended a rationalist view of knowledge. He thought he could establish a foundation for all knowledge by starting with the certain knowledge that he existed. In the passage below, Descartes describes both his methods for acquiring knowledge and expresses his confidence in the power of human reason.*

The first [method] was never to accept anything for true which I did not clearly know to be such; that is to say, carefully to avoid precipitancy and prejudice, and to comprise nothing more in my judgment than what was presented to my mind so clearly and distinctly as to exclude all ground of doubt.

The second, to divide each of the difficulties under examination into as many parts as possible, and as might be necessary for its adequate solution.

The third, to conduct my thoughts in such order that, by commencing with objects the simplest and easiest to know, I might ascend by little and little, and, as it were, step by step, to the knowledge of the more complex; assigning in thought a certain order even to those objects which in their own nature do not stand in a relation of antecedence and sequence.

At the last, in every case to make enumerations so complete, and reviews so general, that I might be assured that nothing was omitted.

The long chains of simple and easy reasonings by means of which geometers are accustomed to reach the conclusions of their most difficult demonstrations, had led me to imagine that all things, to the knowledge of which man is competent, are mutually connected in the same way, and that there is nothing so far removed from us as to be beyond our reach, or so hidden that we cannot discover it, provided only we abstain from accepting the false for the true, and always preserve in our thoughts the order necessary for the deduction of one truth from another.

[Descartes, René. *The Method, Meditations and Philosophy of Descartes,* *translated from the Original Texts, with a new introductory Essay, Historical and* *Critical by John Veitch and a Special Introduction by Frank Sewall.* Washington: M. Walter Dunne, 1901). Available online. Online Library of Liberty. URL: http://oll.libertyfund.org/title/1698/142006. Accessed June 28, 2011.]

Empiricus, Sextus (ca. second century)   *Ancient skeptical philosopher whose writings are responsible for much of what we know about ancient Greek skepticism; he emphasized the suspension of belief. Sextus Empiricus here gives a brief description of Pyrrhonian skepticism.*

Skepticism is an ability, or mental attitude, which opposes appearances to judgments in any whatsoever, with the result that, owing to the equipollence of the objects and reasons thus opposed, we are brought firstly to a state of mental suspense and next to a state of "unperturbedness," or quietude. Now we call it an "ability," not in any subtle sense, but simple in respect of its "being able to." By "appearances," we now mean the objects of sense-perception, when we contrast them with the objects of thought or "judgments."

[Empiricus, Sextus. Outlines of Pyrrhonism: Sextus Empiricus.
Translated by R. G Bury. Buffalo, N.Y.: Prometheus Books, p. 17.]

Hume, David (1711–1776) *Scottish empiricist philosopher famous for expressing skepticism about cause/effect; he argued that we do not experience a necessary connection between cause and effect but expect one kind of event to follow another because we have seen those kinds of events occurring together in the past. In the following passage, Hume claims that we expect kinds of events to occur together (such as one billiard ball to move when struck by another, or the event of a fire's ignition to produce heat), not because we infer through our reason that there is a connection between such events, but rather because we are in the habit of experiencing those events together.*

And it is certain we here advance a very intelligible proposition at least, if not a true one, when we assert that, after the constant conjunction of two objects—heat and flame, for instance, weight and solidity—we are determined by custom alone to expect the one from the appearance of the other. This hypothesis seems even the only one which explains the difficulty, why we draw, from a thousand instances, an inference which we are not able to draw from one instance, that is, in no respect, different from them. Reason is incapable of any such variation. The conclusions which it draws from considering one circle are the same which it would form upon surveying all the circles in the universe. But no man, having seen only one body move after being impelled by another, could infer that every other body will move after a like impulse. All inferences from experience, therefore, are effects of custom, not of reasoning.

Custom, then, is the great guide of human life. It is that principle alone which renders our experience useful to us, and makes us expect, for the future, a similar train of events with those which have appeared in the past. Without the influence of custom, we should be entirely ignorant of every matter of fact beyond what is immediately present to the memory and senses. We should never know how to adjust means to ends, or to employ our natural powers in the production of any effect. There would be an end at once of all action, as well as of the chief part of speculation.

[Hume, David. *Enquiries Concerning the Human Understanding and Concerning the Principles of Morals by David Hume.* 2nd ed. Edited by L. A. Selby-Bigge, M.A. Oxford: Clarendon, 1902. Available online. Online Library of Liberty. URL: http://oll.libertyfund.org/title/341/61956. Accessed June 28, 2011.]

Kant, Immanuel (1724–1804) *German philosopher who made what he called the Copernican revolution, arguing that objects conform to our knowledge, rather than knowledge conforming to objects; he believed that the mind structures experience according to certain categories, and therefore he advocated neither rationalism nor empiricism. Kant here relates the laws of nature to how the mind categorizes experience; he claims that experience is possible at all because the mind structures experience according to certain concepts ("categories"). So, for example, because the mind applies the concept of cause to experience, laws regarding causes are among the laws of nature. (We cannot experience nature without such laws.)*

We shall here . . . be simply concerned with experience, and the universal and *à priori* given conditions of its possibility, and thence determine Nature as the complete object of all possible experience. I think it will be understood, that I do not refer to the rules for the observation of a nature already given, which presuppose experience, or how through experience we can arrive at the laws of Nature, for these would not then be laws *à priori,* and would give no pure science of Nature; but how the conditions *à priori* of the possibility of experience are at the same time the sources from which all the universal laws of Nature must be derived.

We must first of all observe then, that, although all the judgments of experience are empirical, i.e., have their ground in the immediate perception of sense, yet on the other hand all empirical judgments are not judgments of experience, but that beyond the empirical, and beyond the given sensuous intuition generally, special conceptions must be superadded, having their origin entirely *à priori* in the pure understanding, under which every perception is primarily subsumed, and by means of which only it can be transformed into experience.

[Kant, Immanuel. "The Second Part of the Main Transcendental Problem. How Is Pure Science Possible." In *Kant's Prolegomena and Metaphysical Foundations of Natural Science*. 2nd rev. ed. Translated and with a biography and introduction by Ernest Belfort Bax. London: George Bell and Sons, 1891. Available online. Online Library of Liberty. URL: http://oll.libertyfund.org/title/361/54872. Accessed June 28, 2011.]

Locke, John (1632–1704) *British empiricist philosopher who believed there are no innate ideas and that all concepts are derived from experience. Below, Locke succinctly describes one of his main theses: that all knowledge is ultimately based on experience, in the sense that all materials for knowledge (all ideas) are derived from experience. By experience, Locke meant experience not only of the empirical world but also experience of the workings of one's own mind.*

All ideas come from sensation or reflection. Let us then suppose the mind to be, as we say, white paper, void of *all* characters, without any *ideas;* how *comes* it to be furnished? Whence *comes* it by that vast store which the busy and boundless fancy of man has painted on it, with an almost endless variety? Whence has it *all* the materials of reason and knowledge? To this I answer, in one word, *from* experience; in *all* that our knowledge is founded, and *from* that it ultimately derives itself. Our observation employed either about external sensible objects, or about the internal operations of our minds, perceived and reflected on by ourselves, is that which supplies our understandings with *all* the materials of thinking. These two are the fountains of knowledge, *from* whence *all* the *ideas* we have, or can natur*all*y have, do spring.

[Locke, John. "Of Ideas in General, and Their Original." In *The Works of John Locke in Nine Volumes.* 12th ed. Vol. 1. London: Rivington, 1824. Available online. Online Library of Liberty. URL: http://oll.libertyfund.org/title/761/80718/1923200. Accessed June 28, 2011.]

Moore, G. E. (1873–1958) *British philosopher who defended a commonsense view against skepticism, arguing that there are many propositions of commonsense that everyone understands and knows to be true. In the passage below, Moore gives his famous proof of the existence of an external world (a world outside ourselves).*

It seems to me that, so far from its being true . . . that there is only one possible proof of the existence of the things outside of us . . . I can now give a large number of different proofs, each of which is a perfectly rigorous proof . . . I can prove now, for instance, that two human hands exist. How? By holding up my two hands, and saying, as I make a certain gesture with the right hand, "Here is one hand," and adding, as I make a certain gesture with the left, "and here is another."

[Moore, G. E. "Proof of an External World." In *Contemporary Analytic and Linguistic Philosophies*, edited by E. D. Klemke, 98. Amherst, N.Y.: Prometheus Books, 1983.]

Plato (ca. 428–348 B.C.E.) *Ancient Greek philosopher who distinguished between opinion and true knowledge, epistcmc; he thought that true knowledge applied only to concepts called Ideas, not the physical objects of ordinary experience. In the passage below from Plato's* Republic, *Socrates and Glaucon discuss higher Ideas, especially the Idea of the Good, as the objects of true knowledge and that which make all knowledge possible.*

Why, you know, I said, that the eyes, when a person directs them towards objects on which the light of day is no longer shining, but the moon and stars only, see dimly, and are nearly blind; they seem to have no clearness of vision in them?

Very true.

Visible objects are to be seen only when the sun shines upon them; truth is only known when illuminated by the idea of good.

But when they are directed towards objects on which the sun shines, they see clearly and there is sight in them?

Certainly.

And the soul is like the eye: when resting upon that on which truth and being shine, the soul perceives and understands, and is radiant with intelligence; but when turned towards the twilight of becoming and perishing, then she has opinion only, and goes blinking about, and is first of one opinion and then of another, and seems to have no intelligence?

Now, that which imparts truth to the known and the power of knowing to the knower is what I would have you term the idea of good, and this you will deem to be the cause of science, and of truth in so far as the latter becomes the subject of knowledge; beautiful too, as are both truth and knowledge, you will be right in esteeming this other nature as more beautiful than either . . . good may be said to be not only the author of knowledge to all things known, but of their being and essence, and yet the good is not essence, but far exceeds essence in dignity and power.

[Plato. *The Dialogues of Plato translated into English with Analyses and Introductions by B. Jowett, M.A. in Five Volumes.* 3rd ed revised and corrected. Oxford: Oxford University Press, 1892. Available online. Online Library of Liberty. URL: http://oll.libertyfund.org/title/767/93812. Accessed June 28, 2011.]

Pyrrho (ca. 365–270 B.C.E.)   *Ancient Greek philosopher said to have founded Pyrrhonic skepticism, which did not claim that knowledge was impossible but emphasized the suspension of belief in the face of conflicting evidence for the purpose of achieving inner tranquility. There are no writings by Pyrrho; below, Sextus Empiricus describes the goal of Pyrrhonian skepticism.*

We assert . . . that the Skeptic's end is quietude in respect of matters of opinion . . . For the Skeptic, having set out to philosophize with the object of passing judgment on the sense-impressions and ascertaining which of them are true and which false, so as to attain quietude thereby, found himself involved in contradictions of equal weight, and being unable to decide between them, suspend judgment . . .

[Empiricus, Sextus. *Outlines of Pyrrhonism: Sextus Empiricus.* Translated by R. G. Bury. Buffalo, N.Y.: Prometheus Books, p. 23.]

Quine, Willard Van Orman (1908–2000) *Influential American philosopher who defended a form of coherentism about the justification of beliefs, describing a set of beliefs as forming a web, with no individual belief or set of beliefs providing a foundation for all the rest. Here Quine, with coauthor J. S. Ullian, argues that it is best to evaluate the merits of beliefs not individually but instead in the context of other beliefs that one holds; beliefs should somehow fit together as a whole.*

Often in assessing beliefs we do best to assess several in combination. A very accomplished mechanic might be able to tell us something about an automobile's engine by examining its parts one by one, each in complete isolation from the others, but it would surely serve his purpose better to see the engine as a whole with all the parts functioning together. So with what we believe. It is in the light of the full body of our beliefs that candidates gain acceptance or rejection; any independent merits of a candidate tend to be less decisive.

[Quine, Willard Van Orman, and J. S. Ullian. *The Web of Belief*. New York: Random House, 1970, p. 16.]

Russell, Bertrand (1872–1970) *British philosopher who distinguished knowledge by acquaintance and knowledge by description, arguing that knowledge by description is ultimately based on knowledge by acquaintance. In this passage from* The Problems of Philosophy, *Russell comments on the value of knowledge by description, while affirming that we know only truths that are based on acquaintance (direct awareness).*

The chief importance of knowledge by description is that it enables us to pass beyond the limits of our private experience. In spite of the fact that we can only know truths which are wholly composed of terms which we have experienced in acquaintance, we can yet have knowledge by description of things which we have never experienced. In view of the very narrow range of our immediate experience, this result is vital, and until it is understood, much of our knowledge must remain mysterious and therefore doubtful.

[Russell, Bertrand. *The Problems of Philosophy*. Oxford: Oxford University Press, 1912, p. 59.]

Wittgenstein, Ludwig (1889–1951) *Austrian philosopher who argued that claims about what one knows make sense only where what is claimed is genuinely in question. In this passage from* On Certainty, *Wittgenstein illustrates the use and misuse of claims about what one knows by pointing out that it would be nonsensical for someone who is obviously sitting with a sick man he believes to be sick to claim "I know that a sick man is lying there."*

I know that a sick man is lying there? Nonsense! I am sitting at his bedside, I am looking attentively into his face.—So I don't know, then, that there is a sick man lying here? Neither the question nor the assertion makes sense. Any more than the assertion "I am here," which I might yet use at any moment, if suitable occasion presented itself . . . "I know that there's a sick man lying here," used in an unsuitable situation, seems not be nonsense . . . only because one can fairly easily imagine a situation to fit . . .

[Wittgenstein, Ludwig. *On Certainty.* Edited by G. E. M. Anscombe and G. H. von Wright. Translated by Denis Paul and G. E. M. Anscombe. New York: Harper Torchbooks, 1969, p. 3E.]

PART II

Logic

Introductory Discussion Questions

1. Is the sentence "This sentence is false" true or false?
2. If a man with a full head of hair lost one hair every minute, at what point would you say that he is bald? Is that point at which he becomes bald arbitrary?
3. Do numbers exist? Is so, where are they? If not, how can mathematics apply to the world?
4. Is the sentence "Every boy loves some girl" ambiguous (that is, has more than one clear meaning)? If so, what are the meanings?
5. Is there a difference between saying "Snow is white" and saying "Snow is white is true"? If so, what is the difference? If not, why not?
6. For any given sentence, must it be either true or false (even if we do not know which)?

Logic: The Structure of Reason

Logic is often defined as the study of correct reasoning. One aspect of this definition is that logic is concerned not merely with describing how in fact people reason; rather, the emphasis is on *correct* reasoning, according to specific criteria and standards. Sometimes logic is defined as the criteria and standards of the analysis and evaluation of arguments. In this sense, an argument is not a heated debate or discussion; instead, it is a collection of sentences, one of which (the conclusion) is said to follow from the others (the premises). In this definition, the focus is less on people's reasoning, and the inferences that they make, and more on arguments themselves. Yet another definition of logic is that it is the study of the laws of implication. This is related to the notion of arguments, rather than reasoning, in the sense that inferences are a matter of people's thinking, while implications are a matter of sentences that are entailed by other sentences, whether or not people actually make related inferences about those implications. This last definition is the one that most logicians use, and it relates logic directly to some areas of mathematics, such as set theory and Boolean algebra.

The broad study of logic is usually divided into two branches: deduction and induction. From the writings of Aristotle, which are often seen as the first systematic treatment of logic in the West, up to the beginning of the 20th century, most logicians understood the distinction between deduction and induction as this: For deduction, there is a movement from general premises to a more particular conclusion, while, for induction, there is a movement from particular premises to a more general conclusion. For example, the argument

"Since all humans are mortal and Socrates is human, therefore Socrates is mortal" was said to be deductive because it moves from premises about all humans to a conclusion about one human. On the other hand, the argument "Most (or every) piece of metal that has been tested has conducted electricity, therefore all pieces of metal conduct electricity" was said to be inductive because it moves from particular premises about particular cases of tested metal to a more general conclusion about all metal. Today, however, most logicians do not characterize the difference between deduction and induction in this way. For one reason, there are arguments and implications that do not move from general to particular or from particular to general. For instance, the argument "Since all dogs are mammals, therefore all non-mammals are not dogs" has a general premise and an equally general conclusion (but it still shows deductive validity). Another reason that logicians today do not characterize deduction and induction in the traditional way is because deduction and induction are now seen as criteria for evaluating arguments and implications, not as types of arguments. Today, logicians speak of deduction as argument forms in which the conclusion must follow from the premises and induction as argument forms in which the conclusion probably follows from the premises or in which the conclusion is made more probable, given the premises.

Besides the distinction between deduction and induction, logicians distinguish between propositional logic and predicate (or quantificational) logic. Propositional logic investigates the relationships between sentences and takes whole sentences as the basic unit of the investigations. Propositional logic is sometimes also called truth-functional logic. This simply means that the truth (or falsity) of complex sentences is determined by—or is a function of—the truth (or falsity) of the simple sentences that make up that complex sentence. For instance, "Today is Friday" is a simple sentence and is either true or false, depending upon when it is said. Likewise, the sentence "Today is cloudy" is a simple sentence and is either true or false, depending upon the weather conditions. However, the sentence "Today is Friday and cloudy" is a complex sentence that is made up of two simpler sentences: "Today is Friday" and "Today is cloudy." The truth of the complex sentence is said to be a function of the truth of the two simpler sentences that make up that complex sentence. So, "Today is Friday and cloudy" is true only when the two simpler sentences are themselves true at the same time.

Within propositional (or truth-functional) logic, complex sentences are composed of simpler sentences plus some logical connective. A connective is a word or phrase that connects simpler sentences to form a complex sentence. In the example "Today is Friday and cloudy," the connective was the word *and*. This word connected the two simpler sentences ("Today is Friday," "Today is cloudy") into one, complex sentence. Given these connectives and the forms of simple sentences, truth tables can be constructed to display the relationships between sentences and also whether or not a propositional logic argument is valid.

While propositional logic takes whole sentences as the basic unit of study, predicate logic looks at the relationships of sentences by focusing on meaningful units within sentences. The simplest forms of such sentences are called categorical statements, and they are usually treated in the context of syllogisms (argument forms analyzed by Aristotle). Predicate logic is also called quantificational because a primary emphasis is on the notion of quantifiers. A quantifier is basically a word or phrase that is used to refer to all or part of some class of things. For example, in the sentence "All whales are mammals," the entire class of whales is referred to, and the word *all* in this context represents a universal quantifier. In the sentence "Some whales are mammals," the word *some* refers to part of the class of whales and represents a particular (or existential) quantifier. Besides quantifiers, there are other relevant meaningful units within sentences that are important to quantificational logic. These other units are predicates and names. Predicates are words or phrases that refer to qualities or relations of things, such as *sleeps, is tall, enjoys, is north of*, etc. These are words or phrases that in everyday contexts we use to talk about things (such as, "My uncle enjoys chocolate"). Names refer either to specific individuals (such as Albert Einstein) or variables, meaning individuals, but not any specific ones (such as, "Somebody enjoys chocolate"). Where propositional logic would treat the sentence "Albert Einstein was a great physicist" as a single, simple unit, predicate logic would treat this same sentence not as being simple but as containing a quantifier, a name, and a predicate. Predicate logic is said to be a more powerful logical system than propositional logic because it can analyze and evaluate not only whole sentences but also arguments that propositional logic cannot. Most standard logic textbooks demonstrate how.

As noted above, logic is concerned with analyzing and evaluating arguments. There are two primary ways that arguments are evaluated as being good or bad: validity and cogency (or soundness). Validity has to do with the form or structure of arguments, while cogency (or soundness) has to do with the content of arguments, specifically whether or not the sentences in them are true. The difference between form and content is similar to evaluating whether a given sentence is meaningful or not. A sentence might be meaningless (and, so, a bad sentence) because it is ungrammatical. For instance, the sentence "Lead roads to all Rome" is gibberish: It makes no sense grammatically; its form is bad. On the other hand, the sentence "All roads lead to Rome" makes sense grammatically, even though the content is false. Likewise, when it comes to analyzing and evaluating arguments, logic is concerned with the form of arguments—their validity—and with the content of arguments—their cogency, or soundness.

Different philosophers have different views about the importance of logic. Some, such as Bertrand Russell, claim that logic is the essence of philosophy, because it focuses on forms and structures. By doing this, logic allows us and even encourages us to look beyond the immediate, particular things of everyday experience to see underlying essences and commonalities of things. It also encourages us to examine implications of sentences and the beliefs that are expressed by sentences. Logic, and the study of logic, these philosophers say, promotes critical thinking and clarity of thought and expression. It helps us to analyze and evaluate our own thoughts and beliefs as well as those of others. Through such analysis and evaluation, we are led to clearer and better thinking, and from this we are led to clearer and better actions. Other philosophers, such as Søren Kierkegaard, thought that logic is harmful because it focuses on forms and structures. It makes us cold and calculating and moves our attention away from the lived and living particulars of our lives, as well as away from the specific contexts and situations in which we find ourselves. Far from leading to clearer and better actions, these philosophers say, logic and the study of logic emphasize validity and truth over other values, such as care for and connection with others.

Argument

In philosophy, an argument refers not to a heated discussion but to a collection of sentences that are related to each other in such a way that one of those sentences, called the conclusion, is said to follow from the others, called the premises. It is this relationship among the sentences that make them an argument; otherwise, they are simply a collection of sentences. The focus is not on whether or not the conclusion is true, although having a true conclusion is important. Instead, the focus is on whether the conclusion follows from, or is sufficiently supported by, the premises. That is, in the context of an argument, what matters is whether or not the conclusion should be accepted because of, or on the basis of, the premises.

Arguments are collections of related sentences, but not just any sentences. The sentences in an argument must be sentences that are either true or false. The philosophical phrase is to say that an argument's sentences must have a truth-value. This simply means that the sentences can be either true or false, even if we do not know which they are. For instance, "More boys than girls were born in Italy during the year 1250" is either true or false, although we might not know whether it is true or false. So, it has a truth-value (that is, it is either true or false), even if we do not know its specific truth-value. On the other hand, some sentences do not have a truth-value; they are neither true nor false. For example, questions or commands are neither true nor false. If someone asks, "Did you shut the door?" this question is not true or false, although the answer to it is. Likewise, if someone orders, "Shut the door!" that command is neither true nor false. So, arguments contain sentences that have truth-value and are related in such a way that the conclusion is said to follow from the premises.

In everyday speaking, there are words or phrases that indicate which of the sentences in an argument are the premises and the conclusion. These are often called indicator words, because they indicate that the sentence is a premise or a conclusion. For premises, common indicator words are *because, since, assuming that, given that, inasmuch as,* and (sometimes) *for.* With respect to conclusions, common indicator words are *therefore, so, thus, hence, consequently, in conclusion, accordingly,* and *as a result.* Often, even without these indicator words, context will make it clear what the conclusion is and what the premises are.

One distinction to make with respect to arguments is between inference and implication. An inference is a mental or cognitive act made by people (and perhaps other animals). For instance, if someone hears scratching at a door, that person might infer that there is an animal trying to get inside. This is a case of making some cognitive leap based upon some information or evidence. An implication, on the other hand, is not mental or cognitive but is a relationship contained in the information itself. For instance, the sentence "The mayor vetoed yet another bill" contains the implication that the mayor has vetoed at least one other bill in the past. The words *yet another* contain an implication in them, whether or not someone makes an inference based on that information. Technically speaking, then, the relationship between the premises and conclusion in an argument is one of implication, not one of inference. That is, the conclusion might follow from the premises in an argument, which is to say that the conclusion might be implied, whether or not someone made the inference that the conclusion followed (or was implied). However, even common usage within philosophy sometimes blurs this distinction between inference and implication.

There are two broad criteria for evaluating arguments, that is, for determining whether an argument is good or bad (whether the conclusion follows from the premises). Those two criteria are (1) whether the form, or structure, of the argument is good, and (2) whether the sentences in the argument are true. The first criterion focuses on structure, and the second criterion focuses on content. This is analogous to language being meaningful or not; one criterion is whether the grammar is appropriate, and a second criterion is whether the language makes sense. For example, the sentence "Pink carnations sneeze boringly" makes no sense, but the grammar is fine. On the other hand, the sentence "Sneeze pink boringly carnations" is not even grammatically correct. So, with respect to meaningful language, both form and content matter. The same holds for arguments: Both form and content matter.

The forms of arguments are evaluated on the basis of deduction and induction. If the form of an argument meets the criteria of deduction, the argument is said to be deductively valid and if not, it is said to be deductively invalid. If the form of an argument does not meet the criteria for deduction but does meet the criteria for induction, the argument is said to be inductively strong, and if not, it is said to be inductively weak. The most basic sense of the difference between deduction and induction is that for deduction the conclusion is said to follow necessarily from the premises, while for induction the conclusion is said to follow probably from the premises.

Besides an argument just having good form, another important aspect is for it to have good content, which just means having sentences that are true. When the form is deductively valid and the content of the sentences are true, an argument is said to be sound. When the form is inductively strong and the content of the sentences is true, an argument is said to be cogent.

Aristotle and the Beginnings of Logic

Syllogism

The term *syllogism* comes from the Greek word *logos,* meaning "word," and the Greek prefix *syl,* meaning "together." A syllogism is a basic form of argument, and the formal study of syllogisms is most often traced back to the writings of Aristotle (384–322 B.C.E.). The study of syllogisms was treated as the full subject of logic from Aristotle's time up to the end of the 19th century, when it was fit into a larger discipline and seen as being correct, but limited in scope.

Syllogisms are based on a subject/predicate view of language. This view holds that sentences contain a subject and something that is said about that subject (that is, a predicate). For instance, in the sentence "Whales are mammals," the word *whales* is the subject, and the word *mammals* is the predicate. Some sentences do not have a subject/predicate form, and therefore, they are not treated within the study of syllogisms. For instance, the command "Shut the door!" does not have a predicate that says something about a subject. Although there might be an implied subject in this case (namely, whoever is being commanded), there is still nothing being said about that subject.

The technical term for sentences that fall within the study of syllogisms is *categorical propositions.* This means that they are sentences that can be either true or false; they supposedly describe the world. Any sen-

Statue of Aristotle at the University of Freiburg im Breisgau in Germany *(Sculpture by Cipri Adolf Bermann; photograph by Michael Schmalenstroer)*

tence that can be either true or false is said to have a truth-value, where the value is either true or false. For example, the sentence "Whales are mammals" supposedly states a fact, and it does, so its truth-value is "true." The sentence "Whales are dogs" also has the form of stating a fact, but in this case the sentence is false, and its truth-value is "false." However, the sentence "Shut the door" cannot be either true or false; it has no truth-value.

Every categorical proposition has four components. One component is the subject, and another is the predicate. These two components each refer to some class of things. For example, in the sentence "Whales are mammals," the subject refers to the class of whales, and the predicate to the class of mammals. The other two components of categorical propositions are the quantifier and the copula. The quantifier is simply some word or phrase that modifies the subject and indicates whether the subject refers to its entire class of things or just part of that class. For example, in the sentence "All cows have lungs," the word *all* is the quantifier, and it indicates that the subject refers in this case to the entire class of cows. On the other hand, in the sentence "Some fish have lungs," the word *some* is the quantifier, and it indicates that the subject refers only to part of the entire class of fish. For the sake of convenience, quantifiers are said to be either universal, meaning that the subject term refers to its entire class of things, or particular, meaning that the subject term refers to only part of its class of things Finally, the copula is simply some form of the verb to be. A copula is said to be either affirmative, meaning that the predicate does apply to the subject, or negative, meaning that the predicate does not apply to the subject. For instance, "Whales are mammals" contains an affirmative copula, but "Some dogs are not black" contains a negative copula.

Given the four components of any categorical proposition (namely, the quantifier, subject, copula, and predicate), there are four basic forms of categorical proposition that are possible. These forms are: (1) universal affirmative, or any sentence of the form "All A are B," (2) universal negative, or any sentence of the form "All A are not B" (which is also sometimes written as "No A are B") (3) particular affirmative, or any sentence of the form "Some A are B," and (4) particular negative, or any sentence of the form "Some A are not B."

Syllogisms are argument patterns that contain only categorical propositions. Standard form syllogisms contain exactly three categorical propositions. Those three categorical propositions are two premises and a conclusion. A premise is the evidence or warrant that is said to support the conclusion, and the conclusion of a syllogism is said to follow from the premises. For example, in the syllogism "All humans are mortal" and "Socrates is human," therefore "Socrates is mortal," the first two sentences are the premises, and the third sentence is the conclusion. Every standard form syllogism contains exactly two premises and a conclusion.

Each of the three sentences in a syllogism is a categorical proposition, and each categorical proposition can be one of four possible forms. For example, one syllogism might be of this pattern: All A are B, all B are C, therefore all A are C. Another syllogism might be: All A are B, no B are C, therefore all A are C. Yet another syllogism might be: Some A are not B, all B are C, therefore some A are C. As a result, there are 64 different patterns of syllogisms that result from various combinations of categorical propositions. Finally, for each of these patterns, there are four different ways that the two premises can be constructed. For instance, the sentence "All A are B" is a universal affirmative form, and the sentence "All B are A" is also a universal affirmative form, but they are different sentences. Because each of the 64 different patterns of syllogisms can be put into four different combinations, there turns out to be 256 possible syllogisms. Syllogistic logic is the analysis of which of those 256 possible syllogisms are in fact valid, which is to say which of those syllogisms have a conclusion that actually follows from the premises.

Immediate Inferences

Some immediate inferences result from switching the subject and predicate terms within a given sentence. There are three types of immediate inferences that philosophers speak of: conversion, obversion, and contraposition. In a conversion, the subject and predicate terms in a sentence are directly switched. For example, "All cats are mammals," when converted, becomes "All mammals are cats." The converted sentence is called the converse of the original sentence. Some conversions are good inferences; that is, the converse of some sentences result in true sentences, while other conversions are not good inferences; they result in false sentences. In the example just given—"All cats are mammals"—its converse ("All mammals are cats") turns out to be false. However, in the sentence "Some cats are black," its converse—namely, "Some black things are cats"—is true.

An obversion is basically a double negative. For example, for the sentence "All cats are mammals," its obverse is "All cats are not non-mammals." In an obversion, the copula changes (an affirmative becomes a negative or a negative becomes an affirmative) and the predicate is reversed. That is to say, the predicate refers to the opposite of what it originally referred to; for example, if the original predicate is mammals, then the obverse predicate is non-mammals.

Finally, a contraposition involves both conversion and obversion together. For example, the sentence "All cats are mammals" has as its contrapositive in the sentence "All non-mammals are non-cats." For contraposition, not only are the subject and predicate terms switched, but also they are replaced by their opposites.

The value of these three immediate inferences is that they help to reveal some common inferences that people make, and often those inferences are mistaken. For instance, it is not uncommon that stereotypes and guilt by association occur because people make inferences about conversions. For example, if one begins with the sentence "Most Arabs are Muslims" which is true, one ends up with a converse, namely, "Most Muslims are Arabs," which is false. Most of the world's Muslims are not Arabs, but many people make this error of conversion.

Enthymemes/Sorites

Enthymemes and sorites are forms of syllogisms. A standard form syllogism is an argument pattern that contains exactly three sentences: two premises and a conclusion. In addition, in a standard form syllogism, there are exactly three class terms (that is, three words or phrases that refer to classes of things), with each class term occurring twice within the syllogism. For example, in the syllogism, "All humans are mortal," "Socrates is human," therefore "Socrates is mortal," there are three sentences, the first two being premises and the third being the conclusion. There are three class terms: *human, Socrates* (a class of one thing), and *mortal* beings, each occurring twice within this syllogism.

An enthymeme is a syllogism in which at least one of the sentences is missing or not stated explicitly. An example of an enthymeme is: "This banana is not ripe, because it is green." In this case, the conclusion is "This banana is not ripe." There is one premise offered in support of this conclusion, namely, "It [this banana] is green." However, another premise is assumed here, "No green bananas are ripe." Another example of an enthymeme is: "All metals are heat conductors, so no metals are insulators." In this example, the conclusion is "No metals are insulators" and the premise that is stated is "All metals are heat conductors." The missing, or implicit, premise is "No heat conductors are insulators." The two examples of enthymemes just given are ones in which a premise is missing, or implicit, but some enthymemes provide the premises and omit the conclusion. For instance, in the following enthymeme the conclusion is not stated: "Switch hitters are hard to pitch to, and some batters are switch hitters." What is missing is the conclusion that therefore "Some batters are hard to pitch to." An enthymeme, then, is a syllogism in which at least one sentence is not explicitly stated.

A sorites is an argument that combines at least two enthymemes. Lewis Carroll, the author of *Alice in Wonderland,* was known for constructing sorites as games for children and students. One example is: "Babies are illogical," "Nobody is despised who can manage a crocodile," "Illogical persons are despised," therefore "Babies cannot manage crocodiles." In this example, the first enthymeme is: "Babies are illogical" and "Illogical persons are despised," with the missing conclusion that "Babies are despised." Using that missing conclusion and combining it with the remaining premise ("Nobody is despised who can manage a crocodile") leads to the final conclusion, namely, "Babies cannot manage crocodiles." As with enthymemes, some sorites provide all of the premises and omit the final conclusion, as in this example—"All puddings are nice," "This dish is a pudding," and "No nice things are wholesome." The final conclusion is missing, namely, "This dish is not wholesome." A sorites, then, is a single argument that contains two or more enthymemes.

Venn Diagrams

In the late 1800s, the British logician John Venn (1834–1923) developed a way to visually portray syllogistic information. What he developed has come to be known as a Venn diagram. In particular, these diagrams portray information about the relationship between two classes of things. For example, the sentence "All spiders are poisonous" contains two class terms—namely, *spiders* and *poisonous*—that refer to classes of things, the class of spiders and the class of poisonous things. A Venn diagram can portray the information in this sentence in this way:

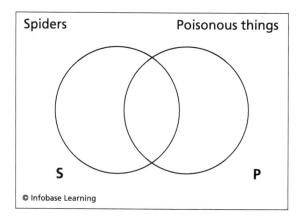

Each circle represents a class of things. In this case, the circle on the left represents the class of spiders, and the circle on the right represents the class of poisonous things. There are four possible relationships between these two classes: (1) all spiders are poisonous, (2) no spiders are poisonous, (3) some spiders are poisonous, and (4) some spiders are not poisonous. Those four possible relationships can be visually represented in the following ways:

(1) All spiders are poisonous (the area that is shaded represents spiders that are outside of the class of poisonous things; this diagram indicates, by the shading, that there are no spiders outside of the class of poisonous things; in other words, all spiders are poisonous).

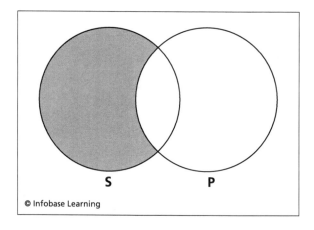

(2) No spiders are poisonous (the area that is shaded represents spiders that are inside of the class of poisonous things; this diagram indicates, by the shading, that there are no spiders inside the class of poisonous things; in other words, no spiders are poisonous).

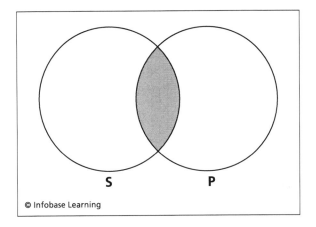

(3) Some spiders are poisonous (the area with an X represents that there is at least one individual thing in that area; this diagram indicates that there is at least one thing that is inside the class of spiders and is also inside the class of poisonous things; in other words, some spiders are poisonous).

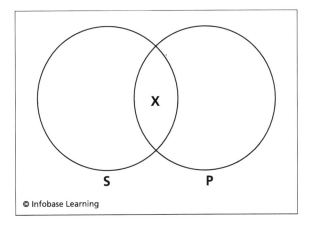

(4) Some spiders are not poisonous (the area with an X represents that there is at least one individual thing in that area; this diagram indicates that there is at least one thing that is inside the class of spiders and is also outside the class of poisonous things; in other words, some spiders are not poisonous).

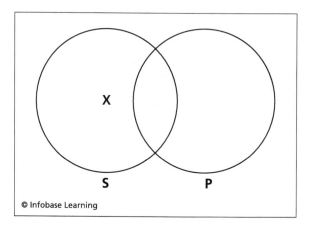

© Infobase Learning

Venn diagrams can be used to display information involving more than two classes. Within syllogisms, they are used to display whether or not a syllogism is valid or invalid. For example, the following Venn diagram portrays this syllogism: All spiders are meat-eaters, and no meat-eaters are poisonous; therefore, no spiders are poisonous.

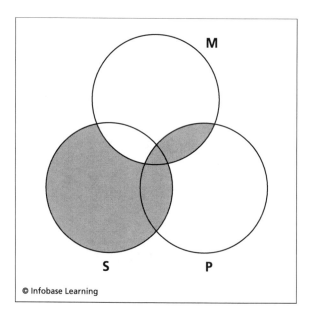

© Infobase Learning

This diagram shows that no things that are spiders are inside of the class of things that are poisonous, and the syllogism is valid.

Deduction

The study of logic is usually divided into two areas: deduction and induction. Traditionally, this distinction was based on two ways of making inferences. One way was said to argue from general premises to a particular conclusion. The following example was often used to illustrate this: "All humans are mortal; Socrates is human; therefore, Socrates is mortal." The inference begins with some general claim or information about all humans and moves on to a more particular claim or information in the conclusion, namely, about one human, Socrates. Induction, on the other hand, was said to argue in the opposite direction, that is, from particular claims or information to some more general conclusion. For example, "Emerald #1 is green; emerald #2 is green; . . . ; emerald #n is green; therefore, all (or most) emeralds are green." In this case, the inference begins with particular claims or information about specific emeralds and moves on to a more general claim or information about all (or most) emeralds.

However, philosophers no longer speak of deduction and induction in this way. One reason is because there are many arguments and inferences that do not show a movement from general claims or information to particular claims or information (or the reverse). For example, "All cats are mammals; therefore, all non-mammals are not cats." In this case, all of the claims or information are equally general, so there is no movement from general to particular (or the reverse). With the traditional view, this argument would be neither deductive nor inductive.

The second reason that philosophers no longer speak of deduction and induction in the traditional way is because they now view deduction and induction not as different *types* of arguments but as different criteria or ways of *evaluating* arguments. So, it is no longer said that a given argument is deductive or inductive, but instead that a given argument satisfies deductive criteria or inductive criteria for being a good or bad argument.

A third reason that philosophers no longer speak of deduction or induction in the traditional way is because they now say that the standard for an argument being good involves the form, or structure, of the argument and not the content of the argument, so, again, what matters is not making an inference from general claims or information to particular claims or information (or the reverse).

Today, philosophers speak of deduction as shorthand for deductive validity. The standard for an argument to be deductively valid is that it is truth-preserving. All this means is that an argument has the kind of form, or structure, such that *if* the premises are true, *then* the conclusion must be true. This is called truth-preserving in the sense that the truth that is contained in the premises is preserved in the inference to the conclusion, or, in other words, the truth in the premises did not lead to a false conclusion. If an argument does have a form, or structure, that moves from true premises to a false conclusion, then the argument is said to be deductively invalid. (To reemphasize, a deductively invalid argument does not mean that the argument is no longer a deductive one; deduction and induction are not types of arguments, rather they are criteria for evaluating arguments.)

An important point to remember is that whether or not a given argument is deductively valid has to do with its form, or structure, not its content. Again, the definition for deductive validity is if the premises are true, then the conclusion must be true. For example, the following argument is deductively valid: "All mammals are warm-blooded; all dogs are mammals; therefore, all dogs are warm-blooded." What makes this argument valid is not the specific content of it (mammals and dogs and warm-blooded things). It is the form, or structure, that matters. The form that this argument has is: All A are B; all B are C; therefore, all A are C. It is the form, or structure, that is valid (or truth-preserving), regardless of the content. The following argument has the same form, even though the sentences in the argument are false: "All mammals are dogs; all rocks are mammals; therefore, all rocks are dogs." In this case, the sentences are all false, but *if* the premises were true, *then* the conclusion would be true. That is, if it were the case—even though it is not—that all mammals were dogs and all rocks were mammals, then it would be the case that all rocks were dogs.

With respect to an argument being deductively valid or invalid, what is important is that its validity (or invalidity) is a matter of the relationship between the premises and the conclusion. The specific sentences themselves do not need to be true, but their relationship needs to be one such that the conclusion follows from the premises. If it does, then the argument is deductively valid; otherwise it is deductively invalid.

Just having a collection of sentences is not necessarily the same thing as having an argument. For instance, the following sentences do not count as an argument: "George Washington was the first U.S. president"; "John Adams was the second U.S. president"; "Thomas Jefferson was the third U.S. president"; "James Madison was the fourth U.S. president." This is just a collection of sentences, not an argument, because there is no conclusion and no premises; none of the sentences is said to follow from the others in the sense that the others are offered as evidence for a conclusion. In addition, even in an argument, simply having a collection of true sentences does not guarantee that the argument is deductively valid. For example, the following argument has all true sentences, but the premises are irrelevant to the conclusion: "George Washington was the first U.S. president"; "James Adams was the second U.S. president"; therefore, "Sacramento is the capital of California." What makes this argument deductively invalid is that it has a form that is not truth-preserving; the conclusion does not follow from the premises, even though the conclusion and the premises are true.

Induction

The study of logic is usually divided into two areas: deduction and induction. Traditionally, this distinction was based on two ways of making inferences. One way was said to argue from general premises to a particular conclusion. The following example was often used to illustrate this: "All humans are mortal; Socrates is human; therefore, Socrates is mortal." The inference begins with some general claim or information about all humans and moves on to a more particular claim or information in the conclusion, namely, about one human, Socrates. Induction, on the other hand, was said to argue in the opposite direction, that is, from particular claims or information to some more general conclusion. For example, "Emerald #1 is green; emerald #2 is green; . . . ; emerald #n is green; therefore, all (or most) emeralds are green." In this case, the inference begins with particular claims or information about specific emeralds and moves on to a more general claim or information about all (or most) emeralds.

Philosophers today do not distinguish between deduction and induction in this way. In part, this is because they now speak of deduction and induction not as different types of arguments but rather as different criteria for evaluating arguments. The basic concern with evaluating any argument is whether or not the conclusion of the argument follows from the premises of the argument. That is, do the premises (the evidence or support for the conclusion) warrant the conclusion? Deductively speaking, the premises would need to guarantee that the conclusion follows in order for the argument to be considered good. Inductively speaking, the premises would need to make the conclusion more likely to be true in order for the argument to be considered good. The difference between deduction and induction, then, is basically the level of support that the premises of an argument provides for the conclusion of that argument. The formal, technical study of inductive logic is the field of probability and statistics.

Although induction is about criteria and standards of evaluating arguments, people continue to speak of various types or patterns of inductive arguments. One such pattern is called inductive generalization. This involves making an inference to some general claim on the basis of some examples or small sample. The following case is such an example: "A random sample of colleges across the nation revealed that most of the students were opposed to a death penalty. Thus, it is likely that most college students feel the same way." Here a somewhat general conclusion about most college students is drawn from evidence taken from a smaller random sample. A particular form of inductive generalization is called simple enumeration. In this kind of case, a somewhat general conclusion is drawn from specific examples provided by the premises. An example of this pattern is the emerald example given above.

Another similar argument is called statistical syllogism. In this pattern of argument, the premises are similar to those in inductive generalization and simple enumeration, but the conclusion is not a general claim. For example, the following is a statistical syllogism: "At a Republican committee meeting, the incumbent prosecuting attorney lost his party's endorsement and, so, considered running as an Independent candidate. His advisers, however, told him not to do this, because hardly any Independent candidate could receive enough votes to win an election in that district." In this pattern, the premises include some statistical information as well as a statement of a specific case; the conclusion that follows relates that specific case to the more general, statistical information.

Another common form of argument that is usually included as being inductive is called an argument by analogy. An analogy is a similarity or likeness between two (or more) things that are not identical. For example, a watermelon is analogous to a ball in the sense of being round; Kansas is like a pancake in the sense of being flat; some particular person is like a cat in the sense of being especially curious. In an argument by analogy, the premises claim that two (or more) things are analogous in various ways, and an inference is then made in the conclusion that, therefore, they are likely to be similar in some other particular way. An example of this pattern of argument is the following case: "Mr. Smith and Mr. Jones both have similar incomes; they both are middle-aged; they both have college degrees; they both live in the suburbs; so, it is likely that they both have the same political views and vote the same way." Many common sayings are arguments by analogy. For instance, the saying you cannot teach an old dog new tricks is really an argument by analogy suggesting that, just like old dogs, old people are unlikely to accept new views or attitudes or ways of doing things.

One area in philosophy where inductive reasoning is especially relevant is in analyzing and understanding evidence. Another area is in analyzing and understanding the concept of cause. In particular, with the issue of cause, various common inductive argument patterns were spelled out by John Stuart Mill and are referred to as Mill's methods.

Responses to Aristotelian Logic

Although the formal study of logic is usually associated with Aristotle and with syllogistic logic, there were other classical philosophers who studied logic. Prior to Aristotle, Euclides of Megara (a city in southeastern Greece), who lived from 430 to 360 B.C.E., was known for analyzing the validity of the arguments of other philosophers. People came to speak of Megarians as skilled in argumentation. One of Euclides' students, Eubulides (fourth century B.C.E.), was said to have developed various logical paradoxes, including the Liar Paradox and the Problem of the Heap (both discussed below). Even more, however, some later Stoic philosophers were renowned for advancing the formal study of logic. *Stoicism* comes from the Greek word *stoa,* meaning "porch." This term became associated with a particular school of philosophy because the philosopher Zeno of Citium (335–263 B.C.E.) delivered lectures in Athens at a public porch. The Stoic philosopher who was especially associated with logic was Chrysippus (280–207 B.C.E.). Chrysippus and other Stoic logicians focused on the logic of conditional sentences, that is, sentences with the form of if . . . , then. . . . What is important about this is that these are sentences of a very different form than sentences analyzed by Aristotle's syllogisms. Syllogisms focus on categorical sentences, that is, sentences of the form "All (or some) S is (or is not) P" (for instance, "All cats are mammals"). In categorical syllogisms, what is important is the relationship between classes of objects (such as cats and mammals), while in conditional sentences, what is important is the relationship between two complete sentences (such as, "I am late" and "I will miss the bus"). The Stoics, then, were investigating the logic of sentences that were outside the realm of syllogisms. In his investigations, Chrysippus formulated five basic valid forms, what he called "the five indemonstrables," meaning that they were basic and did not need to be demonstrated, or proven. These five were: (1) if the first, then the sec-

Sculpted head of Chrysippus, a Stoic logician from the late third century B.C.E. This was bequeathed to the British Museum by Richard Payne Knight.

ond, but the first, therefore the second; (2) if the first, then the second, but not the second, therefore not the first; (3) not both the first and the second, but the first, therefore not the second; (4) either the first or the second, but not the first, therefore the second; and (5) either the first or the second, but not the second, therefore the first. These five basic valid forms are still taught today.

Propositional and Predicate Logic

Logicians distinguish between propositional logic and predicate (or quantificational) logic. Propositional logic investigates the relationships between sentences and takes whole sentences as the basic unit of the investigations. Propositional logic is sometimes also called truth-functional logic. This simply means that the truth (or falsity) of complex sentences is determined by—or is a function of—the truth (or falsity) of the simple sentences that make up that complex sentence. For instance, "Today is Friday" is a simple sentence, and it is either true or false, depending upon when it is said. However, the sentence "Today is Friday and cloudy" is a complex sentence that is made up of two simpler sentences: "Today is Friday" and "Today is cloudy." The truth of the complex sentence is said to be a function of the truth of the two simpler sentences that make up that complex sentence. So, "Today is Friday and cloudy" is true only when the two simpler sentences are themselves true.

Within propositional (or truth-functional) logic, complex sentences are composed of simpler sentences plus some logical connective. A connective is a word or phrase that connects those simpler sentences to form a complex sentence. In the example above, "Today is Friday and cloudy," the connective was the word *and*. This word connected the two simpler sentences into one complex sentence. Given these connectives and the forms of simple sentences, truth tables can be constructed to display the relationships between sentences and also whether or not a propositional logic argument is valid.

While propositional logic takes whole sentences as the basic unit of study, predicate logic looks at the relationships of sentences by focusing on meaningful units within sentences. The simplest forms of such sentences are called categorical statements, and they are usually treated in the context of syllogisms. Predicate logic is also called quantificational because a primary emphasis is on the notion of quantifiers. A quantifier is basically a word or phrase that is used to refer to all or part of some class of things. For example, in the sentence "All whales are mammals," the entire class of whales is referred to, and the word *all* in this context represents a universal quantifier. In the sentence "Some whales are mammals," the word *some* refers to part of the class of whales and represents a particular (or existential) quantifier. Besides quantifiers, there are other relevant meaningful units within sentences that are important to quantificational logic. These other units are predicates and names. Predicates are words or phrases that refer to qualities or relations of things, such as *sleeps, is tall, enjoys, is north of,* etc. These are words or phrases that in everyday contexts we use to talk about things (such as "My uncle enjoys chocolate"). Names refer either to specific individuals (such as Albert Einstein) or variables, meaning individuals, but not any specific ones (such as "Somebody enjoys chocolate"). Where propositional logic would treat the sentence "Albert Einstein was a great physicist" as a single, simple unit, predicate logic would treat this same sentence not as being simple but as containing a quantifier, a name, and a predicate. Predicate logic is said to be a more powerful logical system than propositional logic because it can analyze and evaluate not only whole sentences but also arguments that propositional logic cannot.

Liar Paradox

Suppose someone says, "I am lying right now." Is that sentence true? There seems to be a paradox about this. On the one hand, if that sentence is true, then it says that what is being said is a lie. Since a lie implies that the content is false, it appears that if this sentence is true, then it is false. On the other hand, if this sentence is false, then it seems that the person is not lying but telling the truth. So, it appears that if this sentence is false, then it is true. Such a situation would indeed be a paradox, and it is often called the liar paradox.

The liar paradox has been referred to for centuries. There are various versions of this paradox. Besides the one above, another version is the following: A Cretan (that is, someone from Crete) says, "Cretans are always liars." Since it is a Cretan who is speaking, then, if the sentence is true, it means that the sentence is a lie. So, once again, if the sentence is true, then it is false, and vice versa.

Yet another version of the liar paradox is "This sentence is false." Again, if the sentence is true, then it says that it is false. However, if the sentence is false, then what it says must be wrong, namely, that it is false. As a result, it must be true.

All three of these versions of the paradox rely on the problem of being self-referential. This simply means that the paradox seems to arise because the sentence refers back to itself and ends up contradicting itself. There is another version of the paradox that is not directly self-referential. It involves two sentences:

(1) Sentence (2) is false.
(2) Sentence (1) is true.

In this version, neither sentence refers directly to itself, yet the result is the same: If either sentence is true, then it is false, and vice versa.

This paradox relates to some basic philosophical concepts, such as self-reference and truth. Philosophers have offered various resolutions to this paradox, but none has been universally accepted as having genuinely solved the paradox. For example, one proposed solution is that the sentence(s) in question are neither true nor false (the philosophical phrase is that there is a truth-value gap). However, philosophers generally have been reluctant to say that any sentence that (supposedly) describes some fact about the world would be neither true nor false. We might not know whether it is true or false, but we assume that it must be one or the other. Another proposed solution is to say that there are different levels of language, called object language and metalanguage. The object language is a language used to talk about the world, while a metalanguage is a language used to talk about the object language. For example, to say "Cats have four legs" is to use the object language and say something about cats. But to say "Cats has four letters" is to use the metalanguage to say something about the word *cats* and not to say something directly about cats (objects). So, some philosophers have suggested that the liar paradox is no paradox because the sentence in question is in the object language, while its truth or falsity is a matter of the metalanguage. That is, to say "This sentence is false" is a sentence in the object language, but to say "It is true that 'This sentence is false'" is a sentence in the metalanguage, so there is not a paradox. However, other philosophers reject this proposed solution, because they find the notion of levels of language to be artificial. The result is, again, that there is no universally accepted resolution to this paradox.

Problem of the Heap

The problem of the heap is a paradox in ancient Greek philosophy (sometimes called a sorites paradox). Suppose you have one grain of sand, and you add to this another grain of sand. Two grains of sand clearly do not count as a heap—there are just not enough of them. Adding just one grain of sand would not seem to make a difference. Neither would adding a fourth grain of sand to three grains, adding a fifth grain to four, or adding a sixth grain to five. In fact, it looks as if, at any point—no matter how many grains of sand there are—adding just one single grain of sand would not make the difference between whether there is a heap or not. The problem is this. On one hand, if adding just one grain of sand would not ever make a difference to whether there is a heap, then no matter how much sand one piles up, there would never be a heap. On the other hand, it seems clear that if you continue adding grains of sand to the grains of sand you already have, eventually there will be a heap. Each of these claims seems reasonable, yet they cannot both be true. That is, it cannot be true both that there would never be a heap and that eventually there would be a heap.

What the problem of the heap illustrates is vagueness. A term (a word or phrase) is considered vague if there are cases that it does not clearly apply to, but that the term does not clearly *not* apply to either. One example is the term *bald*. Some people—those who have no hair on their heads—are clearly bald. And some people—those with full heads of hair—are clearly not bald. But some people seem neither clearly bald nor clearly not bald. These are people who have some hair on their heads, but not so much that they are clearly not bald, yet not so little that they are clearly bald. Such people are borderline cases: They are at the borderline of where *bald* applies and where it does not. The term *heap* is also a vague term: There are some collections of sand that are clearly heaps (for instance, 8 million grains of sand in a tall pile), and there are some collections of sand that are clearly not heaps (such as two grains of sand grouped together). But there are also some collections of sand that are neither clearly heaps nor clearly not heaps. With vague terms, it is often said that there is no apparent sharp line between when the term applies and when it does not. One grain of sand does not seem to make a difference between something being a heap and not being a heap, and one hair does not seem to make a difference between someone being bald or clearly not bald. Especially recently there has been much philosophical discussion about the nature of vagueness and how to account for paradoxes such as the problem of the heap.

Medieval Logicians

During the Middle Ages, much of the focus on logic was in applying Aristotle's syllogisms to other philosophical concerns. The emphasis was on using syllogisms to argue for positions about other things, for example, to prove God's existence or whether there really existed universal objects rather than specific, particular objects (that is, whether there existed something corresponding to the essence of dogs as opposed to there existing only specific, particular dogs). Aristotelian logic was so entrenched in medieval academics that names were used to help remember which syllogistic forms were valid. For example, the name "Barbara" was used to refer to the following syllogistic form: "All M are P, all S are M; therefore, all S are P." Any sentence of the form "All X are Y" was said to be an "A" sentence, so this particular syllogistic form contained three "A" sentences. The three vowels in the name "Barbara" are all As, so "Barbara" was used as a simple way to remember that a syllogism of this form was valid. Another example was the name "Darii," which was used to refer to the following syllogistic form: "All M are P, some S are M; therefore, some S are P." Any sentence of the form "Some X are Y" was said to be an "I" sentence, so this particular syllogistic form contained an A sentence and two I sentences. The three vowels in the name "Darii" reveal this form. "Darii" represented a different form than the name "Dimaris" because the vowels in "Dimaris" are (in order): I, A, I, so the corresponding syllogistic form is: "Some M are P, all S are M; therefore, some S are P," which is different than the form represented by "Darii."

Not all work by medieval logicians, however, was merely a matter of applying Aristotle's syllogisms. One advance, in particular, was that of the work of William of Ockham (1280–1349), who investigated general principles of implication of sentences and also what is now called modal logic, that is, the logic of necessity and possibility. He formulated 11 general rules of logic. In some of these rules, he spoke of the antecedent and the consequent. These terms refer to the parts of conditional sentences. A conditional sentence has the form If . . . , then . . . (for example, "If I am late, then I will miss the bus"). The first part of the conditional is called the "antecedent," because it comes before the "then" clause, while the second part of the conditional is called the "consequent," because it follows the antecedent. So, in the example "If I am late, then I will miss the bus," the antecedent is "I am late," and the consequent is "I will miss the bus." Ockham's 11 rules were: (1) The false never follows from the true; (2) the true may follow from the false; (3) if an implication is valid, the negative of its antecedent follows from the negative of its consequent; (4) whatever follows from the consequent follows from the antecedent; (5) if the antecedent follows from any proposition, then the consequent follows from the same; (6) whatever is consistent with the antecedent is consistent with the consequent; (7) whatever is inconsistent with the consequent is inconsistent with the antecedent; (8) the contingent does not follow from the necessary; (9) the impossible does not follow from the possible; (10) anything whatsoever follows from the impossible; and (11) the necessary follows from anything whatsoever. In spite of work such as Ockham's, most philosophers today speak of medieval logic as emphasizing Aristotelian syllogisms and their application. In addition, the fundamental assumption was that deductive logical demonstration was needed to justify a claim to knowledge. This apparent total reliance on deductive justification was a major aspect of Aristotelian logic and science that came to be challenged beginning in the 1400s.

The European Renaissance and the Rise of Inductivism

Most historians speak of the European Renaissance as the time between the mid-1400s and the mid-1600s. It is also the time period that has been called the Scientific Revolution. This time included some of the most famous people in the history of science, such as Nicolas Copernicus (1473–1543), Johannes Kepler (1571–1630), and Galileo Galilei (1564–1642). During this time there were tremendous social and cultural changes. This was the period of the discovery of the New World (from the perspective of Europeans) and the rise of global exploration and colonialism. The influence and authority of the Catholic Church were questioned and challenged by the rise of nation-states in Europe and also by theologians such as Martin Luther (1483–1546). At the same time, new technologies were emerging, such as the printing press, that made information more accessible to more people.

With respect to science (at this time still called natural philosophy), there were a number of fundamental changes and developments. One change was the emergence of scientific societies, that is, groups of people who worked on similar issues. Prior to this time essentially all scientific investigation had taken place by independently wealthy individuals or by clergy (for instance, monks in monasteries), because they were the only people who were literate or had time and opportunity to carry out scientific work. With the emergence of scientific societies, there was a greater flow and cross-checking of scientific research.

Another change at this time was emergence of a mechanical view of the world. That is, more and more there came to be the view that the world was like an enormous, complex mechanism that operated by definite, precise causes and laws. As part of this mechanical picture of the world, the traditional Aristotelian view of final cause was, in large part, dropped. (Final cause was the notion that things must be explained in terms of some purpose or goal or end; things happen for a reason, for some potential goal to be realized.) Scientists began more and more to speak of proximate causes, meaning mechanical, physical causes that could be measured and tested, while setting aside ultimate causes, meaning purposes or goals or even God. Since only proximate causes could be measured and tested, they would be the focus of scientific inquiry and explanation. Along with this new focus on proximate causes, scientists placed more emphasis on inductive reasoning, that is, beginning with particular information and generalizing from that information as they gathered more information. This, they said, was how to read the book of nature rather than assuming that knowledge must be deduced from principles that were assumed to be true (which is what they claimed was the longstanding view derived from Aristotle). One of the most outspoken critics of the reliance on deductions and advocates of this new inductivism was Francis Bacon.

Francis Bacon

The English statesman and philosopher Francis Bacon (1561–1626) claimed that all knowledge was his province. He was highly critical of earlier methods of inquiry and advocated a new method for acquiring knowledge. It had been common for scientists to make use of syllogisms, a special form of logical argument. An example of a syllogism is: "All men are mortal. Socrates is a man. Therefore, Socrates is mortal." Syllogisms proceed deductively; that is, the conclusion is intended to follow logically, not empirically, from the reasons (premises) given for that conclusion. Put another way, the premises lead to the conclusion simply as a matter of logic, not because the natural world behaves one way rather than another or because there is some phenomenon in nature on which the conclusion is based. For example, in the above example, the conclusion that Socrates is mortal follows logically from the premises that Socrates is a man and that all men are mortal. So, *if* the premises are true, then the conclusion *must* be true also. But the conclusion follows from the premises as a matter of logic, not because of the way the natural world is. To see this, consider the syllogism "All men are immortal. Socrates is a man. Therefore, Socrates is immortal." It is

Francis Bacon,

when a boy.

An engraving of 1863 of Francis Bacon as a boy, taken from James Spedding, Robert Leslie Ellis, and Douglas Denon Heath's *The Works of Francis Bacon,* Vol. 11 *(Engraving by H. Wright Smith)*

false, of course, that all men are immortal, and in fact because no man is immortal, the conclusion of this syllogism (that Socrates is immortal) is false as well. However, the conclusion does follow logically from the premises (it just happens to be the case that one of those premises, that all men are immortal, is false).

Bacon charged that the use of syllogisms in science hindered the progress of science for the reason that too often scientists drew general conclusions on the basis of just a few observations and then proceeded to use those general observations in syllogisms to draw more conclusions. But a general conclusion on the basis of just a small number of observations of the natural world is not likely to be a very strong conclusion; for example, the general conclusion that all swans are white is not a very strong conclusion if it is based on observing just a handful of white swans. It would not be surprising if such general statements turned out to be false. In that case, however, using such statements in syllogisms would likely lead to false conclusions (just as, in the example above, the premise that all men are immortal helps lead to the false conclusion that Socrates is immortal). Science, Bacon thought, had relied too little on actual observations of the actual world.

Bacon specifically identified four other problems that weaken methods of inquiry; he dubbed these problems the Four Idols. The Idols of the Tribe are flaws in human perception and reasoning; our senses sometimes deceive us, and sometimes our understanding distorts what is real (we misconstrue the nature of what is real or true). The Idols of the Cave are a person's individual biases and limited perspective. These can occur as a result of what a person is taught, a person's personality, or a person's circumstances. A person who spends most of her life living in a lush landscape, for instance, will have a different perspective regarding plant life than someone who has spent most of his life living in a desert landscape. The mistake would come in assuming that one's own perspective is the only and best perspective or, put another way, that one's own experience is uniquely authoritative. The third kind of idols are the Idols of the Marketplace, which are the concepts and words people use in conversation and communication with each other. Of course, there is nothing wrong with many concepts and words. But, Bacon thought, because sometimes concepts and language are vague, misleading, or even refer to nothing, mistakes in inquiry can arise as a result. For instance (though this is not Bacon's example), it was once thought there must be a special substance called phlogiston, and scientists spent time and energy discussing and attempting to examine the nature of phlogiston. But it turned out there was no such substance; the word *phlogiston* did not refer to anything at all. Finally, the Idols of the Theater are the dogmatic beliefs associated with philosophical theories in particular (the phrase "Idols of the Theater" suggests that various philosophical theories are fictional, like plays).

A good method of inquiry would avoid these Idols. In addition, Bacon had something positive to say about how a good method of inquiry would proceed (not just what it should avoid), describing his preferred method in some detail. Inquiry, he thought, should involve a new kind of induction. Induction, roughly, is the drawing of general conclusions on the basis of individual observations; drawing the conclusion that all crows are black after observing many individual black crows is an example of induction. However, Bacon thought it was a mistake to investigate the world simply by adding up a lot of individual observations. Of course, making individual observations was necessary, and it was necessary to make a lot of them; Bacon criticized earlier ways of science for relying on too few individual observations. Merely making individual observations, however, for Bacon was not enough. To investigate some phenomenon in nature one should not merely observe many instances of that phenomenon and see under what conditions it occurred but also make many observations of cases in which the phenomenon in question did *not* occur and note the conditions in those cases as well. In addition, according to Bacon, one should observe the circumstances under which the phenomenon occurs in greater degrees and when it occurs in lesser degrees. On the basis of such data one should try to determine the essential nature of the phenomenon in question (to test one's hypothesis about that nature, it might be necessary to experiment). For instance, a Baconian investigation of lightning would involve the observation and documentation of when lightning occurred, when it did not occur, the degrees to which lightning occurred (are there just a few lightning flashes in some cases and more in others?), and the circumstances of each case.

The Emergence of Modern Logic: Boole and Frege

George Boole

George Boole (1815–64) was a British mathematician whose work is often credited as the basis for much of modern logic. In particular, he demonstrated that logical sentences could be formulated as algebraic sentences (or formulas). As a result, he is said to have originated the algebra of logic.

Boole came from a lower-class family (his father was a shoemaker), but his mathematical talents were realized early in life, and he published his first paper at the age of 23. Before he was 30, he had been recognized by the Royal Society for his work in mathematics and in 1849 was appointed professor of mathematics at Queen's College, Cork. He died young (at the age of 49), but not before publishing numerous works in mathematics and logic, with his most famous and influential writings being *The Mathematical Analysis of Logic* (published in 1847) and *An Investigation of the Laws of Thought* (published in 1854).

With respect to logic, Boole showed that logical sentences could be formulated as mathematical ones. Taking 0 to represent an empty class (that is, a class with no members) and 1 to represent the universal class (that is, everything), he showed how logical sentences could be phrased in mathematical terms. For example, in the traditional syllogisms of Aristotle, an argument could be given such as "All mammals are warm-

Illustration of George Boole from 1879

blooded, All dogs are mammals, therefore all dogs are warm-blooded."
For Boole, these sentences could be represented in the following way:
"All mammals are warm-blooded" becomes M~W = 0 (that is, the sum
of those things that are in the class of mammals and those things that
are not in the class of warm-blooded things equals zero); D~M = 0;
therefore D~W = 0. The four traditional syllogistic sentence forms are:
All S are P, No S are P, Some S are P, and Some S are not P. These can
be represented thus: S~P = 0, SP = 0, SP ≠ 0, and S~P ≠ 0. For any class
(say, the class of dogs) that can be represented by, say, x, its complement
class (say, all those things that are not dogs) can be represented as 1-x.
By showing that these sentences can be formulated as mathematical
formulas—in particular, algebraic formulas—Boole showed that logical
implications could be demonstrated mathematically. For example, one
algebraic law is called commutation. The law of commutation says that
when adding or multiplying two numbers, their order does not matter: 2+3 = 3+2 (and 2×3 = 3×2). This law of commutation, then, applies
also to logical sentences. So, if the conjunction of two sentences is true,
then the order of the two sentences does not matter or affect the truth
of them. For instance, if it is true that today is sunny and today is dry,
then it is also true that today is dry and today is sunny.

With the advent of set theory, standard logical sentences could be formulated as mathematical sentences in terms of sets. A set of objects is simply a collection of them. For instance, the set of numbers between one and five is {1,2,3,4,5}. The set of dogs includes all things that are dogs. Set theoretic operators can give the relationship between sets. One such operator is called union (represented by the symbol ∪). The union of two sets is the set that contains all the members (or elements) of both of those sets. For example, if there are two sets {1,2,3} and {7,8,9}, then the union of those two sets is {1,2,3,7,8,9}. Another set theoretic operator is called intersection (represented by the symbol ∩). The intersection of two sets is the set that contains all and only those things that are common to the two sets. So, in the two sets above, {1,2,3} and {7,8,9}, there is nothing in common between them, so the intersection is empty. However, in these two following sets, {1,2,3} and {2,3,4}, there is something common to the two sets, so the intersection of them is {2,3}. Sentences using the logical operator disjunction were shown to be equivalent to set theoretical sentences using the union operator, and sentences using the logical operator conjunction were shown to be equivalent to set theoretic sentences using the intersection operator. For instance, the sentence P&Q could be represented as $P \cap Q$. As a result, the mathematical laws that apply to set theory can be applied to logical sentences. One of Boole's colleagues, Augustus DeMorgan (1806–71) is known today for what is called DeMorgan's law, which states $\sim(A \cap B) = \sim A \cup \sim B$. This can be translated into the logical form of DeMorgan's law, which states $\sim(A\&B) \leftrightarrow \sim A \vee \sim B$. (For the logical sentence, this can be understood as saying that if a conjunction is false, this is equivalent to saying at least one part of that conjunction is false. For example, if $\sim[A\&B]$ stands for "It is false that today is sunny and today is mild," then that is equivalent to saying that "Either it is false that today is sunny or it is false that today is mild.") The important point is that Boole showed that logical sentences could be stated in mathematical terms, and this became even more apparent with the advent of the mathematics of set theory.

Gottlob Frege

The German mathematician Gottlob Frege (1848–1925) is often referred to as the father of modern mathematical logic. Even more than the work of George Boole, the writings of Frege shaped the history of logic and provided what is seen as the foundation of modern logic. In particular, he set the course of logic as an axiomatic system and made the case that mathematics was essentially reducible to logic (a view that is often labeled logicism). Although Frege's work is now credited as groundbreaking, it was almost completely ignored during his lifetime. It was only because of the efforts of two other renowned philosophers, Ludwig Wittgenstein (1889–1951) and Bertrand Russell (1872–1970), that his work came to the attention of most other philosophers and mathematicians.

One of the basic developments that Frege made was to treat logic as an axiomatic system. Much like the classical Greek mathematician Euclid did for geometry, Frege set about to establish logic on the basis of certain fundamental axioms (that is, truths that were taken as

Statue of Euclid of Alexandria in the Oxford University Museum of Natural History *(Photograph by Mark A. Wilson)*

given), a set of inference rules (that is, ways of deriving sentences or formulas from those axioms), and theorems (that is, derived sentences or formulas). For example, today logicians speak of certain basic logical axioms, such as the axiom of excluded middle (or for any sentence, either it is true or false, but not both). A common rule of inference is what is called modus ponens. This rule says that if it is the case that a sentence P is true and also that P implies Q, then Q is true (or one can derive Q). Another common rule of inference is called modus tollens. This rule says that if it is the case that a sentence Q is false and also that P implies Q, then P is false (or one can derive not-P). Theorems are any true sentence that can be derived from the set of axioms by using the rules of inference. For Frege, part of the importance of establishing logic as an axiomatic system was that logic could be better seen as objective and independent of people's actual reasoning. His phrase was that he wanted to de-psychologize logic. Logic, he claimed, involved truth, independent of whether or not people recognized that truth. Logically true sentences corresponded, for him, to real objects and facts, not simply to how people thought about things. There is a difference between implication (or what sentences follow from other sentences) and inference (or what people think follows).

Besides making the case that logic is a formal axiomatic system, Frege introduced a fundamental understanding of logical language. He expanded logic to be able to deal with not only objects or classes of objects but also properties, or characteristics, of objects and relations between them. Aristotle's syllogisms dealt with individual objects or classes of objects. For example, the sentence "All whales are mammals" involves a subject term *(whales)* and a predicate term *(mammals)*. Frege introduced formal notation that dealt not only with such classes but also with properties of them and relations between them. For instance, one property of whales is that they are large or that they are marine animals or that they have fins, etc. Frege showed that a logical system could show the form of sentences such as "All whales are large" or even "Plato is large." In addition, he showed that a logical system should show the form of sentences such as "All whales are larger than Plato," where *larger than* refers to a relation between things. Also, by being able to show the logical form of relations, logic can deal with sentences such as "San Francisco is between Seattle and Los Angeles," something that syllogistic logic could not do. As part of this expanded understanding and power of logic, he introduced what is called a quantifier. This allows the form of sentences to be captured by logical notation that goes far beyond what traditional syllogistic logic could do. So, modern logic can formulate the following sentences: "Plato is large" is symbolized as, say: Lp (with the "L" standing for the property "is large," and the "p" standing for Plato); "All whales are large" is symbolized as, say: $(\forall x)(Wx \rightarrow Lx)$ (to be read as "For all x, if x is a whale, then x is large"); "San Francisco is between Seattle and Los Angeles" is symbolized as, say: Bfsl (with "B" standing for the property "is between," "f" standing for San Francisco, "s" standing for Seattle, and "l" standing for Los Angeles). Frege showed that the logical forms of sentences are composed of individuals (either specific individuals such as Plato or San Francisco or variables, such as x, which could stand for unspecified individuals) as well as predicates (which included properties such as "is large" or relations such as "is larger than"). Quantifiers allow the possibility of portraying the logical form of sentences in ways that had not been possible before. Frege's system also allowed for ambiguities and lack of clarity to be resolved. For instance, the sentence "Every boy loves some girl" can be understood in two ways. One such way is that there is one particular girl (call her Mary) who every boy loves, so, in effect, the sentence means that every boy loves Mary. Another way of understanding the sentence, however, is that for each boy there is some girl (not necessarily the same girl) that is loved. Using Frege's logical notation, this ambiguity is easily clarified: The first (Mary) way of understanding the sentence can be written as: $\exists x \forall y$ (Gx & By) $\rightarrow$ Lyx, which would be read as There is something, x, such that for all things, y, if x is a girl and y is a boy, then y loves x. The second way of understanding the sentence can be written as $\forall y \exists x$ ((By & Gx) $\rightarrow$ Lyx).

Frege also formulated the term *truth-value* to speak of the value that a sentence could have in terms of being true or false. So, just as a mathematical sentence can turn out to be true or false depending upon the mathematical value of some variable, the truth-value of a sentence will depend upon the content of some logical variable. For instance, in the mathematical sentence $2x = 8$, the sentence will turn out to be true or false depending upon the value of x. (If the value is 4, then the sentence is true; otherwise, it is false.) The truth value of the logical sentence, Txp (meaning x is the teacher of Plato), depends upon the content, or value, of x. (If the content/value is Socrates, then the sentence is true; otherwise, it is false.)

Finally, Frege is renowned today for promoting the view of logicism, that is, the view that mathematics can be framed in terms of logic. Logic, he held, was the foundation of mathematics. For Frege, the basic components of mathematics, such as numbers or relations or sets, can be formulated in an axiomatic logical system, and consequently, all mathematical sentences can be formulated in terms of logical sentences. This view was endorsed by many philosophers and by some (but not all) mathematicians.

Russell's Paradox

A paradox is a kind of argument in which the conclusion of that argument is unacceptable even though it follows from reasonable and acceptable assumptions. The word *paradox* comes from two Greek words, *para,* meaning "beyond" or "contrary to," and *doxa,* meaning "belief" or "opinion." A paradox is similar to, but distinct from, a contradiction. A contradiction is a sentence, or collection of sentences, that cannot be true. Some, but not all, paradoxes are contradictions; that is, they are unacceptable because they involve a contradiction. Other paradoxes, however, are not straightforward contradictions but have a conclusion that—for reasons outside of pure logic—are not acceptable. Philosophers have wrestled with paradoxes for centuries, in large part because they force people to come face to face with the implications of their beliefs or assumptions. If certain assumptions lead to a paradox, then that might force people to rethink those assumptions or, perhaps, see the implications of their beliefs even when those implications are not pleasing.

Some paradoxes have been known for centuries. For example, there is the famous liar paradox. This paradox has various forms, but it basically involves a claim such as "I am lying right now." (Sometimes it is expressed as "This sentence is false.") The paradox is that if the person who says that she is lying is, indeed, lying, then what she is saying is a lie. But that means that it is a lie that she is lying, so she must be telling the truth. But, if she is telling the truth, then what she says—namely, that she is lying—is the truth. So, she is lying only if she is telling the truth and telling the truth only if she is lying. This form of a paradox is a self-contradiction. (Likewise, if the version is "This sentence is false."

If it is false, then what it says is true; but if what it says is true, and it says that it is false, then it is false. So, it appears to be true only if it is false and false only if it is true.)

A famous early philosopher, Zeno of Elea, constructed a number of paradoxes, all designed to show that reality is permanent and unchanging, so that our commonsense beliefs are mistaken that there are many different things and that they undergo change. One example of his paradoxes is called the paradox of the arrow, and it is intended to show that nothing can change position (or move). Zeno claimed that common sense tells us that an arrow in flight is moving through space. However, at any moment in time, that arrow is at rest. Being at rest, it occupies only the amount of space that it is equal to; it has zero movement (much like a photograph of an arrow shows it to be frozen in space and not moving). This is true for every moment in time; that is, for every given moment, the arrow is at rest. So, although it appears to be moving, it is always at rest, since its apparent movement is just a collection of moments in time, during each of which it is at rest. It is like adding up a bunch of zeroes; the total is still zero. The movement of the arrow, then, is just an illusion.

Another famous paradox is called the problem of the heap, or sometimes, the sorites paradox. This is another case of a conclusion that follows, or at least appears to follow, from certain assumptions, but the conclusion is unacceptable. The problem of the heap is this: A single grain of sand is not a heap of sand (it is just a single grain). Adding one more grain of sand, so that there are two grains, is also not a heap. In fact, for any given number of grains of sand, to simply add one more grain does not result in a heap. If these assumptions are correct—and they seem to be reasonable assumptions—then it follows that there can never be a heap, no matter how many grains of sand there are.

Yet another paradox is one that comes from the 20th-century British philosopher Bertrand Russell (1872–1970). Russell was one of the most influential philosophers of the 20th century, especially in logic, but also in other areas of philosophy. A three-volume work in logic, which he cowrote with Alfred North Whitehead (1861–1947), called *Principia Mathematica,* is considered the most important work in deductive logic since Aristotle.

Russell's paradox resulted from Russell showing that the work of Frege rested on a fundamental problem, in which mathematical sets could be defined in such a way as to lead to a contradiction. His paradox has several forms or versions; one is called the barber's paradox. The paradox is this: In a certain town, there is a barber who shaves all and only those people who do not shave themselves. The question is: Does the barber shave himself? Given the assumption that he shaves all and only those people who do not shave themselves, then, if he does shave himself, then he does not shave himself (and vice versa). This is similar to the liar paradox, but the focus of this for Russell was not directly about truth but rather about some assumptions in the mathematical field of set theory. In particular, he formulated his famous paradox in this way: "The set of all sets that are not members of themselves is a member of itself if and only if it is not a member of itself." (This is exactly like the barber paradox, but phrased in terms of mathematical sets.) Efforts by Russell and others to resolve this paradox constituted a major focus of the work of logicians for much of the early 20th century.

Necessary/Sufficient Conditions

A sufficient condition is a condition that is sufficient, or enough, for some state of affairs to be the case. We can think of a condition as a circumstance—for example, the circumstance of being rich, or that the city of Syracuse is in New York, or that it is raining. So a sufficient condition for some state of affairs is a circumstance that, as long as it is the case, guarantees that that state of affairs will exist. For example, having four quarters is sufficient for having a dollar. It is sufficient because one does not need anything else in order to have a dollar: As long as one has four quarters, one has a dollar. So, possessing four quarters is a sufficient condition for having a dollar. A necessary condition for some state of affairs, on the other hand, is a condition that *must* hold for that state of affairs to be the case. For instance, in order for someone to be a mother, it is necessary to be female. That is because the very concept of mother involves the characteristic of being female. Since to be a mother is roughly, to be a female parent, it is not possible to be a mother without being female. So being female is a necessary condition for being a mother.

Sometimes a condition is sufficient but not necessary. For example, having four quarters is sufficient for having a dollar, but it is not necessary for having a dollar. It is not necessary because there are other ways of having a dollar than having four quarters; someone might have 10 dimes or 100 pennies. Sometimes a condition is necessary but not sufficient. Although it is necessary to be female to be a mother, for instance, it is not sufficient to be female to be a mother. It is not sufficient because there is more to being a mother than just being female (many people who are female are not mothers). To be a mother also requires having a child (or children). Since the condition of being female does not guarantee being a mother, being female is not a sufficient condition for being a mother. In addition, sometimes a condition is both necessary and sufficient. That is, sometimes a condition is essential for some state of affairs and also guarantees that that state of affairs is the case. For instance, consider the condition of being composed of H_2O. Being composed of H_2O is sufficient for being water because it guarantees that something is water. That is, anything composed of H_2O is water. Being composed of H_2O is also necessary for something to be water. This is because nothing can be water without being composed of H_2O. So the condition of being made of H_2O is both necessary and sufficient for something to be water. Finally, sometimes philosophers talk of conditions as being jointly sufficient and necessary. What this means is that certain conditions, taken together, are both necessary and sufficient.

With respect to logic, when a sentence is of the form $P \rightarrow Q$ (or if P, then Q), the P represents a sufficient condition, and the Q represents a necessary condition. So, $P \rightarrow Q$ says that if P happens (or is the case), then Q happens (or is the case); that is, P being the case is sufficient for Q to follow. On the other hand, $P \rightarrow Q$ says that P being the case implies that Q is the case; without Q being the case, P would not be the case (or Q is necessary for P).

The distinction between necessary and sufficient conditions has played an important role in philosophy. In part, this is because philosophers have often tried to understand what something is by analyzing a concept, and sometimes philosophers have analyzed concepts by attempting to give sets of necessary and sufficient conditions. The idea here is when we know when a concept applies to something and when it does not, then we know what that concept is. For example, if we knew when the concept of knowledge applies and when it does not, it seems we would understand the nature of knowledge. So, in analyzing the concept of knowledge, philosophers might try to establish a set of conditions that are necessary and sufficient for something to count as knowledge. In order for a belief to count as knowledge, for instance, that belief must be true. So a necessary condition for a belief to count as knowledge is that the belief is true. Yet truth is not sufficient for a belief to count as knowledge. For example, suppose someone believed that a particular team would win the World Cup one year, but she believed it just because she guessed, not because she knew anything about the teams. Even if her belief turned out to be true, it was a lucky guess, not a case of knowledge.

However, other philosophers have denied that it is possible to analyze all concepts by giving sets of necessary and sufficient conditions. One suggestion is that we should understand concepts instead in terms of family resemblance—that is, roughly, by looking at what things that a concept applies to have in common (for instance, by looking at what beliefs that seem to count as knowledge have in common). On this view, some of those things a concept applies to might have one feature in common, and other things might have another feature in common. But there might be no or few features that *all* things have in common that the concept applies to.

Semantic Logic: Tarski, Hilbert, Gödel

Truth Tables

Formal logic can be thought of as being genuinely formal, that is, concerned with the form of sentences, as opposed to the content of sentences. Speaking of the form of sentences is sometimes said to be speaking of the syntax of sentences. Syntax is like grammar, where the emphasis is on the form rather than the content. For example, the sentence "Joe is late for work" has good syntactic form, while the sentence "Joe late work for is" does not have good syntactic form (at least in English). One way to view formal logic is that the emphasis is on form, or syntax. That is, regardless of content, a logical system can have axioms and rules of inference; these, in effect, are the syntax of a system. However, when a formal system is given content—what logicians call an interpretation—then it is said that the system now has semantics. With a semantic interpretation, it now makes sense to speak of sentences in that formal system as having truth-value, because now those sentences have content. One of the tools that logic uses to speak of assigning truth-values to sentences is with what is called a truth table.

One branch of logic is called propositional logic (sometimes called sentential logic). Propositional logic investigates the relationships between sentences and takes whole sentences as the basic unit of investigations. For example, a sentence such as "Saturn is larger than Venus" is treated as a single, indivisible unit. We might just use the letter *S* to stand for the sentence "Saturn is larger than Venus." In such a case, the sentence "Jupiter is larger than Venus" is a different sentence, and we might use the letter *J* to stand for it. Likewise, the sentence "Saturn is larger than Mars" is yet another different sentence, and we would use some other letter to represent it.

Propositional logic is sometimes also called truth-functional logic. This simply means that the truth (or falsity) of complex sentences is determined by—or is a function of—the truth (or falsity) of the simple sentences that make up that complex sentence. For instance, "Today is Friday" is a simple sentence, and it is either true or false, depending upon when it is said. Likewise, "Today is cloudy" is a simple sentence and is either true or false, depending upon the weather conditions. However, "Today is Friday and cloudy" is a complex sentence that is made up of the two simpler sentences. The truth of the complex sentence is said to be a function of the truth of the two simpler sentences that make up that complex sentence. So, "Today is Friday and cloudy" is true only when the two simpler sentences are themselves true.

Within propositional (or truth-functional) logic, complex sentences are comprised of simpler sentences plus some logical connective. A connective is a word or phrase that connects those simpler sentences to form a complex sentence. In the example above—"Today is Friday and cloudy"—the connective was the word *and*. This word connected the two simpler sentences into one complex sentence. Logicians usually speak of five basic logical connectives: (1) negation (such as the word *not*); (2) conjunction (such as the word *and*); (3) disjunction (such as the phrase *either-or*); (4) conditional (such as the phrase *if-then*); and (5) biconditional (such as the phrase *if and only if*). This chart gives examples of each of these connectives:

Simple sentence #1: Whales are mammals (symbolized as *M*).
Simple sentence #2: Whales are warm-blooded (symbolized as *B*).

COMPLEX SENTENCE	CONNECTIVE	MEANING	SYMBOL
Whales are not mammals	Negation	Not	~ M
Whales are not warm-blooded	Negation	Not	~ B
Whales are mammals and warm-blooded	Conjunction	And	M & B
Either whales are mammals or warm-blooded	Disjunction	Either-or	M v B

COMPLEX SENTENCE	CONNECTIVE	MEANING	SYMBOL
If whales are mammals, then they are warm-blooded	Conditional	If-then	M → B
Whales are mammals if and only if they are warm-blooded	Biconditional	If and only if	M ↔ B

With these logical connectives as a starting point, the truth (or falsity) of complex sentences can be determined by what is called a truth table. A truth table displays how the truth (or falsity) of a complex sentence is a function of the truth (or falsity) of the simpler sentences that make up the complex sentence. To do this, a truth table gives columns that define when a given sentence is true or false. For example, any simple sentence can be either true or false. We might not know whether it is true or false, but it is one or the other. For instance, the sentence "Socrates liked spinach" is either true or false (even if we do not know which it is). So, there are two possible truth-values for that sentence, which simply means that it can have the value of being true or the value of being false. For any simple sentence, the negation of that sentence has the opposite truth-value of it. Using the sentences in the chart above, this merely means that if the sentence "Whales are mammals" is true, then its negation "Whales are not mammals" is false. A conjunction is true only when the two simpler sentences that make up that conjunction are both true. For instance, the sentence "Whales are mammals and warm-blooded" is true only if both of the simpler sentences are true. If either of those two sentences were false, then the conjunction would turn out to be false.

A disjunction is true whenever at least one (and perhaps both) of the simpler sentences that make it up is true. Sometimes when we say "either A or B," we mean that they cannot both be the case. For instance, if we say "My pet is a cat or a dog," it cannot be both a cat and a dog; one option excludes the other. For logic, this is called an exclusive disjunction. However, most of the time when logicians speak of disjunction, they mean an inclusive disjunction, which means that a true disjunction can include the possibility that both simpler sentences are true. For instance, if we say "My car will not start; it must be a dead battery or a bad spark plug," then an inclusive disjunction would be true even if both things were true (that is, even if the battery were dead and there was a bad spark plug).

A conditional sentence, such as "If whales are mammals, then they are warm-blooded," is true in any situation, except when the first simple sentence is true and the second simple sentence is false. That is, because conditional sentences are hypothetical the "if" sentence does not need to be true in order for the whole complex sentence to be true. For example, the sentence "If today is Friday, then tomorrow is Saturday" is true even if today is not Friday, even if we said it on a Monday. Because a conditional sentence expresses a condition, then the only time the sentence is false is when the "if" part is true and the "then" part is false.

A biconditional is a conjunction of two conditional sentences, basically saying that the condition goes in both directions. In other words, with a biconditional if one sentence is true, then a second sentence is true, and also if the second sentence is true, then the first sentence is true. Using the above sentences about whales, this says that if whales are mammals, then they are warm-blooded (or $M \rightarrow B$) and also if whales are warm-blooded, then they are mammals (or $B \rightarrow M$). This is really another way of saying that each sentence implies the other one.

As mentioned above, the relationships between these types of sentences can be displayed on a truth table. For any two simple sentences, call them P and Q, the following truth table gives the truth-values for complex sentences that are made up from the simple sentences plus connectives:

P	Q	~P	~Q	P & Q	P ∨ Q	P → Q	P ↔ Q
true	true	false	false	true	true	true	true
true	false	false	true	false	true	false	false
false	true	true	false	false	true	true	false
false	false	true	true	false	false	true	true

The complex sentences that are represented in this truth table each contain two simple sentences and one connective. However, complex sentences could be even more complex. For instance, there could be a sentence such as "If whales are mammals, and they are warm-blooded, then they will bear live offspring." In this case, there are three simple sentences and two connectives all together in one complex sentence. Taking the simple sentences to be represented as M ("Whales are mammals"), B ("Whales are warm-blooded"), and O ("Whales bear live offspring"), this sentence would be symbolized in this way: $(M \& B) \rightarrow O$. Again, this complex sentence is said to be truth-functional, because its truth is determined by the truth of the simpler sentences that make it up.

Because the two simple sentences, P and Q, represent any two different simple sentences and not any particular, specific sentences, it is more correct to speak of these as sentence forms (because they represent the form of any sentences). The truth table here is one that contains just two different simple sentence forms, P and Q, and the complex sentence forms that are made up from them. As seen with the example of (M & B) → O, some complex sentence forms contain more than two simple sentences. As a result, a more complex truth table is needed to represent them. Such tables can be found in any standard logic textbook.

Alfred Tarski

Bertrand Russell and other philosophers pointed out that paradoxes are not merely quirky puzzles but important because they indicate that there is some fundamental logical flaw in a system (or in one's thinking). Russell's paradox showed that Gottlob Frege's attempt to develop a good formal foundation of mathematics was flawed. The famous liar paradox showed that philosophers did not have a good foundation for what it means to say that a sentence is true, since the liar paradox involves a sentence that is true just in case it is false. One attempt to resolve these concerns was to say that there are (at least) two levels of language: the object language and the metalanguage. The object language is the language(s) we use to talk about objects, things in the world. For example, "Cats have four legs" is a sentence about objects in the world. On the other hand, if one says "*Cats* has four letters," then this sentence is not about cats but about the word *cats*. Philosophers say that this second sentence is "in the metalanguage," meaning that it is speaking about a word, not about objects in the world. So, in effect, it is a language that speaks about the object language. (It just happens that both sentences are in English, but they function differently; the first sentence is about objects, while the second sentence is about words.) With respect to the liar paradox, then, one could say that the sentence "I am now lying" or "This sentence is false" is a sentence in the object language. However, if we want to say that "This sentence is false" is itself true, then we have moved to the metalanguage. In other words, what we are doing is saying, "The sentence 'This sentence is false' is true."

This last sentence is in the metalanguage. So, they claim, the paradox is resolved because what is true is one sentence at a different level, so to speak, than the original sentence. To put it another way, it is one thing to speak *in* a language, and it is another thing to speak *about* a language.

One of the philosophers who was especially important in working on this issue and on showing how logic relates to language was the Polish philosopher and mathematician Alfred Tarski (1901–83). Tarski attended the University of Warsaw, where he received his doctorate in 1924. As a young man he converted from Judaism to Catholicism but was forced nonetheless to flee Poland to the United States with the rise of Hitler and Nazism. During World War II, he taught at various American universities and in 1942 began teaching at the University of California, Berkeley, where he remained until his retirement in 1968. Even after retirement, he continued to teach and work with students until his death.

For philosophers, Tarski is best known for establishing what is called the semantic theory of truth and for his work in formal languages, such as logic. In a nutshell, his semantic theory of truth was a way of showing that a formalized language can be given an interpretation in which sentences can be said to be true or false by showing how sentences can be systematically related to the objects they speak about. A result of this was that logical paradoxes, such as the liar paradox, could be avoided or resolved because the issue of the truth (or falsity) of a sentence was shown to be in the metalanguage. His famous example was to say "Snow is white" is true just in case snow is white. This might seem obvious and trivial, but the point was that the issue of truth could be dropped out (or, "moved" to the metalanguage) for the sentence to still be true. So, a sentence ("Snow is white") is connected up with a fact about the world (the fact that snow is white) in a formal way that avoids or resolves paradoxes about its truth. With respect to logic in particular, this was seen as establishing a firm grounding for showing that a rigorous formal axiomatic system could be given an equally rigorous semantics.

Hilbert's Program

At the turn of the 20th century, Bertrand Russell's paradox showed there were basic problems with set theory and led many philosophers and mathematicians to turn to the issue of the very foundations of mathematics. One such person was the German mathematician David Hilbert (1862–1943). Hilbert, along with others, began explicitly not just to do mathematics but to ask about the nature of mathematics. For instance, what exactly is a proof? What does it mean to say that a mathematical claim is true? What exactly is a number? These fundamental questions led Hilbert to focus on what he called metamathematics, that is, the philosophy of mathematics. For example, among the metamathematics issues is the question of what things or kinds of things are mathematical. Mathematicians speak of numbers, sets, functions, relations, etc. For example, numbers include integers (such as 1, 2, 3, etc.). Of course, these include negative, as well as positive integers (so, -1 as well as 1). Today, zero is included as a number, but for many centuries it was not (likewise, for many centuries negative numbers were not accepted by mathematicians as being "real"). There are also numbers that are not simple integers, such as 17/32 or $\sqrt{3}$ or the number designated by π (that is, 3.14. . .) or even a number designating infinity.

A basic question about numbers is are they real, that is, do they exist? Philosophers and mathematicians have held different views about the nature and reality of numbers (and other mathematical objects, such as sets and functions). Some have claimed that numbers are real, but they are abstract objects, not concrete, physical objects (like trees or cats). This view is sometimes referred to as realism (because numbers are said to be real) and also as Platonism (because the Greek philosopher Plato argued that they are real). Realists about numbers claim that numbers must be real because mathematics is the language of science. Scientists use mathematics to describe the world, and those mathematical formulae must be real in order for them to be so accurate. That is, it cannot simply be a happy accident or mere coincidence that mathematics matches up so well with the physical world; the objects of mathematics must be real if they describe the features and behavior of physical objects so well. In addition, mathematicians continually discover things about mathematical objects (for example, they discover new theorems in geometry). This fact of discovery must mean that they are finding out facts about something that is real. Other philosophers and mathematicians disagree. They claim that mathematical objects do not exist and are not real, at least not real in the sense of anything else that is considered existing or real. Mathematics, according to this view, is a formal system of rules and structures but not a collection of things that exist in the world. As a system of rules and structures, mathematics might, indeed, describe facts about the world, but that in itself does not prove that numbers are real. This view is often referred to as formalism, and this is the view that Hilbert embraced.

Hilbert argued that all of mathematics is fundamentally a matter of setting out an axiomatic system that has some basic given axioms and then rules for showing what is a legitimate kind of sentence (or formula) in that system and how to derive other sentences (or formulae) from those axioms. In this way, he said, one could establish several features of the system and of mathematics as a whole (including logic). One feature was decidability, that is, an algorithm (or set of procedures) for determining the truth or falsity for any sentence in the system. That is, there would be a formal, rigorous way of deciding for any sentence whether it was true or false in the system. Deciding was understood to be proving, using the axioms and rules of deduction for that system. Another feature was consistency, that is, showing that the system did not contain any contradictions within it. A third basic feature was completeness, meaning that any and all statements that could be formulated in the system could be proven to be either true or false in that system. This goal and effort came to be called Hilbert's Program, and Hilbert (along with others) saw this as a fundamental concern for mathematics and logic.

Kurt Gödel

For most logicians and mathematicians, Hilbert's Program came to an end with the publication of several papers in the 1930s by a young Austrian mathematician, Kurt Gödel (1906–78). In several very technical papers, Gödel showed that a formal axiomatic system (in this case, simple arithmetic) could not be both complete and consistent. In effect, what he showed was that there are sentences (or formulas) that are true in arithmetic (or a formal axiomatic system) but cannot be proven within that system. Any sentence (or formula) in such a system can be assigned a unique number that came to be called a Gödel number. These Gödel numbers could be said to arithmeticize a formal system. In other words, there is a way of relating each and every Gödel number to specific components in that formal system. In addition, metamathematical sentences (that is, sentences outside the formal system, but about that formal system) could also be assigned Gödel numbers, so sentences *about* arithmetic could be expressed *in* arithmetic. So, for example, the following sentence (call it *G*) is metamathematical: "The formula with Gödel number *h* is not demonstrable." This very sentence can be assigned a Gödel number, which then claims its own indemonstrability, although it is a legitimate sentence within the system. Even more, the very claim that arithmetic is consistent, said Gödel, can be shown to be indemonstrable. That is, the metamathematical claim of arithmetic's consistency can be assigned a Gödel number and, so, shown not to be provable within the system even though it can be stated in the system. As a result, arithmetic (and any formal axiomatic system) is shown to be incomplete, that is, shown to include some sentence(s) that cannot be proven in that system. In effect, this resurrected the old liar paradox at the very core of the foundations of mathematics. Hilbert's Program, then, said Gödel, was fundamentally flawed. Philosophers and mathematicians can continue to do logic and mathematics, but the goals of establishing a complete and consistent language on the basis of some axioms and rules of implication cannot work. It is the axiomatic method, not logic or mathematics, that is flawed.

Vienna Circle and Logical Positivism

Logical Positivism

Logical positivism, also called logical empiricism, was a philosophical movement that originated in the 1920s. It was born out of the Vienna Circle, a group of intellectuals (mathematicians, scientists, philosophers, and others) who met regularly in Vienna to share and discuss ideas. The philosophers Moritz Schlick (1882–1936), Rudolf Carnap (1891–1970), Friedrich Waismann (1896–1959), Otto Neurath (1882–1945), Carl Hempel (1905–97), and A. J. Ayer (1910–89) are all considered positivists. W. V. O. Quine (1908–2000) met with the Vienna Circle and is also associated with logical positivism; however, some of his ideas later helped undermine the movement.

According to the classical logical positivist program, science is the only source of knowledge about the world, and most of the claims of religion, metaphysics, ethics, and aesthetics are neither true nor false but simply meaningless. Logic and science, the positivists observed, had advanced even as philosophers continued to discuss the same metaphysical questions without ever arriving at answers. The problem was that these metaphysical questions were nonsense, and philosophy ought to dispense with them. Instead, positivists viewed the purpose of philosophy as using logic to analyze the concepts and the claims of science. Influenced by the logical work of Gottlob Frege, Alfred North

Whitehead, and Bertrand Russell, positivists thought that they could clarify what concepts and claims mean. Science, in this view, tells us about the world, and philosophy makes it clear precisely what science tells us.

Fundamental to logical positivism was the principle of verifiability. Positivists formulated this principle in different ways, but in each case the idea was that, according to the principle of verifiability, metaphysical claims were meaningless. In one version of the principle, sentences are meaningful only if they are either analytically true or if they are in principle verifiable through sensory experience. That is, meaningful sentences are true either because they are true in virtue of the meaning of the words (or the grammar of the sentence) or because it is, in principle, possible to verify the truth of the sentence through experience based on the five senses. For instance, the sentence "Babies are young" is analytically true because part of the definition of the term *babies* is that they are young. So, the sentence is meaningful. The sentence "The cat Happy Jack has black fur" is verifiable through sense experience because in principle it is possible to see Happy Jack and his black fur. So, that sentence is meaningful too. However, according to positivists, a metaphysical sentence such as "Everything that exists is One" is neither analytic nor verifiable through sense experience. So, the sentence has no meaning: It is not false, it is just literally nonsense. On the basis of this reasoning, most ethical, aesthetic, and religious claims are also nonsense; it is not possible to verify, for example, the claim "The Mona Lisa is a good painting." Also associated with positivism is the view that ethical claims express a speaker's attitude but do not express anything true or false. In this view, to say that "Cruelty is bad" is just to express one's own negative attitude about cruelty; it is not to say anything true (or false).

Influenced by the early work of Ludwig Wittgenstein, positivists thought the structure of language mirrored the structure of the world. As a very simple example, consider the sentence "Happy Jack is black." It is composed of a name for a cat and a predicate *(black)* that identifies the color black. Corresponding to the name is a cat, and corresponding to *black* is the color black, which Happy Jack is. It is as if the sentence "Happy Jack is black" mirrors the actual state of affairs that Happy Jack is black. This is a very simple and rough example, but positivists thought that any true, meaningful, nonanalytic sentence similarly mirrors a state of affairs in the world. In addition, according to positivism, any meaningful, nonanalytic sentence can be reduced to a more basic statement about sensory experience. That is, any meaningful, nonanalytic sentence can ultimately be understood as saying something about sensory experience. For instance, "Happy Jack is happy" might be reducible to sentences that are about observing Happy Jack behave in certain ways (such as purring). Exactly how to understand such more basic reports was controversial among logical positivists. Some positivists argued that basic statements should be about sense data—that is, information about individual sensory experiences, such as the sensation of seeing a patch of black color when looking at Happy Jack. Other positivists rejected this view on the grounds that it made scientific claims too subjective. The concern was that scientific claims are more objective than the sense data view suggests; scientific claims should not be understood as being about individual sensations.

A persistent challenge for logical positivists was how to understand the meaningfulness of the principle of verifiability itself. Of course, they believed the principle was meaningful. Yet by its own lights it was not obvious how. After all, the principle was not verifiable by sensory experience: No observation of the empirical world would seem to verify it or not verify it. Ayer claimed that it was analytically true, but this seemed unsatisfactory. First, it was not obvious that the definition of the term *meaningful* involved verifiability. Second, if the verifiability principle was analytic, it was not clear how the principle could be informative. An analytic sentence such as "Babies are young" does not tell us anything new; it is just true by definition. Similarly, if the principle of verifiability were analytic, it would not seem to tell us anything new either. In part because of concerns over how to understand the principle of verifiability, logical positivism fell out of favor by the 1960s. Quine's rejection of the analytic/synthetic distinction was also influential, casting doubt on the notion that any sentences were analytic at all. Although logical positivism as a movement is now widely considered defunct, logical positivists were very influential in areas such as philosophy of science, philosophy of language, and analytic philosophy.

Logic and Computers

In the 1800s and early 1900s, mathematicians showed that logic and mathematics (in particular, set theory) were closely related. George Boole (1815–64) developed what came to be called the algebra of logic, showing that logical sentences could be formulated as algebraic equations. Later, Gottlob Frege (1848–1925) worked to show that logic and set theory were the basis for all of mathematics. In addition, other thinkers attempted to show that calculating machines could be created, at least in theory, to perform mathematical (and, so, logical) calculations. Perhaps the most famous of these thinkers prior to the 20th century was Charles Babbage (1791–1871), who developed a crude machine to carry out mechanically basic mathematical calculations. In the 20th century, this goal was fully realized with the creation of the modern digital computer. Fundamental to this accomplishment was the work of the English engineer Alfred Turing (1912–54). Turing's work on the nature of computability was instrumental in the development of the modern computer and in showing the relationship between logic as philosophers had developed it over the years and computability. He is especially known today for what has come to be called a Turing machine. A Turing machine is a hypothetical machine or abstract representation that illustrates how a computer functions. Turing machines function by scanning symbols printed on an infinitely long strip of paper and either replacing those symbols with new ones or scanning a different symbol on the paper, depending on the machine's internal state, the symbol it scans, and the set of instructions it follows. In effect, Turing showed the conceptual nature and structure of the modern computer.

With respect to the connections between logic and computers, there is a simple interrelation between how computers function and how logic functions. The very structure of modern computers is often spoken of in terms of the logic circuits involved in their working. A computer works by having electronic circuits perform various functions in various ways. This involves gates opening or closing to allow or prevent an electronic current to flow. For instance, a circuit could be designed so that when a key is pressed, then an electrical current flows in a certain desired manner. (As an example, one might want a light to go on when one flips a switch.) So, a circuit is designed and built so that when the switch is in one direction, a gate is closed so that it allows the electric current to flow and illuminate the lightbulb. In effect, the input is a closed gate, and the output is an illuminated bulb. In addition, when the switch is in a different direction, the input is an open gate, and because the electric current cannot flow past that gate—that is, there is now an open space where contact needs to be made—the output is a dark (nonilluminated) bulb. This can be represented in the following way:

INPUT	OUTPUT		INPUT	OUTPUT
closed	on	or	1	1
open	off		0	0

That is, rather than saying open or closed or on or off, numerical values can be assigned to represent those situations. Likewise, with a more complex circuit (say, one wanted two different light switches to be able to turn the lightbulb on or off), a circuit could be designed and built such as the following:

INPUT A	INPUT B	OUTPUT		INPUT A	INPUT B	OUTPUT
closed	closed	on		1	1	1
closed	open	on	or	1	0	1
open	closed	on		0	1	1
open	open	off		0	0	0

It turns out that circuits such as this perfectly mirror truth tables that are part of standard logic. If the 1s and 0s in the tables above are replaced by truth-values (Ts and Fs), then one has the standard logic truth tables. For instance, the table immediately above is equivalent to what is called disjunction in logic. Disjunction is like either/or, meaning that it involves two sentences and for it to be true one or other of those sentences (possibly both) must be true. For example, if my car will not start, I might think *either* the car is out of gas *or* the battery is dead. When is that sentence ("Either the car is out of gas or the battery is dead") true? It is true when either of the two smaller sentences—"The car is out of gas" and "The battery is dead"—is true (or even if both of them are true). However, if both of those smaller sentences are false, then it will be false that "Either the car is out of gas or the battery is dead." The point is that how logicians have understood the truth-values of sentences mirrors how logic circuits function in computers. The table above is simply a disjunction, but rather than involving truth-values of sentences, it involves numerical values that represent whether or not a gate is closed or open. Any circuit, no matter how complex, can be represented by a corresponding table of values, which can either be framed as a table of numerical values or truth-values. The even broader point is that the logic of sentences matches up exactly with the logic of computer circuitry and has shown (again) the close interrelationship between logic, mathematics, and computability.

Analysis of Induction

Goodman and the New Riddle of Induction

The word *grue* was made up by the American philosopher Nelson Goodman (1906–98) in order to raise a concern about induction as a reliable form of reasoning. Goodman's concern is often called the new riddle of induction. The original riddle of induction was raised by the 18th-century British philosopher David Hume. Hume's riddle, or problem, was the following: How can induction, or inductive inferences, be justified? The very nature of induction is that the conclusion of an argument is not guaranteed, given its premises. For example, based on past experience, we might notice a pattern of events, and as a result, we might infer that this event will happen again tomorrow. However, it is not guaranteed that it will happen tomorrow, even if it is highly probable that it will. For instance, every day for millions of years the Sun has risen in the east each morning, so we infer that tomorrow the same thing will happen. While it is highly likely that it will, there is always the (extremely remote) possibility that tonight the Earth will explode, so tomorrow the Sun will not rise in the east. Hume's question, again, was: How can induction, or inductive inferences, be justified?

Hume said that we cannot use induction itself to justify inductive inferences, as that would be arguing in a circle; it would be assuming the very thing that we are questioning, namely, the reliability of induction. On the other hand, Hume said, we cannot use deduction (in which the conclusion of an argument *is* guaranteed, given its premises) because induction is, by definition, not deductively valid! The only justification for induction, then, for Hume, was that it seemed to work much of the time. But, he said, that was a weak justification.

In the mid-1900s, Goodman introduced the term *grue,* a blend of the words *green* and *blue.* It is defined this way: Something is grue just in case it is green prior to, say, January 1, 3000, and also just in case it is blue after January 1, 3000. So, for instance, someone who speaks English would say that grass is green. Someone who speaks a Gruesome language would say that grass is grue, but after January 1, 3000, that person would say that grass is not grue, but that the sky is grue. Goodman also coined the word *bleen,* as: Something is bleen just in case it is blue prior to, say, January 1, 3000, and also just in case it is green after January 1, 3000. (So, to the Gruesome speaker, prior to January 1, 3000, grass is grue and after that date grass is bleen.)

Goodman suggested that we might make this example of an inductive inference: Since every emerald that has been observed in the past was green, the next emerald we observe will be green. However, one could also say that since every emerald that has been observed in the past was grue, the next emerald that we observe will be grue. Of course, as we expect that the green inductive inference will be correct (because we expect that after January 1, 3000, the next emerald will, indeed, be green, but as we expect the grue inductive inference will be incorrect (because we do not expect that after January 1, 3000), the next emerald will be blue.

The riddle here is that, while it appears that *grue* is a strange concept because it is defined by some point in time, Goodman claimed that actually *green* could be defined in terms of *grue* and *bleen.* So, *green* means something is green just in case it is grue prior to January 1, 3000, and also just in case it is bleen after that date. Goodman's point is that there is no reason to assume that *green* and *blue* are more natural than *grue* and *bleen,* since each pair of words can be defined in terms of the other pair. So, again, there is a riddle about justifying inductive inferences, since two different inferences result in this case depending upon which pair of words is taken as better. But, even if we say that one pair (green and blue) gives us a better inference, the only justification seems to be that it works in this case (which lands us right back to the original riddle of induction).

Counterfactuals

Philosophers call some sentences categoricals. This means that they purport to state a fact. For example, the sentence "Cats are mammals" is a categorical sentence. Categorical sentences might be false, however, as in the sentence "Cats can fly." The point is that categorical sentences (even if they turn out to be false) are of the form S is P. Philosophers call some other sentences conditionals. These are sentences that contain some condition or hypothetical component. For instance, the sentence "If I sleep in too late, I will miss class" is a conditional sentence. The sentence does not state that I will sleep in too late, but rather states a hypothetical situation or a condition: "*If* I sleep in too late, *then* I will miss class." Conditional sentences are of the form: If S, then P.

One kind of conditional sentence is called a material conditional. This kind of conditional sentence involves a straightforward if-then structure, as in the sentence "If cats are mammals, then they are warm-blooded." Another kind of conditional sentence is called a subjunctive conditional. Often in subjunctive conditionals we use words like *could* and *were,* as in the sentence "If I could flap my arms and fly, then I would be happy" or "If I were to break this window, then I would be in trouble." These are often called contrary-to-fact, or counterfactuals, by philosophers. This is because they are not factual claims. In particular, the "if" part of the sentence is contrary to the facts of the world.

Philosophers have wrestled with conceptual problems about counterfactuals. One concern for philosophers is how counterfactuals relate to the notion of dispositions. Some features of things are said to be dispositions, meaning that things have a likelihood to behave in certain ways, even if they do not actually behave that way. For example, if one said that glass is fragile, then that means that glass is likely to break (or has the disposition to break) if it is struck and it has that disposition even if it is never struck. Counterfactuals are also related to the notion of natural laws. For instance, if one said that it is a law that metals conduct electricity, then that means that if one *were* to give an electric current to a metal, then it would conduct that current. Counterfactuals also relate to the issue of cause. For example, if one said that smoking causes lung cancer, then that means that if one *were* to smoke, then one would get lung cancer.

The reason that philosophers are concerned with counterfactuals is that they are difficult to analyze in terms of what makes them true and also in terms of how to distinguish them from other conditionals. Because by their very nature they are contrary to facts, they are false; yet we have very good reasons for taking them to be true. So, the sentence "If cats were birds, then they could fly" states a truth, even though it is not obvious why. For instance, if that sentence were true, would the following sentence thereby be false: "If cats were birds, then not all birds could fly"? This difficulty of knowing how to analyze counterfactuals is important to philosophers because, as noted above, they are so basic to issues about how to understand dispositions and laws and cause. In addition, as Goodman pointed out, they make the distinction blurry at best between sentences that express genuine laws (of nature) and mere lawlike sentences that express accidental generalizations.

Evidence/Bayes

A basic issue in epistemology (the study of knowledge) concerns the justification of our beliefs. That is, what justifies the beliefs that we have? Occasionally, we say that a belief is self-justified (or needs no justification). For example, I might claim that I like chocolate ice cream more than I like vanilla ice cream. If asked to justify this belief (that is, if someone asked me how I know that I prefer chocolate ice cream to vanilla), I would not know what to say; it is just obvious! Also, occasionally, we say that a belief is justified simply by our intuition or gut feeling. For instance, I might claim that people should get what is due to them. If asked why (that is, if asked to justify my claim), I would simply appeal to my sense that it just seems right; I would not know what else to say to justify my belief.

Most of the time, however, justifying a claim involves providing some evidence for it. Philosophically, however, the concept of evidence is not straightforward. First, there is the question of what exactly evidence is. That is, what does the word *evidence* mean? In terms of metaphysics (the study of reality), nothing is inherently evidence. In other words, the world contains lots of things (such as cats and trees), events (such as sneezes and hurricanes), processes (such as physical interactions and ceremonies), even abstract relations between things (such as being older than or being married to), but nothing just *is* evidence. For example, a pencil is just a pencil. Things or events or processes, etc., might come to be taken as evidence of something or evidence for some hypothesis; a pencil might come to be taken as evidence that someone had the means to write a letter. By itself, however, the pencil is just a pencil. So, one philosophical question is: How does something come to be evidence?

In addressing this question, philosophers have noted that if anything is evidence, it is always evidence *of* something or evidence *for* something (and never simply evidence in itself). That is, there is some fact that something else is evidence of, or there is some hypothesis that something else is evidence for. For example, the presence of certain noises might be evidence of a small animal running across someone's roof, or the absence of fingerprints on a murder weapon might be evidence that the killer wore gloves and even evidence for the hypothesis that the murder was premeditated.

However, what makes the presence of these noises or fingerprints evidence of something or for something? One answer is that these noises or fingerprints are consistent with other facts or hypotheses. This simply means that the truth of beliefs about these noises or fingerprints does not contradict the truth of these other facts or hypotheses. (If the truth of beliefs about the noises and fingerprints did contradict those other facts or hypotheses, then they would not be evidence for them!) A problem with this notion of evidence—namely, something, call it A, is evidence of or for something else, call it B, if A is consistent with B—is that something could be consistent with something else, but be completely irrelevant to it, or, at least, not clearly relevant. For instance, certain noises on the roof of my house are consistent with the theory of evolution (that is, those noises do not contradict the theory), but we certainly do not think that those noises are evidence for the theory of evolution (or evidence against the theory).

A second answer to the question of what makes one thing evidence for something else is that the first thing makes the second thing more likely or more probably true. The philosophical phrase for this view is called Bayesianism, named for the work of an 18th-century British theorist, Thomas Bayes (1702–61). Bayes constructed a mathematical formula to measure how some thing or event would affect the probability of another thing or event being the case. For example, suppose that the probability of Joe being at some party is one out of two (that is, it is just as likely that he went to the party as it is that he did not). Also, suppose that the probability of his car being parked outside the house of the party is three out of four if he went to the party but only one out of four if he did not. Bayes's formula showed that the hypothesis of Joe being at the party is increased, given that his car is parked outside the house. Therefore, Bayes said, Joe's car being parked there is evidence for the hypothesis that Joe went to the party; it is evidence because it increased the probability of the hypothesis being true (the probability is now stronger than one out of two that Joe went to the party).

Not all philosophers think that Bayes's formula explains the concept of evidence. They claim that it gives a measure of evidence, but it still ignores the prior question of what makes something evidence at all. In this case, what makes Joe's car being parked in a particular place evidence at all? Is Joe's car being parked there evidence for the theory of evolution? Once again, there is the assumption that this fact (where Joe's car is parked) is relevant to the given hypothesis, but whether or not it is relevant is not determined by the simple fact that it is parked there.

An additional complication is that of negative evidence, that is, when there is the absence of consistent data. For instance, is the lack of fingerprints at a crime scene evidence that some person is not guilty? A common saying is that the absence of evidence is not the evidence of absence; in other words, not having data that is consistent with some hypothesis does not in itself mean that the hypothesis is false. In spite of these conceptual, philosophical concerns, scientists, lawyers, and people in everyday situations continue to speak of things and events as evidence of other facts or for hypotheses.

Expansion of Modern Logic

Modal Logic

People often speak of things or events as being possible or as being necessary. For example, we might claim that it is possible that there is life on Jupiter; it might be the case that there is life on Jupiter, even if we do not know. Similarly, we might claim that a father is necessarily older than his daughter; it *must be* the case that he is older than she is. These notions of necessity and possibility (what might be or must be) are what philosophers call modalities (modes, or ways, that something is). We often distinguish possibility and necessity not only from each other but also from two other concepts, actuality and contingency. That is, we sometimes distinguish something as being possible from something as being actual. For instance, it was possible that Babe Ruth could have run for governor of New York, but in actuality he did not. Likewise, while it in fact happened that Babe Ruth hit more than 700 home runs, he might not have; it did not have to happen, so it was contingent (not necessary) that it happened. Philosophers also speak of sentences as being contingent (for example, "Bachelors are ugly"), which means that those sentences are true sometimes, but not always, as well as other sentences being necessary (for example, "Bachelors are unmarried"). In the latter case (sentences being necessary), they can be either necessarily true, such as "Bachelors are unmarried" (also called tautologies) or necessarily false, such as "Bachelors are married" (also called contradictions).

These notions seem common and mundane. However, a closer look at them shows that they raise a number of conceptual and philosophical issues. One such issue is that there are different kinds of necessity and possibility. For example, philosophers speak of logical possibility as opposed to physical possibility. To say that something is logically possible simply means that it does not involve a contradiction. For instance, it is logically possible that a person could jump from the Earth to the Moon, but it is not physically possible. The law of gravity is relevant to physical possibility, but not to logical possibility. However, it is logically impossible for a square to be round but not physically impossible (at least, if we take geometrical figures to be nonphysical, abstract things, so physical possibility or impossibility is irrelevant). People also speak of other kinds of possibility (or necessity), such as technological possibility (it might be logically and physically possible to fly faster than light, but it is not now technologically possible). In addition, we might speak of temporal possibility (or necessity), that is, possibility or necessity related to time and a sequence of events. Philosophers even speak of epistemic possibility (or necessity), meaning what might or must be known.

Another issue about modalities, besides the various kinds of possibility and necessity, that philosophers deal with is whether or not necessity and possibility are properly spoken of as "in the world" or as only as "in language." For example, if we say that something is possible—for example, it is possible that there is life on Jupiter—does that simply mean that the sentence "There is life on Jupiter" is not a contradiction or does it mean that there is actual possible life on Jupiter? The first case could be restated as "It is possible that there is life on Jupiter." In this case, the possibility is about the truth of the sentence, that is, that the sentence is possibly true (and not a contradiction). The second case could be restated as "It is the case that there is possible life on Jupiter." In this case, the possibility is about life-forms, not about the sentence. Philosophers refer to the first case as *de dicto* (from the Latin words, meaning "of language") and they refer to the second case as *de re* (from the Latin words, meaning "of things"). The reason this distinction is made is because there are conceptual questions about claiming that there are possible things, that is, that there are actually things that are possible. For instance, the 20th-century American philosopher W. V. O. Quine (1908–2000) asked: Are there more possible thin men in the doorway than possible fat men? His point was that the notion of *de re* possibility raises questions and concerns that lead philosophers astray, while *de dicto* possibility does not; however, some other philosophers disagree.

Modal logic deals with the logic of sentences involving possibility and necessity (as well as contingency). Standard, nonmodal logic includes what are called logical operators, such as negation, conjunction, and conditional. They operate, as it were, on sentences, so that sentences can be combined, and the truth of them is determined by how these operators work. For instance, negation reverses the truth of the sentence that it operates on. If the sentence "Today is Tuesday" is true, then negating that sentence (that is, using the negation operator on it) makes that sentence false. Modal logic uses the logical operators of standard logic but also adds two additional logical operators, the possibility operator and the necessity operator. This simply means that there is a way to express a sentence as being possibly or necessarily true (or false). Two symbols are used for these operators: ◊ (for possibility) and □ (for necessity). For example, the sentence "It is possible that Plato was seven feet tall" can be expressed as: ◊ Plato was seven feet tall. The sentence "It is necessary that 2+2=4" can be expressed as: □ 2+2=4. Sometimes philosophers use a contingency operator (represented by the symbol: ▽) to express a contingent sentence when they are using modal logic. Both possibility and necessity can be defined in terms of each other. To say that a sentence is possibly true means that it is not necessary that it is false. Symbolically, this can be represented as follows: ◊ P is the same as ~ □ ~ P. Likewise, to say that a sentence is necessarily true means that it is not possible that it is false (□ P is the same as ~ ◊ ~ P).

There are theorems and implications that are involved in modal logic. For example, if a (contingent) sentence P is true, then it follows that P is possibly true (that is, if it is actually true that cats have four legs, then it is certainly possibly true that they do). Using logical symbols, this can be represented as: P ⇒ ◊ P. Furthermore, if a sentence is necessarily true, then it follows that it is actually (contingently) true, or: □ P ⇒ P.

Modal logic was investigated by medieval logicians, but the modern formal treatment of it is attributed first to the work of the American philosopher C. I. Lewis (1883–1964). Lewis was concerned that standard logic did not adequately capture the notion of implication. The standard conditional sentence, of the form "If P, then Q," was too weak, he claimed, to capture what he called "strict implication." Strict implication involves a conditional sentence being necessarily the case. Since the work of Lewis in the early years of the 20th century, many philosophers have focused on developing formal systems of modal logic, in part to help address basic philosophical questions that involve modality, for example, how to assess sentences about God as a necessary being.

Deontic Logic

Deontic logic is the field of philosophy that attempts to formulate and formally analyze sentences involving permission and obligation. The term *deontic* comes from the Greek word *deon,* meaning "duty." A long-standing tradition in ethics is called "deontological ethics," because the focus is on moral duties and obligations. Deontological views of ethics are views that evaluate the rightness or wrongness of some actions (or kinds of actions) in terms of a person's moral duties. Such views are usually contrasted with consequentialist views, which evaluate the moral rightness or wrongness of an action (or kind of an action) just in terms of an act's consequences. For instance, in a case where telling a lie might make a lot of people very happy and just one person a little sad, a consequentialist view might hold that telling the lie is the morally right thing to do. This is because what matters (most) for the morality of an action is its consequences, and in this case the consequences are more good than bad. However, the deontologist is likely to disagree. Deontologists typically believe that it is intrinsically right to do some things and intrinsically wrong to do other things, even if the consequences turn out to be (apparently) unpleasant. Lying is usually taken in deontological views to be an action that is intrinsically wrong. So, one has a duty not to lie, even if telling a lie will make a lot of people very happy and just one person a little sad. The most famous philosopher often associated with deontological ethics is Immanuel Kant (1724–1804).

Deontic logic includes standard logic plus two additional logical operators, the permission operator and the obligation operator. To say that an action is permitted, of course, means that it may be done but does not need to be done. For instance, it is permitted to give a stranger directions on how to find a local gas station. To say that an action is obligated means that it must be done (that is, morally must be done). Permission and obligation can be defined in terms of each other. To say that an action, *a*, is permitted is the same as saying that it is not obligated not to do *a*. To say that an action, *a*, is obligated means that it is not permitted not to do *a*. Using P and O to represent the deontic operators of permission and obligation, these notions can be symbolically represented as: Pa (meaning action *a* is permitted) and Oa (meaning action *a* is obligatory). Because some actions are permissible or obligatory in certain contexts but not in others, P(a/c) can be used to mean action *a* is permitted in context *c*. Philosophers who have worked on deontic logic have claimed that there are some formal theorems or implications that follow from basic concepts of permission and obligation. For example, they claim that if one action, *a*, implies another action, *b*, then if *a* is permitted, then it follows that *b* is permitted (symbolically: [a → b] → [Pa → Pb]). On the other hand, some theorems and implications have been questioned. For instance, some deontic logicians have claimed that ∼ Pp → P ∼p, in other words, if action *p* is not permitted, then it is permitted not to do action *p*. Some other deontic logicians have argued that such theorems fail to distinguish between acts of commission (that is, acts that are committed, or actually done) and acts of omission (that is, acts that are omitted, or not done), because, they claim, a person might be morally responsible for not having acted as opposed to being morally responsible only for having acted.

Epistemic Logic

Epistemic logic deals with the formal analysis of sentences involving knowledge and belief. The term *epistemic* refers to the subject of philosophy called epistemology, the study of knowledge. The rules and implications of standard logic, however, sometimes lead to questionable results. For example, normally if two things are identical, one can be substituted for the other without any controversy. If Bill is Bob's brother, then if it is true that Bill went to the store, then it is true that Bob's brother went to the store. However, in epistemic contexts (that is, in cases involving knowledge and belief), this simple substitution might not work. For instance, Lois Lane believes that Superman can fly, and it is the case (at least in the stories) that Clark Kent is Superman, so it would seem that Lois Lane believes that Clark Kent can fly; but she does not.

A standard assumption in epistemology is that knowing something entails believing it. That is, if someone knows that Sacramento is the capital of California, then certainly that person must believe it. It would be strange, indeed, for that person to say, "I know that Sacramento is the capital of California, but I do not believe it." As philosophers put it, believing x is a necessary condition for knowing x. Epistemic logic, then, includes logical operators for knowledge and belief. These are typically represented as follows: K stands for *knows that,* and B stands for *believes that.* So, using *a* to stand for some agent or person and *p* to stand for some proposition or sentence, Kap means agent a knows that p and Bap means agent a believes that p. A standard theorem of epistemic logic is Kap → Bap, that is, if a knows that p, then a believes that p. Another assumption in epistemology is that if someone knows p, then p must be true. We cannot know something that is false; for instance, no one can know that Plato was 10 feet tall. People might believe it, but they do not (and cannot) know it. That is one of the major differences between knowledge and belief; we can have false beliefs, but not false knowledge. So, a theorem of epistemic logic is Kap → p.

As with other logical systems, there are questions that arise for epistemic logic. For example, if one sentence implies another (that is, if p → q), then if one knows the first sentence (that is, if Kap), does it follow that one knows the second sentence, Kaq?

Deviant Logic

Deviant logic consists of simply logical systems that deviate from the standard two-valued systems. Traditional logic is said to be bivalent, which simply means that it involves two values. The two values for traditional logic are called truth-values. These two truth-values are true and false. Traditional logic deals with sentences that have truth-values; that is, it deals with sentences that can be either true or false (as opposed to sentences, such as commands or questions, that are neither true nor false). Traditional logic is concerned with the relationship between sentences, primarily with respect to their truth-values. For example, traditional logic focuses on the issue of the validity of arguments. An argument is said to be valid if the conclusion of the argument follows from the premises, or evidence, given in support of that conclusion (or if the premises are true, the conclusion that follows must be true).

As opposed to traditional bivalent logical systems, some philosophers have developed multi-valued systems. In these systems, they allow more than two logical values. A simple three-valued system, for example, might allow the values of true, false, and undetermined. In these systems, sentences that turn out to be true in standard bivalent logic might turn out not to be true. For instance, in standard bivalent logic, a conditional sentence, such as "If P, then Q," will turn out to be true even if the antecedent (the "If P" part) is false. In some multi-valued logics, this might turn out to be indeterminate, because the antecedent was false.

One particularly significant system of deviant logic is called fuzzy logic. This is because it deals with the fact that for some sentences it is difficult to say whether they are true or not. The difficulty is not a matter of not knowing certain facts but of having vagueness concerning what the sentence is about. For example, the sentence "Bill is tall" is not obviously true or false, in part because being tall is vague. If Bill stands seven feet high, we would probably say it is true that Bill is tall. However, if it turns out that Bill is not a human but is an elephant, then it is not clear whether or not it is true that Bill is tall.

There is another complication for traditional bivalent logic beyond the vagueness in some sentences. This additional complication is sometimes called a sorites paradox or the problem of the heap, from the Greek word *soros,* which means "heap." For instance, suppose that Bill is bald. If we add just one hair to Bill's head, we would still say that he is bald. If Bill has one hair and we add just one more hair (so he has two), we would still say that he is bald. So, at any time if we add a single hair to someone's head, it would not seem to change the status of that person being bald or not. However, if we keep adding hairs to Bill's head, at some point Bill will have, say, a million hairs, and surely would not be bald. So, with zero hairs on his head, it is true that Bill is bald, and with one hair on his head, it is true that Bill is bald, and with two hairs on his head, it is true that Bill is bald. At some point, it is false that Bill is bald, but at what point?

Because these concerns about truth-values and vagueness arise, philosophers speak of fuzzy logic. Fuzzy logic is not necessarily bivalent but might have many truth-values. As a result, some sentence (such as "Bill is tall") might be true or false or, say, indeterminate. Or we might speak of some sentence as more or less true or true to some degree. Philosophers have developed many fuzzy logic systems, and these have been applied to some technologies where degrees of clarity matter (for instance, in designing toasters for toasting bread to various degrees of crispness).

Concluding Discussion Questions

1. What is the difference between inference and implication?
2. What is the difference between deduction and induction?
3. What is the difference between an argument being valid and an argument being sound (or cogent)?
4. What is the difference between an object language and a meta-language? How do they relate to the liar paradox?
5. What is a formal axiomatic system?
6. What is the difference between a syllogistic logical system and a propositional logic system?

Further Reading

Bonevac, Daniel. *Simple Logic.* Oxford: Oxford University Press, 1998.

Clark, Michael. *Paradoxes from A to Z.* 2nd ed. New York: Routledge, 2007.

Copi, Irving M., and James A. Gould, eds. *Readings on Logic.* New York: Macmillan, 1964.

———, eds. *Contemporary Readings in Logical Theory.* New York: Macmillan, 1967.

Haack, Susan. *Deviant Logic, Fuzzy Logic: Beyond the Formalism.* Chicago: University of Chicago Press, 1996.

Hausman, Alan, Howard Kahane, and Paul Tidman. *Logic and Philosophy: A Modern Introduction.* 11th ed. Belmont, Calif.: Wadsworth, 2009.

Kneale, William, and Martha Kneale. *The Development of Logic.* Oxford: Clarendon, 1962.

Priest, Graham. *Logic: A Very Short Introduction.* Oxford: Oxford University Press, 2001.

Read, Stephen. *Thinking about Logic: An Introduction to the Philosophy of Logic.* Oxford: Oxford University Press, 1995.

Robbin, Joel W. *Mathematical Logic: A First Course.* Mineola, N.Y.: Dover, 2006.

Shapiro, Stewart. *Thinking about Mathematics: The Philosophy of Mathematics.* Oxford: Oxford University Press, 2000.

Skyrms, Brian. *Choice and Chance: An Introduction to Inductive Logic.* 4th ed. Belmont, Calif.: Wadsworth, 1999.

Glossary

algebra of logic   the view of logic that it is equivalent to, or translatable into, a system of algebraic formulas (for example, the logical sentence $P \rightarrow Q$ is treated as $PQ = 0$).

argument   a set of sentences, one of which (the conclusion) is said to follow from (or be implied by) the other sentences (the premises).

axiomatic system   a system, or collection of sentences, in which some sentences, the axioms, are taken as basic or as true, with other sentences being derived from those foundational axioms.

completeness   a property of a set of sentences in which every logically true sentence is derivable within that set of sentences.

conclusion   the component of an argument that is said to follow from the other components of that argument, the premises.

consistency   a property of a set of sentences in which all of the sentences, taken together, are true (that is, no one of the sentences contradicts any of the others).

deduction   initially understood as a branch of logic involving information in the conclusion as being already contained in the premises; now also understood as particular criteria for evaluating the formal correctness of an argument, with the standard for correctness being that the truth of the premises guarantees the truth of the conclusion (see also induction).

deviant logics   logical systems other than the standard two-valued logic, where two-valued refers to sentences having a value of either true or false (such as fuzzy logic); also logical systems with nonstandard operators, meaning, logical relationships between sentences other than if-then, either-or, and and (such as modal logic).

induction   initially understood as a branch of logic involving information in the conclusion that goes beyond information contained in the premises; now also understood as particular criteria for evaluating the formal correctness of an argument, with the standard for correctness being that the truth of the premises makes the truth of the conclusion more likely (see also deduction).

induction, problem of   the problem of justifying an inference about the future on the basis of past and present phenomena; often associated with the inductivist model of scientific change as well as concerns about evidence and confirmation; associated with the writings of David Hume and Nelson Goodman.

liar paradox   a paradox that states "I am now lying" (or, for example, if a Cretan says, "All Cretans are liars"); if the sentence is true, then it appears that it is false and vice versa.

logical positivism   philosophical model of science, often associated with inductivism, emphasizing the criterion of empirical observation as the basis for meaningfulness and embracing a sharp division between facts and values.

logicism   the view that logic is the basis for mathematics (or all of mathematics can be reduced to logic).

necessary condition   a condition that is needed or required for the status of something (for example, being female is a necessary condition, as opposed to a sufficient condition, for being a mother).

paradox   literally "against belief," a set of sentences in which each sentence by itself seems plausible but taken together do not (some paradoxes are stated as a single sentence, such as "This sentence is false").

predicate logic   the branch of logic that takes individuals and properties or classes as its basic unit (as opposed to propositional logic, which takes whole sentences, or propositions, as its basic units); for example, in the following sentence: "Happy Jack eats cheese," the term *Happy Jack* refers to an individual, and *eats cheese* refers to a predicate.

premise   a sentence within an argument that is taken as the information from which a conclusion is derived or said to follow.

propositional logic   the branch of logic that takes whole sentences (or propositions) as its basic units (as opposed to predicate logic, which takes individuals and properties or classes as its basic units); for example, in the formal sentence: "If P, then Q," the *P* and the *Q* represent whole propositions.

Russell's paradox   a paradox of set theory: a set of all sets that are not members of themselves; the paradox is that if this set is a member of itself, then (by definition) it is not a member of itself and vice versa.

soundness   the property of an argument in which the sentences in that argument are true (as opposed to validity, which is a property of the form or structure of an argument).

sufficient condition   a condition that is enough to guarantee the status of something (for example, having 100 pennies is a sufficient condition, as opposed to a necessary condition, for having a dollar).

syllogism   a specific form of logic, developed by Aristotle, that demonstrates the logical relations of certain classes of objects.

truth table   a chart that displays how the truth values of complicated sentences are derived from the truth values of the simpler components of them; a basis for propositional logic.

Turing machine   a simplified form of computer (named for its originator Alan Turing), sometimes claimed as a conceptual foundation of modern artificial intelligence.

vagueness   the property of an expression in which there are multiple meanings or in which there are no definite necessary and sufficient conditions (for example, "tall").

validity   a property of form or structure (as opposed to content) of an argument, in which the conclusion necessarily follows from (or is implied by) the premises.

Venn diagram   a means of visually portraying information involving different classes of objects and often used to display the validity or invalidity of syllogisms; developed by the British mathematician John Venn.

Key People

Aristotle (**384–322 B.C.E.**)　*Greek philosopher who greatly influenced philosophy and science. Among his accomplishments is that he established the discipline of logic. In particular, he formulated and developed the systems of syllogisms as a means of demonstrating knowledge and inferential reasoning. The selection below is from Aristotle's work entitled* Posterior Analytics.

All instruction given or received by way of argument proceeds from pre-existent knowledge. This becomes evident upon a survey of all the species of such instruction. The mathematical sciences and all other speculative disciplines are acquired in this way, and so are the two forms of dialectical reasoning, syllogistic and inductive; for each of these latter make use of old knowledge to impart new, the syllogistic assuming an audience that accepts its premises, inductive exhibiting the universal as implicit in the clearly known particular . . .

We suppose ourselves to possess unqualified scientific knowledge of a thing, as opposed to knowing it in the accidental way in which the sophist knows, when we think that we know the cause on which the fact depends, as the cause of that fact and of no other, and, further, that the fact could not be other than it is . . . Consequently the proper object of unqualified scientific knowledge is something which cannot be other than it is.

. . . What I now assert is that at all events we do know by demonstration. By demonstration I mean a syllogism productive of scientific knowledge, a syllogism, that is, the grasp of which is *eo ipso* [i.e., by that very fact] such knowledge. Assuming then that my thesis as to the nature of scientific knowledge is correct, the premises of demonstrated knowledge must be true, primary, immediate, better known than and prior to the conclusion, which is further related to them as effect to cause . . .

Now since the required ground of our knowledge—i.e., of our conviction—of a fact is the possession of such a syllogism as we call demonstration, and the ground of the syllogism is the facts constituting its premises, we must not only know the primary premises—some if not all of them—beforehand, but know them better than the conclusion: for the cause of an attributes inherence in a subject always itself inheres in the subject more firmly than that attribute . . .

Now it has been shown that the positing of one thing—be it one term or one premise—never involves a necessary consequent: two premises constitute the first and smallest foundation for drawing a conclusion at all and therefore *a fortiori* [i.e., with more force] for the demonstrative syllogism of science.

[*The Works of Aristotle*. Vol.1. Translated and edited by W. D. Ross. Oxford: Clarendon, 1913.]

Bacon, Francis (1561–1626)   *English statesman and philosopher who argued in favor of a rigorous form of induction (the drawing of general conclusions on the basis of many individual observations) and the social nature of science. The following selection is from his most influential work,* The New Organon.

There are, and can be, only two ways to investigate and discover truth. The one [based on deduction] leaps from sense and particulars to the most general axioms, and from these principles and their settled truth, determines and discovers intermediate axioms; this is the current way. The other [based on induction] elicits axioms from sense and particulars, rising in a gradual and unbroken ascent to arrive at last at the most general axioms; this is the true way, but it has not been tried.

[Bacon, Francis. *The New Organon*. Edited by Lisa Jardine and Michael Silverthorne. Cambridge: Cambridge University Press, 2000.]

Boole, George (1815–1864)   *English mathematician who formulated what is called the algebra of logic, the foundation of modern symbolic logic. The following passage is taken from his book* An Investigation of the Laws of Thought.

Logic is conversant with two kinds of relations—relations among things, and relations among facts. But as facts are expressed by propositions, the latter species of relation may, at least for the purposes of Logic, be resolved into a relation among propositions. The assertion that the fact or event of *A* is an invariable consequent of the fact or event *B* may, to this extent at least, be regarded as equivalent to the assertion, that the truth of the proposition affirming the occurrence of the event *B* always implies the truth of the proposition affirming the occurrence of the event *A*. Instead, then, of saying that Logic is conversant with relations among things and relations among facts, we are permitted to say that it is concerned with relations among things and relations among propositions. Of the former kinds of relations we have an example in the proposition—"All men are mortal"; of the latter kind in the proposition—"If the sun is totally eclipsed, the stars will become visible." The one expresses a relation between "men" and "mortal beings," the other between the elementary propositions—"The sun is totally eclipsed"; "The stars will become visible." Among such relations I suppose to be included those which affirm or deny existence with respect to things, and those which affirm or deny truth with respect to propositions. Now let those things or those propositions among which relation is expressed be termed the elements of the propositions by which such relation is expressed. Proceeding from this definition, we may then say that the *premises* of any logical argument express *given* relations among certain elements, and that the *conclusion* must express an *implied* relation among those elements, or among a part of them, i.e., a relation implied by or inferentially involved in the premises . . .

General Rule for the Symbolical Expression of Primary Propositions

1st. If the proposition is affirmative, form the expression of the subject and that of the predicate. Should either of them be particular, attach to it the indefinite symbol v, and then equate the resulting expressions.

2ndly. If the proposition is negative, express first its true meaning by attaching the negative particle to the predicate, then proceed as above.

One or two additional examples may suffice for illustration. Ex.—"No men are placed in exalted stations, and free from envious regards." Let y represent "men," x, "placed in exalted stations," z, "free from envious regards." Now the expression of the class described as "placed in exalted station," and "free from envious regards," is xz. Hence the contrary class, i.e., they to whom this description does not apply, will be represented by $1\text{-}xz$, and to this class all men are referred. Hence we have $y = v\,(1\text{-}xz)$.

[Boole, George. *An Investigation of the Laws of Thought.* London: Walton and Maberly, 1854.]

Frege, Gottlob (1848–1925)   *German logician and mathematician who is generally considered one of the founders of modern symbolic logic and of what is called logicism, the view that logic is the foundation of mathematics. For Frege, logic and mathematics are objective and independent of people's thoughts or beliefs. Logic, then, is not about people's reasoning but about real laws and rules of implication. In the passage below, Frege rejects the view that logic is psychological (that is, concerned with how people actually reason or what they think the laws of logic are).*

It has often been said that arithmetic is only a more highly developed logic; but that remains disputable as long as the proofs contain steps that are not performed according to acknowledged logical laws, but seem to rest on intuitive knowledge. Only when they are resolved into simple logical steps can we be sure that arithmetic is founded solely upon logic . . .

I must give up hope of securing as readers all those mathematicians who, when they come across logical expressions like "concept," "relation," "judgment," think: *Metaphysica sunt, non leguntur* [It is metaphysics; one does not read that]; and those philosophers who at the sight of a formula call out: *Mathematica sunt, non leguntur* [It is mathematics; one does not read that] . . .

One might just as well make a lazy pupil diligent by a mere definition. Confusion easily arises here through our not making a sufficient distinction between concept and object. If we say: "A square is a rectangle in which the adjacent sides are equal," we define the concept *square* by specifying what properties something must have in order to fall under this concept. I call these properties "marks" of the concept. But it must be carefully noted that these marks of the concept are not properties of the concept. The concept *square* is not a rectangle; only the objects which fall under this concept are rectangles; similarly the concept *black cloth* is neither black nor a cloth.

. . . [What] stands most in the way of psychological logic is that its exponents have such a high opinion of psychological profundity, which is, after all, nothing but a psychological falsification of logic. And that is how our thick books of logic came to be; they are puffed out with unhealthy psychological fat which conceals all finer forms. Thus a fruitful collaboration of mathematicians and logicians is made impossible. While the mathematician defines objects, concepts, and relations, the psychological logician watches the becoming and changing of ideas, and at bottom the mathematicians' way of defining must appear to him just silly, because it does not reproduce the essence of ideation. He looks into his psychological peepshow and says to the mathematician: "I cannot see anything at all of what you are defining." And the mathematician can only reply: "No wonder, for it is not where you are looking for it."

[Frege, Gottlob. "The Fundamental Laws of Arithmetic." In *Grundgesetze der Arithmetik,* translated by Johann Stachelroth and Philip E. B. Jourdain. *The Monist,* Vols. 25 (October 1915): 481–494 and 26 (April 1916): 182–199.]

Gödel, Kurt (1906–1978)   *Austrian mathematician and logician who proved that arithmetic is undecidable, meaning that there are true arithmetical sentences that cannot be proven or disproven, given the axioms of arithmetic. For many logicians, this result was seen as a significant shock to the view that mathematics had a solid logical foundation. Gödel's writings are very technical and the passage below is a brief summary statement of his conclusion.*

> If to the Peano axioms we add the logic of *Principia Mathematica* (with the natural numbers as the individuals) together with the axiom of choice (for all types), we obtain a formal system S, for which the following theorems hold:
>
> I. The system S is *not* complete; that is, it contains propositions A (and we can in fact exhibit such propositions) for which neither A nor *not-A* is provable and, in particular, it contains (even for decidable properties F of natural numbers) undecidable problems of the simple structure *(Ex)Fx*, where x ranges over the natural numbers.
>
> II. Even if we admit all the logical devices of *Principia Mathematica* (hence in particular the extended functional calculus and the axiom of choice) in metamathematics, there does *not* exist a *consistency proof* for the system S (still less so if we restrict the means of proof in any way). Hence a consistency proof for the system S can be carried out only by means of modes of inference that are not formalized in the system S itself ...

> [Gödel, Kurt. "Some Metamathematical Results on Completeness and Consistency." In *From Frege to Gödel: A Source Book in Mathematical Logic, 1879–1931,* edited by Jean van Heijenoort. Cambridge: Harvard University Press, 1967.]

Goodman, Nelson (1906–1998)   *American philosopher who formulated the new riddle of induction, in which he claimed that what counts as confirmation for some hypothesis is not simply determined by facts in the world and, indeed, the same facts can support different, even contradictory, hypotheses. The passage below is from his book* Fact, Fiction, and Forecast. *In this book he introduces the following problem: If we observe a green emerald that observation seems to (help) confirm the hypothesis* *that all emeralds are green. However, a green emerald also seems to (help) confirm the hypothesis that all emeralds are grue, where grue means that something is green if it is examined before some specified time (say, January 1, 3000) and blue if it is examined after that time.*

> The odd cases [such as grue] that we have been considering are clinically pure cases that, though seldom encountered in practice, nevertheless display to the best advantage the symptoms of a widespread and destructive malady.
>
> We have so far neither any answer nor any promising clue to an answer to the question what distinguishes lawlike or confirmable hypotheses from accidental or nonconfirmable ones; and what may at first have seemed a minor technical difficulty has taken on the stature of a major obstacle to the development of a satisfactory theory of confirmation. It is this problem that I call the new riddle of induction.

[Goodman, Nelson. *Fact, Fiction, and Forecast.* Cambridge: Harvard University Press, 1955.]

Hilbert, David (1862–1943)   *German mathematician whose work was fundamental in the foundations of mathematical logic; he was famous for identifying, at the beginning of the 20th century, basic questions that mathematicians needed to address as well as for trying to spell out basic axioms of logic. In the selection below, from his paper "Foundations of Logic and Arithmetic," Hilbert remarks that not only is arithmetic part of logic but that it can be axiomatized.*

> It is my opinion . . . that we can provide a rigorous and completely satisfying foundation for the notion of number, and in fact by a method that I would call *axiomatic* and whose fundamental idea I wish to develop briefly in what follows.
>
> Arithmetic is often considered to be a part of logic, and the traditional fundamental logical notions are usually presupposed when it is a question of establishing a foundation for arithmetic. If we observe attentively, however, we realize that in the traditional exposition of the laws of logic certain fundamental arithmetic notions are already used, for example, the notion of set and, to some extent, also that of number. Thus we

find ourselves turning in a circle, and that is why a partly simul-
taneous development of the laws of logic and of arithmetic is
required if paradoxes are to be avoided.

[Hilbert, David. "Foundations of Logic and Arithmetic." In *From Frege to Gödel:*
A Source Book in Mathematical Logic, 1879–1931, edited by Jean van Heijenoort.
Cambridge: Harvard University Press, 1967.]

Hume, David (1711–1776)   *Scottish philosopher who formulated the*
problem of induction (that is, how inductive reasoning can be justified).
Hume claimed that inductive reasoning cannot be justified; at best we
can only say that some inductions in the past have satisfied our inquiries.
Even the notion of cause and effect cannot be justified beyond the fact that
we accept certain events as usually following other events. The passage
below presents his problem of induction.

All reasonings may be divided into two kinds, namely, demonstrative [deductive] reasoning, or that concerning relations
of ideas; and moral [inductive] reasoning, or that concerning
matter of fact and existence . . . May I not clearly and distinctly
conceive, that a body, falling from the clouds, and which in all
other respects resembles snow, has yet the taste of salt or feeling of fire? Is there any more intelligible proposition than to
affirm, that all the trees will flourish in December and January,
and will decay in May and June? Now, whatever is intelligible,
and can be distinctly conceived, implies no contradiction, and
can never be proved false by any demonstrative argument or
abstract reasoning a priori.

   If we be, therefore, engaged by arguments to put trust in past
experience, and make it the standard of our future judgment,
these arguments must be probable only, or such as regard matter of fact and real existence, according to the division above
mentioned. But that there is no argument of this kind, must
appear, if our explication of that species of reasoning be admitted as solid and satisfactory. We have said that all arguments
concerning existence are founded on the relation of cause and
effect; that our knowledge of that relation is derived entirely
from experience; and that all our experimental conclusions
proceed upon the supposition, that the future will be conform-

able to the past. To endeavor, therefore, the proof of this last supposition by probable arguments, or arguments regarding existence, must be evidently going in a circle, and taking that for granted which is the very point in question.

[*The Philosophical Works of David Hume.* Vol. 4. London: Little, Brown, 1854.]

Lewis, Clarence Irving (1883–1964) *American philosopher whose writings spanned logic, the theory of knowledge, and ethics; with respect to logic, his work on modal logic (dealing with necessity and possibility) was especially groundbreaking. In the selection below, he criticizes how modern symbolic logic uses the notion of implication, saying that it fails to fit the purposes that (most) people use it for.*

The development of the algebra of logic brings to light two somewhat startling theorems: (1) a false proposition implies any proposition, and (2) a true proposition is implied by any proposition. These are not the only theorems of the algebra which seem suspicious to common sense, but their sweeping generality has attracted particular attention. In themselves, they are neither mysterious sayings, nor great discoveries, nor gross absurdities. They exhibit only, in sharp outline, the meaning of "implies" which has been incorporated into the algebra. What this meaning is, what are its characteristics and limitations, and its relation to the "implies" of ordinary valid inference, it is the object of this paper briefly to indicate.

. . . One of the important practical uses of implication is the testing of hypotheses whose truth or falsity is problematic. The algebraic implication has no application here. If the hypothesis happens to be false, it implies anything you please. If one find facts, *x, y, z,* otherwise unexpected but suggested by the hypothesis, the truth of these facts is implied by one's hypothesis, whether that hypothesis be true or not—since any true proposition is implied by all others. In other words, no proposition could be verified by its logical consequences. If the proposition be false, it has these 'consequences' anyway. Similarly, no contrary-to-fact conditionals could have any logical significance, whether one happen to know that it *is* contrary to fact or not. For if the fact *is* otherwise, the proposition which states the supposition implies anything and everything. In the ordinary and "proper"' use of "implies" certain conclusions can validly be inferred from contrary-to-fact suppositions, while certain others cannot. Hypotheses whose truth is problematic have logical consequences *which are independent of its truth or falsity.* These are the vital distinctions of the ordinary meaning of "implies"— for which *"p* implies *q"* is equivalent to *"q* can validly be inferred from *p"*—from that implication which figures in the algebra . . .

Nothing that has preceded should be taken to imply that the algebra of logic is necessarily unequal to the task of symbolizing such logical processes as those of inference and proof, or the more general processes which the algebra itself has the value of bringing to light. Our conclusions militate not against symbolic logic in general, but against the calculus of propositions in its present form.

[Lewis, C. I. "Implication and the Algebra of Logic." In *Mind* 21, no. 84 (1912): 522–531.]

Russell, Bertrand (1872–1970) *English philosopher and mathematician, whose multivolume work,* Principia Mathematica *(cowritten with Alfred North Whitehead), was a landmark in modern symbolic logic. Russell wrote both highly technical works and many books and articles for nonprofessionals, culminating in his winning the Nobel Prize in literature in 1950. The following passage illustrates his view that logic, because it focuses on general form, is the essence of philosophy.*

In every proposition and in every inference there is, besides the particular subject-matter concerned, a certain *form,* a way in which the constituents of the proposition or inference are put together. If I say, "Socrates is mortal," "Jones is angry," "The sun is hot," there is something common in these three cases, something indicated by the word "is." What is in common is the *form* of the proposition, not an actual constituent. If I say a number of things about Socrates—that he was an Athenian, that he married Xantippe, that he drank the hemlock—there is a common constituent, namely Socrates, in all the propositions I enunciate, but they have diverse forms. If, on the other hand, I take any one of these propositions and replace its constituents, one at a time, by other constituents, the form remains constant, but no constituent remains. Take (say) the series of propositions, "Socrates drank the hemlock," "Coleridge drank the hemlock," "Coleridge drank opium," "Coleridge ate opium." The form remains unchanged throughout this series, but all the constituents are altered. Thus form is not another constituent, but is the way the constituents are put together. It is forms, in this sense, that are the proper object of philosophical logic.

. . . In order to understand a sentence, it is necessary to have knowledge both of the constituents and of the particular instance of the form. It is in this way that a sentence conveys information, since it tells us that certain known objects are related according to a certain known form. Thus some kind of knowledge of logical form, though with most people it is not explicit, is involved in all understanding of discourse. It is the business of philosophical logic to extract this knowledge from its concrete integuments, and to render it explicit and pure.

In all inference, form alone is essential: the particular subject-matter is irrelevant except as securing the truth of the premises. This is one reason for the great importance of logical form. When I say, "Socrates was a man, all men are mortal, therefore Socrates was mortal," the connection of premises and conclusion does not in any way depend upon its being Socrates and man and mortality that I am mentioning. The general form of the inference may be expressed in some such words as, "If a thing has a certain property, and whatever has this property has a certain other property, then the thing in question also has that other property." Here no particular things or properties are mentioned: the proposition is absolutely general. All inferences, when stated fully, are instances of propositions having this kind of generality. If they seem to depend upon the subject-matter otherwise than as regards the truth of the premises, that is because the premises have not been all explicitly stated. In logic, it is a waste of time to deal with inferences concerning particular cases: we deal throughout with completely general and purely formal implications, leaving it to other sciences to discover when the hypotheses are verified and when they are not.

[Russell, Bertrand. *Our Knowledge of the External World*. London: Allen & Unwin, 1914.]

Strawson, Peter (1919–2006)   *British philosopher who argued that the problem of induction (that is, how inductive reasoning can be justified) is the result of a misunderstanding by David Hume and other philosophers. Justification of experiences presupposes inductive reasoning and a uniformity of nature, for Strawson. The selection below is taken from Strawson's book* Introduction to Logical Theory.

> [The] rationality of induction, unlike its "successfulness," is not a fact about the constitution of the world. It is a matter of what we mean by the word "rational" in its application to any procedure for forming opinions about what lies outside our observations or that of available witnesses. For to have good reasons for any such opinion is to have good inductive support for it . . .
>
> So it is a contingent, factual matter that it is sometimes possible to form rational opinions concerning what specifically happened or will happen in given circumstances (I); it is a non-contingent, *a priori* matter that the only ways of doing this must be inductive ways (II). What people have done is to run together, to conflate, the question to which I is an answer and the quite different question to which II is an answer. . . .
>
> [Strawson, P. F. *Introduction to Logical Theory.* New York: John Wiley & Sons, 1952.]

Tarski, Alfred (1901–1983)   *Polish logician and mathematician whose writings on formal semantics led many philosophers to claim that truth (at least for a formal logical system) could be made fully clear and unambiguous. The selection below is from his article "The Concept of Truth in Formalized Languages"; he states that his formal concept of truth is valuable even if it seems artificial.*

> Philosophers who are not accustomed to use deductive methods in their daily work are inclined to regard all formalized languages with a certain disparagement, because they contrast these "artificial" constructions with the one natural language—the colloquial language. For that reason the fact that the results obtained concern the formalized languages almost exclusively will greatly diminish the value of the foregoing investigations

in the opinion of many readers. In my opinion the consider-
ations [here] prove emphatically that the concept of truth (as
well as other semantical concepts) when applied to colloquial
language in conjunction with the normal laws of logic leads
inevitably to confusions and contradictions.

[Tarski, Alfred. *Logic, Semantics, Metamathematics Papers from 1923 to 1938.*
Translated by J. H. Woodger. Oxford: Clarendon, 1956.]

Turing, Alan (1912–1954) *British mathematician who played an
important role in the development of modern computers and computer
science, by showing the connections between logic and computability.
While his writings are very technical, the passage below, from his essay
"Systems of Logic Based on Ordinals," briefly states his view that comput-
ing machines can carry out logical operations.*

A function is said to be "effectively calculable" if its values can be
found by some purely mechanical process . . . We may take this
statement literally, understanding by a purely mechanical process
one which could be carried out by a machine. It is possible to give
a mathematical description, in a certain normal form, of the structures of these machines. The development of these ideas leads to the
author's definition of a computable function, and to an identification
of computability with effective calculability. It is not difficult, though
somewhat laborious, to prove that these three definitions [function,
calculability, and computability] are equivalent.

[*The Essential Turing: The Ideas That Gave Birth to the Computer Age.*
Edited by B. Jack Copeland. Oxford: Clarendon, 2004.]

Vienna Circle *The name used for a group of philosophers and other
academics who met and worked in Vienna at the beginning of the 20th
century; they formed the core of the school of thought called logical positivism, advocating the view that philosophy needed to be more scientific
and that the only meaningful claims are ones that can be verified. The
passage below is from a manifesto authored by three members of the
Vienna Circle (Hans Hahn, Rudolf Carnap, and Otto Neurath), in which
they state their scientific world conception.*

The scientific world conception is characterized not so much by theses of its own, but rather by its basic attitude, its points of view and direction of research . . . We have characterized the scientific world conception essentially by two features. First it is empiricist and positivist: there is knowledge only from experience, which rests on what is immediately given. This sets the limits for the content of legitimate science. Second, the scientific world conception is marked by application of a certain method, namely logical analysis. The aim of the scientific effort is to reach the goal, unified science, by applying logical analysis to the empirical material. Since the meaning of every statement of science must be statable by a reduction to a statement about the given, likewise the meaning of any concept, whatever branch of science it may belong to, must be statable by step-wise reduction to other concepts, down to the concepts of the lowest level which refer directly to the given.

[Neurath, Otto. *Empiricism and Sociology.* Dordrecht, Netherlands: Kluwer Academic, 1973.]

PART III

Philosophy of Science

Introductory Discussion Questions

1. What makes something a fact of nature?
2. What makes something a law of nature?
3. Is there a difference between asking *how* something happened (or is the way it is) and asking *why* it happened (or is the way it is)? If not, why not? If so, what is the difference?
4. Are there correct rules for how science should proceed? If so, what are they? If not, why not?
5. Some people claim that Darwinian evolution is just a theory. What does that mean to say that it is just a theory? Are other scientific theories just theories?
6. Can the same fact support two different, perhaps even conflicting, theories? Why or why not? If it can, then what would determine that one theory is better than another?

Philosophy of Science

The philosophy of science is the philosophical analysis of basic concepts and practices within science, such as theories and observation, and about science, such as its relation to religion or technology. As a philosophical analysis, rather than a sociological or historical one, the emphasis is on the metaphysics of science (that is, basic components of what constitutes science), the epistemology of science (that is, how science proceeds), and the axiology of science (that is, values related to science).

One example of a basic concept within science that philosophers examine and analyze is the concept of explanation. A fundamental aspect of any science, whether it is physics or psychology, is that scientists attempt to explain things and events and processes in the world rather than simply describe them. Physicists explain why objects fall (or rise), biologists explain why organisms have certain features, psychologists and sociologists explain why people behave in certain ways. However, none of these specific sciences analyze the concept of explanation. They provide explanations but do not ask what is an explanation (or what does it mean to give an explanation). The question, what is an explanation? is a philosophical one, involving the analysis of a concept. Other examples of basic concepts within science that philosophers examine include: observation and measurement, theories and models, experiments, realism, evidence, and reductionism.

Besides questions about basic concepts within science, a major focus of philosophical analysis has been on the broad issue of change and progress in science. Science in the 21st century is dramatically different in many ways from science in the 19th century and even more so from science in the 10th century or third century b.c.e. It is different in terms of content; for example, astronomers today claim that the universe is expanding and that stars have a life cycle, but these claims were not held prior to the 1900s. In addition, besides the content of science, many of the methods that are often used in science today are different than methods used prior to the 1900s; for example, many experiments are done today via computer simulation. Beyond content and methods, even some of the values related to science are different today than in the past; for example, one value within science is to be as quantitative as possible, but this was not always seen by scientists as necessary or even desirable. So, while it is obvious that science has changed over time in terms of its content and methods and values, there are questions about how and why science has changed as well as in what ways science can be said to involve progress.

Philosophers have addressed these issues of change and progress by proposing various models of how science works (and, hence, how it changes and progresses). One such model is called inductivism, sometimes associated with the work of Francis Bacon (1561–1626). Inductivism is the view that science proceeds by starting with straightforward observations, noting any patterns among the observations and proposing some hypothesis to account for those observations and patterns (if there are any); these hypotheses are then tested against future observations and, if the patterns turn out to be general enough, perhaps constructing a theory to account for those observations and hypotheses. For instance, we might notice that heavy objects fall when they are not supported by something else; furthermore, with careful observation and experimentation, we notice that they fall at certain velocities; after enough testing of various hypotheses, we might formulate a theory of gravity to explain all of these observations and experimental results. This view sees science as relying on the mode of reasoning of induction, going from a collection of observations up to an overarching theory, with scientific knowledge being the accumulation of more and more (observed) facts that finally get grouped together within theories.

Although this inductivist view of science seems like common sense, many philosophers (and scientists) have questioned it as an overall view of how science proceeds. One philosopher who questioned it was Karl Popper (1902–94). First, he said that we can find inductive support for just about anything, so induction does not prove to be very helpful in characterizing science. For example, we could find observations that support the view that evolutionary theory is right and also that evolutionary theory is wrong. Second, he said that what makes something truly good science (indeed, what makes something scientific at all) is that it might be shown to be false. In other words, scientific hypotheses take risks; they provide information to us because they might turn out to be wrong. His term for this is *falsifiability*. By this term, he meant that a good scientific hypothesis is an educated guess about the world; by testing it, we will learn some information, but we will only learn some information if it were possible that the hypothesis could have been shown to be wrong (that is, could have been falsified). For instance, if I predict that a piece of copper will either conduct electricity or it will not, then that is a safe prediction, and any observation will support it or at least not contradict it. On the other hand, if I predict that a piece of copper will conduct electricity and will do so at a particular rate and strength, then future observations could well show this hypothesis to be false. So, the hypothesis is truly testable, and the results give us information about the world. For Popper, what distinguishes science from nonscience is exactly this point of falsifiability. Science involves hypotheses that are genuinely testable, which is to say, that are genuinely falsifiable. Good hypotheses could be tested and falsified, but if these hypotheses are truly good in the sense of capturing the way the world is, they will pass those tests and not be falsified. So, a good hypothesis is falsifiable, but (we hope) not falsified, and it proceeds and makes progress by passing more and more tests. Of course, some hypotheses pass many tests, but eventually they fail. For example, Newton's laws of physics were supported by observations for centuries, but as physicists were able to experiment on subatomic particles traveling at extremely high velocities, then Newton's laws failed to hold up. As a result, for Popper, we can never say for sure that our hypotheses or theories are true (meaning that they fully describe how the world is). At best we can say that our best hypotheses and theories have passed many tests and have good support, but they might turn out in the future to be shown false.

Another important view of the nature of scientific change and progress comes from Thomas Kuhn (1922–96). Kuhn argued that scientific change is a matter of a change of paradigms. The term *paradigm* is rather vague, but he meant it to include a broad notion of how we understand the world. Within science, a paradigm includes assumptions about what things are real and how science should investigate them, even what concepts make sense for thinking about the world. For example, within an evolutionary paradigm, scientists assume that species will vary over time and as a result ask certain kinds of questions (for instance, about the rate of variation or the pace of variation of species). Within a non-evolutionary paradigm, different assumptions are held, and so, different questions will be asked, and different hypotheses will be formulated and tested. An important feature of scientific paradigms, for Kuhn, is that these assumptions are not questioned; they are assumed. Because scientists do not challenge these assumptions but build upon them, the accumulation of knowledge is always within some paradigm. However, if that paradigm is challenged and perhaps eventually rejected, then a new paradigm replaces it, along with new assumptions and new hypotheses and questions. For example, people often speak of the Ptolemaic paradigm in astronomy, in which the Earth was seen as being at the center of the universe and everything else circulating around it, while they speak of a Copernican paradigm, in which the Earth is one planet among others, not at the center of the universe, but itself circulating around the Sun. For Kuhn, science proceeds via a series of replacements of paradigms. The change in paradigms is connected to scientific revolutions, in which old assumptions are rejected and new assumptions are accepted, guiding future scientific practice. Science proceeds, then, not by slow accumulation of observed facts but by scientific revolutions and changes in paradigms.

Besides questions about basic components of science, such as explanation, and the broad issue of change and progress in science, another major focus for philosophy of science is the relation between science and society, especially with respect to values. One topic within this focus is the relation between science and religion. Some people see science and religion, or at least specific claims made in the name of science and religion, as being in conflict with each other. For example, if scientists say that the Earth is 4 billion years old and a theist says that the Earth is 6,000 years old, those claims appear to be in clear conflict with one another. On the other hand, other people argue that scientific claims and religious claims are not meant in the same way and, so, are not necessarily in conflict. So, some people argue that scriptural religious claims should not be understood literally, but rather they should be understood figuratively, or in terms of giving people meaning to their lives. For instance, these people argue, the biblical story of creation is not meant to be understood in the same way that scientists understand observational claims about the age of the universe. Scientific claims and religious claims are not in conflict because they are not talking about the same thing, even if on the surface they seem to be. These people claim that science and religion lie within different spheres of discourse.

Another issue within the topic of science and society is the relation between science and technology. Most people think of technology when they are asked about science. For example, they think of computers or automobiles or even nuclear weapons, rather than the theory of relativity or the theory of plate tectonics or genetics. It is clear that science and technology are interrelated in many ways, but many philosophers (as well as scientists and technologists) see definite differences between science and technology. For one thing, the goal of science is often said to be an understanding of the world—an understanding that is, ultimately, complete and true—while the goal of technology is action in the world, being able to manipulate things and processes in ways we want. In addition, science is concerned with developing theories that explain aspects of the world, while technology is concerned with developing mechanisms that change aspects of the world. There are, of course, overlapping concerns and interrelations between science and technology (for example, science uses computers, and technology uses scientific theoretical information), but the nature of the two, including how they relate and do not relate, are broad philosophical concerns.

Beyond issues such as the relation of science to religion and technology, there is a broad topic of the value of science itself in society. Some social critics have argued that a scientific perspective leads to dehumanizing people and leads to the view that the only legitimate way of approaching the world is via science. Critics call such a view scientism. However, others claim that science has given us a much better handle on important human problems. For example, science has led to improved medicines and health care. Also, for instance, by knowing more about the workings of the brain, we can understand and treat mental and emotional problems much better.

Description/Explanation

On the surface, there is a difference between describing some thing or some event and explaining it. For example, it is one thing to describe the changing of the colors of leaves on some trees during different seasons, but simply describing what happens does not explain how or why it happens. Description and explanation, then, are not the same thing, but they are related, since an explanation of some thing or event will rely on further information that itself will involve some description. For instance, when we explain how or why leaves change colors we do so by pointing out certain physical and chemical facts about leaves and how they respond to changes in their immediate environment and conditions. Philosophers have long asked what exactly a description or explanation is. That is, not only have they sought particular descriptions or explanations of things, but also they have pondered the very nature of description and explanation: What does it mean to describe something or to explain it?

One issue that arises is the difference between *a* description and *the* description (or *an* explanation versus *the* explanation) of something. For instance, with respect to description, different people might give different descriptions of the same thing or event. In the case of describing, say, a lamp, one person might describe it by saying what features it has (that is, its color[s], shape, height, weight, etc.). Someone else might speak of its function or its placement in a room or perhaps even its history (that is, when it was made, where, by whom, etc.). These are different descriptions, but the question is: Is there *the* description of the lamp? That is, is there a single, correct description of the lamp? Obviously, there can be incorrect descriptions, for example, if someone says that the lamp weighs two tons but it weighs only two pounds. But, is there one, single correct description? This question points to a large debate within philosophy between those who say yes, there is a correct description of things and events, and those who say no, there is no single, correct description, even though both groups agree that there are incorrect descriptions. The same holds for explanation; philosophers disagree on whether, for any thing or event, it makes sense to say that there is "the" explanation, that is, one, single correct explanation.

A similar way of asking this question of *a* versus *the* (that is, *a* description or explanation versus *the* description or explanation) is the question of what is a good description or explanation versus what is a correct description or explanation. Would it be reasonable to say that there could be a good explanation for something even if it turned out to be wrong (or incorrect)? For example, for thousands of years people thought that the Earth was stationary and the rest of the universe revolved around it. They gave very accurate descriptions of the movements of planets and stars and often made very accurate predictions based on these movements. It seems that they gave good descriptions and—it seems reasonable to say—they gave good explanations. However, today we say they were wrong; their explanations were incorrect and, to some extent, their descriptions were also incorrect. This leads back to the question: Is there only one, single correct description or explanation, with all others being incorrect, that is, being not good?

One aspect of this issue is the claim that what counts as a correct, or even as a good, description or explanation seems to be determined at least in part by goals and interests. For instance, suppose a person is found dead and the question arises: Why/how did this person die? One answer might be: He was shot. Another answer might be: He double-crossed a partner in crime. Another answer might be: He lived a life of sin and God (or karma) caught up with him. Each of these is an explanation and, depending upon the context—that is, depending upon what kind of information is wanted—each provides (perhaps) a correct explanation. For many philosophers, then, although not for all, what could count as a (or the) correct description/explanation, or even as an (or the) incorrect description/explanation, depends upon what kind of information is relevant to the goals or interests in asking the question.

While philosophers have not focused a great deal of attention on the issue of description, they have done so on the issue of explanation. This is especially true with respect to scientific explanation, that is, what it means to explain something scientifically. Although there is no uniform agreement among philosophers about scientific explanation, they have suggested various models of how science explains things. One view is that what it means to give an explanation is to identify the cause(s) of the thing to be explained. This is often called the causal model. For instance, if we want to explain how or why leaves change colors on certain trees, then we would identify the relevant causes; we would describe, say, what physical forces and interactions are involved in causing color change in those leaves. Or if we were to explain why someone died, it would not be enough to simply say that the person was shot; we would need to identify and describe the underlying physical forces and interactions that relate being shot with dying (since not everyone who is shot dies and not everyone who dies is shot). Another view of scientific explanation is that what is needed to truly explain things is what is often called the unification model. This is the view that explaining things is a matter of showing how the particular thing or event in question connects with knowledge and information that we already know and understand. Every thing or event has a multitude of causes that led up to it, and some of those causes seem to be unimportant and perhaps irrelevant to understanding the thing or event in question. So, what is needed, according to this view, is showing how the particular thing or event is relevantly related to information that we already understand. There are other accounts of explanation, and this is a lively area within the broader topic of the philosophy of science.

Theories

The notion of theory usually relates to philosophy in the context of the philosophy of science. Because theories are so much a part of science, when philosophers look at the nature of science and philosophical issues connected to science, one of the things they focus on is theory. One thing to note at the beginning is that the word *theory* is usually contrasted with a number of different terms. For example, *theory* is sometimes contrasted with *fact*. When this contrast is being made, the point is that facts are definite, proven knowledge or information, whereas theories are not (they are merely theories). However, *theory* is also contrasted with *guess*. That is, simply guessing about something is not at all the same thing as having a theory about it.

Besides *fact* and *guess*, the term *theory* is distinguished from other terms. For example, we contrast *theory* with *assumption*. While a theory might serve among assumptions we have about something, a theory is not simply an assumption because there is always evidence and facts that are part of theories. Likewise, *theory* is more inclusive and encompassing than the terms *hypothesis*. A hypothesis is fairly precise and particular. A theory, on the other hand, is broader than that; theories include hypotheses and are meant to explain things, not simply hypothesize about them. The point, of course, is not that the word *theory* is

Portrait of Sir Isaac Newton from Arthur Shuster and Arthur E. Shipley's *Britain's Heritage of Science*

vague or means whatever anyone wants it to mean, but that we use that word in various contexts and usually to contrast it with some other notion.

A basic philosophical question is what is a scientific theory? There is no single definition that philosophers (or scientists) all use, but there are some features they generally point to: theories (at least scientific theories) relate to observation and evidence; theories involve principles, in the sense that they are generalized statements or conceptions rather than specific particular claims and hypotheses; theories have the function of explaining, predicting, verifying, etc. For example, evolutionary theory is said to encompass lots of specific information and provide a basis for predicting future observations, as well as give an explanation for things that are observed. In addition, as a theory, it is not simply dreamed up by someone to account for things but is closely connected with evidence and facts. Likewise, the Newtonian theory of motion and gravitation was much more than simple guesswork and far broader than a simple hypothesis or assumption.

Besides features of what theories are, there are also standards and criteria for what counts as a good theory. For example, a theory should be extensive, or connect and explain a large amount of information. For instance, Newton's theory of gravity and motion explains events throughout the entire universe, not just on the Earth. In addition, a good theory is said to be fecund, or fruitful. In other words, a good theory should stimulate and generate new questions and new research; it not only accounts for information we are already aware of but also it is forward looking in the sense of nudging us toward further information. A third criterion of a good theory is that it is predictive and explanatory. Theories do not simply describe things but give a basis for making predictions and provide a basis for explaining those things that we encounter. For instance, evolutionary theory not only explains why different organisms and species have certain features, but it predicts that particular changes in environments will lead to particular changes in the features of organisms and species.

Another criterion for a good theory is simplicity. That is to say, everything being equal, a simpler theory is better than a more complex theory. Some things and events in the world, of course, are complex, so simplicity in and of itself, then, is not crucial. Rather, if two different theories can account for the same things, the simpler theory is preferable to the more complicated theory. One of the reasons that Newton's theory of gravity and motion was so powerful is that it explained so many things with just three laws of motion and the law of gravity. Along with simplicity, another criterion of a good scientific theory is *plasticity*, or how well a theory can accommodate new information. For instance, although Darwin thought that evolution was gradual, with small changes taking place over many generations of organisms, other evolutionary biologists have said that evolution can function in less gradual ways than Darwin thought. For these biologists, the broad theory is fine, but it can be refined from some parts that Darwin supported.

Yet another criterion of a good theory is that it is coherent. This means that the theory is internally consistent—it does not contradict itself—and also that it is externally consistent—it fits with other established facts, laws, and theories. As with simplicity, this criterion is not crucial, since some good theories do in fact run counter to what is taken at the time to be established knowledge. But, on the whole, being consistent with other aspects of science is important. Finally, many philosophers and scientists take a criterion of a good theory to be that it is quantitative. In other words, the content of the theory should be expressible in quantitative, mathematical formulae. Although it is not obvious that all theories are like this, it is usually assumed that the more quantitative a theory is, the better it is. Now, the point of all of this is that there are widely accepted features of theories that certainly indicate that theories are far more important than simple guesswork, broader than hypotheses, and more comprehensive than facts. Finally, one important philosophical issue about theory is how theory influences people's understanding of things and even how it influences what observations and facts are accepted.

Classical and Medieval Science

Pre-Socratic Natural Philosophy

The term *pre-Socratic* philosophy refers to thinkers in the Mediterranean area, stretching from modern-day Italy to modern-day Turkey, roughly between 600 B.C.E. and 400 B.C.E. They are grouped together for two major reasons. First, they focused largely on the same sorts of conceptual and philosophical concerns, and, second, because Socrates had such a significant influence on subsequent philosophical thought that he is seen as a turning point between those who preceded him and those who followed him.

The pre-Socratic philosophers primarily focused their attention on issues of natural philosophy, that is, fundamental knowledge of nature, as opposed to, say, society. Today we might well think of them as early scientists as much as early philosophers. Their concerns were metaphysical (asking about what is real), epistemological (asking about how we know), and axiological (asking about what is important). In particular, their concerns were about the basic underlying nature of the physical world, what means we can use to know about it, and why such knowledge matters.

Pre-Socratic philosophy is characterized by four overlapping fundamental themes: (1) appearance versus reality, (2) change versus permanence, (3) accident versus essence, and (4) the many versus the one. The theme of appearance versus reality has to do with questioning whether or not the way things appear to be to us is, in fact, the way they really are. Is the real nature of trees or water or anything in the world the same as how we experience them? Today, for example, we would say that water is composed of two gases, and even those gases are composed of molecules and atoms and subatomic particles. So, what we experience on an everyday basis—a wet liquid—is not what we would take to be an experience of gases or atoms. If everyday knowledge of things as we experience them is not necessarily the same thing as knowledge of things as they really are (knowledge of an underlying reality), then it is important, said the pre-Socratics, to go beyond or beneath everyday experience—that is, beyond appearances—to come to know reality. This relates directly to the theme of change versus permanence. In our everyday experience, we note that things often change, or at least they appear to change: acorns become oak trees, kittens become cats, bananas ripen and change color and texture, things come into being and go out of existence. Is there, asked the pre-Socratics, anything that is permanent, that does not change or that remains the same beneath the apparent change? This was asking whether there is a permanent substance, or thing, that stands under the changes we experience.

The third theme of accident and essence gets at much of the same concern. Things have different properties or features. For example, a cat has physical properties, such as fur and eyes, as well as behavioral properties, such as purring and running. Some properties are said to be essential, meaning that if those properties changed or were different, then the thing itself that had those properties would be different. If a particular cat lost an ear, it would not necessarily be a different cat but would be the same cat with one fewer ear. But if a given cat had a different set of genes, then it might well be taken as a different cat, not the same cat that had somehow changed. Essential properties, then, are taken as properties that are defining of what something is. Accidental properties, however, are taken as features of something that happen to be characteristic of that thing but are not necessary for that thing to be what it is. Having claws of a certain length can be a feature of some cat, but if those claws are trimmed, it is still the same cat; having a certain set of genes, however, can be necessary for some cat to be that particular cat. Pre-Socratic philosophers saw essential features as the underlying permanent reality of things in the world.

Finally, the theme of the many versus the one also connects with issues of what is real and permanent and essential. The question here is: Are the things that are real (as opposed to mere appearances) consti-tuted by many basic kinds of things or are they ultimately constituted by one kind of thing? At the level of appearance, the answer seems to be: many kinds of things. Cats are not the same things, or kind of things, as oak trees and neither is the same kind of thing as water. But, the ques-tion is whether at the level of what is real there are many fundamental kinds of things or just one.

The focus on this last theme in particular led to several basic schools of thought among the pre-Socratic philosophers. One school of thought is called monism, because it holds the view that all things are ultimately constituted by one kind of thing. The other school of thought is called pluralism, because it holds the view that there is more than one ultimate kind of thing that constitutes things in the world. The pre-Socratic phi-losophers understood things in the world to be composed of four basic elements: earth, water, air, and fire. These four elements were associated with two basic characteristics: heat and moisture. Earth was said to be cold and dry; water, cold and wet; air, hot and wet; and fire, hot and dry. The monists argued that ultimately things could be understood as being composed of one of these basic elements, while the pluralists argued that all four were necessary and no element could be accounted for in terms of any of the other three.

Earliest among the monists was Thales (fl. 580 B.C.E.). Thales argued that water was the source of all things. Commonsense observation shows that living organisms require water to survive. In addition, the natural landscape itself is shaped by water, or at least moisture. Even the air contains water. This view, however, was immediately criticized by Anaximander (610–546 B.C.E.), who argued that no element could generate its opposite. Since fire is the opposite of water (fire is dry and hot, water is wet and cold), it could not be generated by or composed of water. Furthermore, Anaximander argued, no basic element could be generated by another. Rather, there is an even more basic reality, which he labeled the *apeiron,* meaning boundless or unlimited. The world, for Anaximander, is a "war of opposites" in which the basic elements are separated from the apeiron by a whirling motion. A third pre-Socratic monist was Anaximenes (fl. 545 B.C.E.), who claimed that air was the fundamental element and source of all things. Anaximenes thought that Anaximander's notion of the apeiron did not resolve the problem of opposites, or how one element could be generated by another with opposite features. Rather, he said, the apeiron ignores the problem and simply offers a label to explain it away. Like Thales, Anaximenes thought that one of the material elements was basic and only a material explanation would suffice to resolve the problem of opposites. As a result, he offered such an explanation by saying that air was basic and the other elements were generated by air being condensed or rarefied. As air condensed, clouds could form and eventually moisture/water would be created. If this were condensed even further, silt and mud—that is, earth—would be generated. On the other hand, by rarefying air, fire would be produced. This process could be demonstrated, he claimed, by blowing air out of one's mouth. If the opening in one's lips is small (that is, condensed), then the air coming out feels cool to the touch, but if one opens one's mouth wide (that is, rarefied) and blows air out, then the air coming out feels warm. The important conceptual point is that qualitative features (that is, features of things that we experience every day, such as heat or color) are accounted for in terms of quantity and nothing extra-material, such as the apeiron, is needed.

Other pre-Socratic monists were not convinced of the fundamental nature of the four material elements of earth, water, air, and fire. Pythagoras (571–497 B.C.E.) claimed that what was basic and most real is quantity itself, number. The world is ultimately accounted for in

In this painting from 1662, Pythagoras astounds fishermen with his accurate count of the fish in their nets. *(Painting by Salvator Rosa)*

In this 1477 fresco (trans-
ferred to canvas), a cry-
ing Heraclitus sits beside
a laughing Democritus.
*(Fresco by Donato Bra-
mante)*

terms of quantity and proportion. Besides his famous work on mathematics and musical harmony, Pythagoras argued for the basic essence
of reality less in terms of some material content, such as water, but in
terms of quantitative form or structure. Another monist was Heraclitus
(fl. 500 B.C.E.), who spoke of fire as the basic element. But even more
important, he viewed the basic underlying reality and unity as a unity
of pattern, rather than of things. Change itself is the most basic reality. Heraclitus is famous for having said that one cannot step into the
same river twice, because whatever constitutes the river is in constant
motion and change. Finally, with the opposite view was Parmenides (fl.
485 B.C.E.), who claimed that Being was the one underlying permanent
reality. We cannot even think of or speak of nonbeing, because to think
or speak of something is to think or speak of some *thing*. There must
be something—even if it is not a material thing—that is being referred
to even when we deny that it exists; otherwise, for Parmenides, what
we say is simply nonsense. Change is impossible, even inconceivable,
he argued. In addition, whatever is—whatever exists—must be uncre-
ated (otherwise, there was a time when a thing was nothing) and inde-
structible (otherwise, there will come a time when a thing is nothing).
Likewise, Being is One, since if two separate things existed, both would
Be, but they would both be Being, which is one unity. So, all change
and motion is mere appearance, not actual reality, for Parmenides. His
student, Zeno of Elea (fl. 465 B.C.E.), presented various arguments to
show that motion and change and plurality were mere illusions and not
really possible. One such argument was offered to show that motion was

impossible. It is called the flying arrow paradox. At any instant in time, Zeno claimed, an arrow occupies an exact set of points in space. At that instant, there is no motion, or movement through space. However, time is just a collection of instants. So, for any and every given instant, the arrow is not moving (it occupies just an exact set of points in space). So, there is zero motion at any instant in time. But to add up a collection of zeroes—that is, a collection of instants in time—is still to come up with zero. Motion, then, is only apparent, not real.

The pre-Socratic pluralists included Empedocles (484–424 B.C.E.), Anaxagoras (500–428 B.C.E.), and the atomists, Democritus (460–370 B.C.E.) and Leucippus (fl. 440 B.C.E.). Empedocles claimed that what Parmenides showed was only that monism and motion were incompatible, not that monism was true. Instead, Empedocles rejected monism and accepted the four material elements of earth, water, air, and fire. The different things that we experience in the world are the result of varying proportions of those elements. In addition, he claimed, while Anaximenes spoke of material causes for change in the world, via condensation and rarefaction, he did not provide any explanation for them. Empedocles claimed that Love and Strife (or attraction and separation) were fundamental forces in nature, just as basic and ultimate as the four material elements. Change and appearance, for him, were the result of these forces acting on the basic material elements. Anaxagoras agreed with Empedocles that the four basic elements were indeed basic, and he argued that those elements were eternal: They could not be created or destroyed. Instead, the varying mixtures and proportions of those elements that accounted for different things in the world could alter. Common things, then, could be created or destroyed, but the elements that made them up could not. An additional fundamental component of the world was Mind (or *nous*). Finally, the atomists argued that all things are composed of countless atoms. The Greek word *atomos* meant that which could not be cut or divided. The atomists argued that there must be some smallest material entity, which takes up some amount of space, no matter how small. Whatever this smallest thing was could not be divided any farther, hence was *atomos*. The variation we experience in the world, such as cats and trees and water, are the result of the different combinations of atoms. While this sounds modern, it must be remembered that this pre-Socratic notion of atoms is strictly conceptual and not the result of physical observation or experimentation. Nonetheless, it played an important role in subsequent natural philosophy and even moral philosophy.

Aristotle

The Greek philosopher Aristotle (384–322 B.C.E.) claimed that there were two basic spheres in the universe. One sphere he called the terrestrial sphere, and the other he called the celestial sphere. The terrestrial sphere included the Earth up to the Moon; the celestial sphere, the Moon and onto the rest of the heavens. Aristotle observed that on the Earth, things moved either naturally or unnaturally (what he called "violently"). Natural motion depended upon the nature of the thing that was moving. Heavy objects naturally fell to the ground, while light objects either fell much more slowly or, in the case of, say, a balloon, rose into the sky. Aristotle argued that things moved naturally depending upon their nature, where their nature was a function of the four classical elements: earth, water, air, and fire. Heavy things tended to fall to the ground, for Aristotle, because that is their natural place. Being made primarily of the element earth, they would seek their natural place in the world. Light objects, on the other hand, would seek their natural place, which might be to rise if they were made of air or fire. Unnatural (or violent) motion was when things moved contrary to their natural motion. For example, if someone threw a rock into the air, being made of earth, it would seek its natural place on the ground. Having been thrown, while it was moving upwards, its motion would be unnatural, but because of its nature, it would seek to return to the ground, and so, it would slow down and eventually fall back to the ground. All of this discussion was about the terrestrial sphere, where things come into existence and go out of existence. The celestial sphere, however, for Aristotle, was a place of perfection. In the heavens (not the religious sense of Heaven, but where the planets and stars are), things are "incorruptible" or eternal. Aristotle claimed that heavenly objects must be made up of some fifth element (the later Latin word was *quintessence*, meaning "fifth essence"), because if they were made up of any of the four terrestrial elements, they would seek their natural place and fall into the terrestrial sphere. So, they are composed of something incorruptible, and they move only by natural motion, which, he said, was circular; this is why they move in circular orbits around the Earth (which he thought was stationary and at the center of the universe). Although today we say that Aristotle's views about physics were wrong, they were the basic conception of the physical world for many centuries.

Theoria/Praxis/Techné

The terms *theoria,* praxis*,* and *techné* are Greek words for different kinds of knowledge. They are usually associated with the writings of Aristotle. Aristotle's writings and thinking were very systematic. He often wrote on classifying and categorizing subjects before then analyzing them. For example, with respect to knowledge, broadly speaking, he claimed that there were three fundamental kinds of knowledge: *theoria,* praxis, *techné. Theoria* is theoretical knowledge, with the goal of theoretical understanding. For Aristotle, this type of knowledge included mathematics and physics, but also theology (the study of God). Praxis is practical knowledge, with the goal of practical action and conduct. For Aristotle, this type of knowledge included ethics, economics, even social and political philosophy. *Techné* is technical knowledge, with the goal of making or producing something. For Aristotle, this type of knowledge included art and rhetoric; while we might think this focused on the sorts of things that today we would consider technology, it even more had to do with the notion of technique (in various fields, not just technology). A major aspect of this division of different types of knowledge was that Aristotle was more concerned with describing and explaining the many kinds of things (in this case knowledge) that there are rather than looking for one underlying essence of things. Whereas his teacher, Plato, had focused on discovering and identifying the core features of whatever he studied, Aristotle was more comfortable with looking at the many kinds and variations of those things he studied, without assuming that there were some core features to them.

Plato famously asked, "What is knowledge?" and answered this question by saying that there is a single kind of thing that knowledge is. There are all sorts of cases in which we claim to have knowledge. For example, I know my name; I know that two plus two equals four; I know that the Sun is larger than the Earth; I know I am awake right now; I know George Washington was once the president of the United States. Plato said that if these cases are all truly cases of knowledge, then they must have something in common in order for them to be knowledge. In addition, things that I do not know (that is, cases where I do not have knowledge, but perhaps an opinion or just a belief) must lack something in order for them not to be knowledge. For Plato, the core essence of knowledge was justified true belief. That is, for him, knowledge was a true belief that had some justification to back it up. Aristotle, however, did not assume or look for some core essence to all cases of knowledge. Rather, he said that what counts as knowledge depends in part on the goal of inquiry. In other words, what we count as a case of knowledge depends in part, at least, on what we want to know and why we want to know it. Sometimes we want a basic theoretical understanding of how and why things are the way they are (such as a scientific theory); this is *theoria*. Other times we want more of a practical application of information in order to solve some problem or give us a way to get along in the world (such as building a bridge); this is praxis. Yet other times we want some technique for accomplishing some goal or creating something, but it is not necessarily a practical application of information (such as crafting a moving speech or song); this is *techné*. These different kinds of knowledge are similar to, though not exactly the same as, today's notions of knowledge that something is the case (like knowing that cats are mammals) and knowledge how to do something (like knowing how to ride a bike).

Aristotle died in 322 B.C.E., but his influence lived on for centuries, especially in the area of natural philosophy (or science). In large part, how people thought of the natural world was in Aristotelian terms for nearly 2,000 years! Although his influence waned around the year 1500, there were still many scientists, even into the 1700s, such as the renowned biologist Carl Linnaeus (1707–78), who conceived of the world in ways that Aristotle laid out. Those ways included the notion that function and teleology (or goal-directedness) were necessary for explaining things and events. This focus on understanding things in terms of teleology included the concept of final cause, which meant that things happened for a reason, or for some purpose, that purpose being to fulfill some particular goal. Aristotle was said to have claimed that nature did nothing in vain, and this was taken to mean that things happened for some purpose.

With respect to the universe as a whole, the Aristotelian view—which, for the most part, held sway until the 1600s—was that the Earth was at the center of the universe and everything revolved around it.

While this view was questioned and even challenged by some medieval thinkers, such as Nicole Oresme (1323–82), it was the prevailing view until the 1600s. Along with this view was the belief that the universe was made up of two spheres or regions: the terrestrial sphere and the celestial sphere. The terrestrial sphere included the Earth and space up to the Moon, while the celestial sphere was the rest of the universe. In the terrestrial sphere, things can come into existence and go out of existence (sometimes said as: Things are generable and corruptible). In the celestial sphere, however, the view was that things are not generable or corruptible; they are permanent and fixed.

The terrestrial sphere was said to be composed of four fundamental elements, out of which all things arose. Those elements were earth, water, air, and fire. Things in the celestial sphere were said to be composed of some fifth element, later identified by the Latin term *quintessence,* from "quint" (or five) and "essence" (or being). These four terrestrial elements were associated with two basic features: heat and moisture. Earth was said to be cold and dry; water, cold and wet; air, hot and wet; fire, hot and dry. Everyday things in the world, such as trees and rocks and horses, were made up of these various four elements in different proportions. The seasons of the year were associated with the different elements; for example, spring was seen as hot and wet; summer, hot and dry; autumn, cold and dry; winter, cold and wet. In addition, a person's health was associated with these basic elements. It was said that there were four humours (or four fluids) in the body, with each humour being associated with a particular element. For instance, if someone had a fever, this was seen as the person having too much heat and being too wet. The person was considered to be ill because there was an imbalance of the humours; in this case, the humour associated with being hot and wet was blood. So, the treatment for a fever was to try to make the person cooler and drier. One way of doing this, they thought, was to reduce the level of blood, since that was thought to be causing the person to be too hot and wet. This view, what came to be called the "four humours" view of health, continued as the basic understanding of health for centuries.

Besides the content of Aristotle's scientific views, his notions of method, or how to investigate the world, held sway for centuries as well. Today, many people label this approach as deductivism. The notion was that one should explain the broadest and most basic aspects of nature first and then later focus on particulars and specific differences among things. As part of this approach, Aristotle developed a system of logic called syllogisms. The point was to show that, on the basis of some information, one could arrive at a conclusion about other information. This was done by showing that two things are related to each other because they both are known to be related to a third thing. For example, if someone knew that all mammals are warm-blooded and also knew that some things in the sea are mammals, then one would know that some things in the sea are warm-blooded. This deductive approach was seen as providing a more secure ground for knowledge than just observation or personal experience. Although Aristotle himself wrote a great deal about observation and made very detailed observational studies of nature, this deductive method was seen as the standard for genuine knowledge about the world. The work of the Greek mathematician Euclid, who lived shortly after Aristotle, was seen as the crowning example of this. Mathematics was taken as the best example of deduction, in which one could prove a conclusion and the result was guaranteed. Euclidean geometry was used to make careful measurements

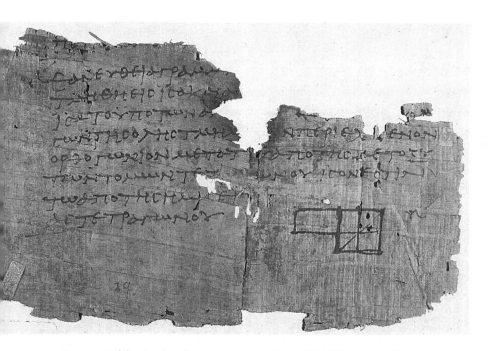

Fragment of the Oxyrhynchus papyrus showing Euclid of Alexandria's *Elements*

and predictions about the natural world, and these successes further secured the belief that deductivism was the best method of inquiry, at least for explaining things if not for exploring them.

In the Middle Ages (roughly 400–1400), the Aristotelian world-view was taken for granted, at least with respect to natural philosophy. Although there were some criticisms of specific claims of Aristotle, the basic assumptions of his views were taken as given. Historically, it turned out that much of his actual writings were lost to the West (that is, Europe) for a long time, but they were known in the Middle East, where scientific inquiry thrived during much of the Middle Ages. Only in the 1100s and 1200s did his writings become widely known again in the West. At that time, some scholars, such as Thomas Aquinas (1225–74) attempted to blend Aristotle's thought with Christian doctrine. His influence was great enough that for a while he was referred to simply as The Philosopher. One such medieval scholar was William of Ockham (1280–1349). Today, Ockham is best known for what has come to be called Ockham's razor. Ockham's razor is a reference to the principle that explanations should be as simple as possible, but not too simple! In Ockham's own writings, he frequently remarked that "plurality is not to be posited without necessity" and "what can be explained by the assumption of fewer things is vainly explained by the assumption of more things." So, there are two ways that this has been understood. One way is in terms of what is real. In this case, Ockham's razor is said to suggest that one should not assume the existence of things unless their assumption is necessary (or at least reasonable). We might be able to explain noises in the attic by claiming that there are goblins up there who are stomping around, but we could probably explain those noises without assuming the existence of goblins. The second, and related, way that Ockham's razor has been understood is more explicitly about explaining (and not about what things there are to be explained). So, even if the noises in the attic are made by, say, squirrels and not by goblins, we should explain this by, say, claiming that the squirrels are looking for food or shelter, not that they are having a dance party.

This notion of Ockham's razor was not created by Ockham; many others, including Aristotle, had expressed a similar sentiment about making explanations as simple as necessary, but the term has become common over the centuries. Later, it was associated somewhat with a view called reductionism, which is the notion that things and explanations can be reduced, or made simpler, and that this is a goal of science.

Reductionism

Usually when people think of reduction or reducing, they think of something getting smaller. In philosophy, the notion of reduction is a special sense of something getting smaller. It is not the notion that some particular thing actually gets smaller, but rather it is the notion that a concept refers to something simpler. For example, philosophers (and people in general) say that water just is H_2O or that heat just is molecules in motion. Philosophers speak of this as saying that the concept of water is reduced to the concept of H_2O or that the concept of heat is reduced to the concept of molecules in motion. Reductionism is the view that more complex things can be reduced to simpler, less complex things.

There are various types of reduction, or various ways in which we can speak of reduction. One way is called ontological reduction. This simply means that one thing, or kind of thing, really just is a simpler thing, or kind of thing. So, again, water (one kind of thing) is said really just to be H_2O (another kind of thing). By saying that water is one kind of thing and H_2O is another (simpler) kind of thing, what is meant is that water is a complex thing, with various features or properties, such as being wet, quenching people's thirst, having some color or taste or smell, etc. H_2O, on the other hand, is another kind of thing, namely, a molecule composed of different atoms bonded together in a certain way, also with various features or properties. But, given what we have learned from science, we now say that water just is H_2O; it is not anything other than H_2O. Take away the hydrogen and the oxygen, and there is nothing left of water.

A second type or sense of reduction that philosophers investigate is called epistemological reduction or, sometimes, theoretical reduction. This sense of reduction has to do, not with the physical features or nature of things, but with how we understand and explain things. For example, in physics, physicists say that Newton's theory can be reduced to Einstein's theory. What this means is that Einstein's theory can explain everything that Newton's theory can, and even more (but not the reverse; that is, Newton's theory cannot explain everything that

Albert Einstein during a lecture in Vienna in 1921 *(Photograph by Ferdinand Schmutzer)*

Einstein's theory can). Another example is that many scientists, but not all, claim that—at least, in theory—psychology can be reduced to biology. What this means is that anything that psychology can explain could, in principle, be explained by biology, because, after all, people are biological organisms and if we just knew enough about biology we could ultimately explain all human actions (including mental and cognitive actions) biologically. In effect, then, psychology would just be part of biology; it would be reduced to biology. The laws and models and theories that biology uses to explain things could ultimately be used to explain everything that psychology now explains (and more). Just as water really just is H_2O, so, too, psychology really just is biology; this is the view of theoretical reduction.

An additional kind or sense of reduction that philosophers speak of is called methodological reduction. This is similar to theoretical reduction, but slightly different. Methodological reduction says that the methods used to study simpler things can ultimately be used to study more complex things. For theoretical reduction, the focus is on one theory explaining another theory (or the theories in one science explaining the things that a theory in another science explains), while for methodological reduction, the focus is on one approach or process or practice being used for exploring those things that another approach or process or practice does. For example, we might think that we can use techniques in physics (such as X-rays or brain-scanning physical equipment) to study things associated with psychology (such as thinking or memory). Or, we might use techniques from biology to study social behavior of people, usually associated with sociology.

These various kinds or senses of reduction are supported by many people (including many philosophers) because, they say, the world is a certain way and therefore ultimately there is a single, correct description of the way the world is. As we learn more about science and about the world, we find that we can describe and explain and study things on the assumption that things can be reduced to simpler and simpler aspects. These people say, for instance, that if physics studies the fundamental nature of all physical things, then, at least in principle, physics could be able to explain all physical things, including all biological organisms and people and their behavior.

Not all people (or philosophers) agree with reductionism. Each of the three kinds or senses of reduction has been criticized. Ontological reduction has been criticized because some philosophers have said that some things have features or properties that are not reducible to their physical nature. For example, economics deals with money and exchanging money. But money is abstract; a dollar is not the physical piece of paper that is a dollar bill. It is also not the bundle of electronic signals that go back and forth when someone's credit card is swiped at the store. So, these critics say, dollars simply cannot be reduced to any simpler physical thing because dollars themselves are not physical.

If these critics are right, that speaks also to theoretical reduction, because no physical theory could then explain economic interactions. After all, these critics say, economic interactions are, like dollars, abstract. Completely explaining the behavior of electrons and electricity would never explain economic exchange, they say. Likewise, methodological reduction does not apply here, they argue. No matter how well physical theories and laws work for studying physical things and events, those techniques are irrelevant to economics, say these critics. Among these critics, many of them do not reject reduction altogether. Rather, they say, some things can be reduced to other things, but some things cannot. Also, among these critics, some say that reduction might make sense in principle, but it could never be fully possible in practice. For instance, some claim that the notions of function and teleology, or being goal-directed, are so basic in biology that they could never be reduced to physical laws and theories that do not explain things in a goal-directed way. For example, the lungs or immune system each can be understood only in terms of its function of keeping an organism alive, but physical laws and theories do not speak of functions but only of interactions. So, although biological organisms are physical, and therefore subject to physical laws and theories, these critics claim that these physical laws and theories are not capable of explaining all aspects of biological organisms in actual practice.

Renaissance and Early Modern Science

Most historians speak of the European Renaissance as the time between the mid-1400s and the mid-1600s. It is also the time period that has been called the Scientific Revolution. This time included some of the most famous people in the history of science, such as Nicolas Copernicus (1473–1543), Johannes Kepler (1571–1630), and Galileo Galilei (1564–1642). During this time there were tremendous social and cultural changes. This was the period of the discovery of the New World (from the perspective of Europeans) and the rise of global exploration and colonialism. The influence and authority of the Catholic Church were questioned and challenged by the rise of nation-states in Europe and also by theologians, such as Martin Luther (1483–1546). At the same time, new technologies were emerging, such as the printing press, that made information more accessible to more people.

With respect to science (at this time still called natural philosophy), there were a number of fundamental changes and developments. One change was the emergence of scientific societies, that is, groups of people who worked on similar issues. Prior to this time essentially all scientific investigation had taken place by independently wealthy individuals or by clergy (for instance, monks in monasteries), because they were the only people who were literate or had time and opportunity to carry out scientific work. With the emergence of scientific societies, there was a greater flow and cross-checking of scientific research.

Another change at this time was emergence of a mechanical view of the world. That is, more and more there came to be the view that the world was like an enormous, complex mechanism that operated by definite, precise causes and laws. As part of this mechanical picture of the world, the traditional Aristotelian view of final cause was, in large part, dropped. (Final cause was the notion that things must be explained in terms of some purpose or goal or end; things happen for a reason, for some potential goal to be realized.) Scientists began more and more to speak of proximate causes, meaning mechanical, physical causes that could be measured and tested, while setting aside ultimate causes, meaning purposes or goals or even God. Since only proximate causes could be measured and tested, they would be the focus of scientific inquiry and explanation. Along with this new focus on proximate causes, scientists placed more emphasis on inductive reasoning, that is, on beginning with particular information and generalizing from that information as they gathered more information. This, they said, was how to read the book of nature rather than assuming that knowledge must be deduced from principles that were assumed to be true (which is what they claimed was the long-standing view derived from Aristotle). One of the most outspoken critics of the reliance on deductions and advocates of this new inductivism was Francis Bacon.

Francis Bacon

The English statesman and philosopher Francis Bacon (1561–1626) was highly critical of earlier methods of inquiry and advocated a new method for acquiring knowledge. It had been common for scientists to make use of syllogisms, a special form of logical argument. An example of a syllogism is: "All men are mortal. Socrates is a man. Therefore, Socrates is mortal." Syllogisms proceed deductively; that is, the conclusion is intended to follow logically, not empirically, from the reasons (premises) given for that conclusion. Put another way, the premises lead to the conclusion simply as a matter of logic, not because the natural world behaves one way rather than another, or because there is some phenomenon in nature on which the conclusion is based. For example, in the above example, the conclusion that Socrates is mortal follows logically from the premises that Socrates is a man and that all men are mortal. So, *if* the premises are true, then the conclusion *must* be true

ono:ᵐ Franciſcus Bacon. Baro de Verulam. Vice-
ount; Sᵗ Albani. mortuus 9 Aprilis, Aᵒ 1626.
Annoq. Ætatis ſuæ, 66.

Illustration of Francis Bacon *(Wenzel Hollar)*

also. But the conclusion follows from the premises as a matter of logic, not because of the way the natural world is. To see this, consider the syllogism: "All men are immortal. Socrates is a man. Therefore, Socrates is immortal." It is false, of course, that all men are immortal, and in fact because no man is immortal, the conclusion of this syllogism (that Socrates is immortal) is false as well. However, the conclusion does follow logically from the premises (it just happens to be the case that one of those premises, that all men are immortal, is false).

Bacon charged that the use of syllogisms in science hindered the progress of science for the reason that, too often, scientists drew general conclusions on the basis of just a few observations and then proceeded to use those general observations in syllogisms to draw more conclusions. But a general conclusion on the basis of just a small number of observations of the natural world is not likely to be a very strong conclusion; for example, the general conclusion that all swans are white is not a very strong conclusion if it is based on observing just a handful of white swans. It would not be surprising if such general statements turned out to be false. In that case, however, using such statements in syllogisms would likely lead to false conclusions (just as, in the example above, the premise that all men are immortal helps lead to the false conclusion that Socrates is immortal). Science, Bacon thought, had relied too little on actual observations of the actual world.

Bacon specifically identified four other problems that weaken methods of inquiry; he dubbed these problems the Four Idols. The Idols of the Tribe are flaws in human perception and reasoning; our senses sometimes deceive us, and sometimes our understanding distorts what is real (we misconstrue the nature of what is real or true). The Idols of the Cave are a person's individual biases and limited perspective. These can occur as a result of what a person is taught, a person's personality, or a person's circumstances. A person who spends most of her life living in a lush landscape, for instance, will have a different perspective regarding plant life than someone who has spent most of his life living in a desert landscape. The mistake would come in assuming that one's own perspective is the only and best perspective or, put another way, that one's own experience is uniquely authoritative. The third kind of idols are the Idols of the Marketplace, which are the concepts and words people use in conversation and communication with each other. Of course, there is nothing wrong with many concepts and words. But, Bacon thought, because sometimes concepts and language are vague, misleading, or even refer to nothing, mistakes in inquiry can arise as a result. For instance (though this is not Bacon's example), it was once thought there must be a special substance called phlogiston, and scientists spent time and energy discussing and attempting to examine the nature of phlogiston. But it turned out there was no such substance; the word *phlogiston* did not refer to anything at all. Finally, the Idols of the Theater are the dogmatic beliefs associated with philosophical theories in particular (the phrase Idols of the Theater suggests that various philosophical theories are fictional, like plays).

A good method of inquiry would avoid these Idols. In addition, Bacon had something positive to say about how a good method of inquiry would proceed (not just what it should avoid), describing his preferred method in some detail. Inquiry, he thought, should involve a new kind of induction. Induction, roughly, is the drawing of general conclusions on the basis of individual observations; drawing the conclusion that all crows are black after observing many individual black crows is an example of induction. However, Bacon thought it was a mistake to investigate the world simply by adding up a lot of individual observations. Of course, making individual observations was necessary, and it was necessary to make a lot of them; Bacon criticized earlier ways of science for relying on too few individual observations. Merely making individual observations, however, for Bacon was not enough. To investigate some phenomenon in nature one should not merely observe many instances of that phenomenon and see under what conditions it occurred but also make many observations of cases in which the phenomenon in question did *not* occur and note the conditions in those cases as well. In addition, according to Bacon, one should observe the circumstances under which the phenomenon occurs in greater degrees and when it occurs in lesser degrees. On the basis of such data one should try to determine the essential nature of the phenomenon in question (to test one's hypothesis about that nature, it might be necessary to experiment). For instance, a Baconian investigation of lightning would involve the observation and documentation of when lightning occurred, when it did not occur, the degrees to which lightning occurred (are there just a few lightning flashes in some cases and more in others?), and the circumstances of each case.

The Newtonian World

Without question, Isaac Newton (1642–1727) was one of the most important and influential scientists of all time. The English poet Alexander Pope once wrote: "Nature and Nature's laws lay hid in night; God said, 'Let Newton be!' and all was light." His point, which was shared by many people, was that Newton had uncovered and explained the most fundamental laws of physics. The laws of motion that Newton described and calculated are taught today in nearly every physics class: the law of inertia (that a body will continue either at rest or in uniform motion until and unless it is changed by some outside force), the law of acceleration (stated as the formula F=ma, or force is mass times acceleration), and the law of recoil (every action evokes an equal and opposite reaction). In addition, he formulated the law of universal gravitation. Besides laying out these fundamental laws of physics, Newton created the mathematics of calculus (at the same time that the German philosopher Gottfried Leibniz [1646–1716] also formulated it) and did groundbreaking work in optics and other sciences. His work explained wide-ranging phenomena, for example, why the planets have their particular orbits and why the tides on Earth happen when they do and why apples fall.

Along with accomplishing significant scientific work, Newton also wrote explicitly about scientific method. He claimed to follow four rules of reasoning. The first is a restatement of Ockham's razor: "We are to admit no more causes of natural things than such as are both true and sufficient to explain their appearances." All else being equal, a simpler answer and explanation is better than a more complex one (but, of course, one should avoid an answer or explanation that is too simple, that is, that fails to truly explain). His second rule of reasoning is the assumption of same effects coming from the same cause: "Therefore to the same natural effects we must, as far as possible, assign the same causes." This is a working assumption, for Newton. Of course, it might turn out that there are different causes for what appear to be the same effects. For instance, on two different occasions one might find that the grass outside is wet. This might be because on both occasions, it rained last night; so, the same effect (wet grass) from the same cause (rain). However, wet grass on two separate occasions might have two different causes; one time because it rained and another time because someone watered the lawn. Still, scientists should begin with the assumption that same effects result from same causes.

His third rule of reasoning was the assumption that, with appropriate experimentation, one could infer general, perhaps even universal, features or qualities of things: "The qualities of bodies, which admit neither intensification nor remission of degrees, and which are found to belong to all bodies within the reach of our experiments, are to be esteemed the universal qualities of all bodies whatsoever." So, if we find that all bodies that we observe exhibit inertia or behave according to the law of gravitation, etc., then we can infer that these are features of the world at large, perhaps even universal laws of nature. Finally, his fourth rule was the claim that a given hypothesis or theory that seems to work should be assumed to be correct until and unless we can formulate a better hypothesis or theory: "In experimental philosophy we are to look upon propositions inferred by general induction from phenomena as accurately or very nearly true, notwithstanding any contrary hypotheses that may be imagined, till such time as other phenomena occur, by which they may either be made more accurate, or liable to exceptions." In other words, if we have a theory or model or hypothesis that makes sense and has been supported by evidence in the past, we should infer that it holds generally until and unless future evidence leads us to revise or reject it. Further, until and unless future evidence leads us to revise or reject it, we should not adopt other theories or models or hypotheses to try to explain the same phenomena. Stick with what works!

Laws of Nature

One important aspect of Newton's work was its emphasis on generalization and universalization. That is, he claimed that the laws of physics were not different in America than they were in Europe (or anywhere else); they were universal. All bodies behave according to the law of gravitation and the law of inertia. Indeed, it was this identifying and mathematically formulating laws of nature that was seen as the success and glory of Newton's work. However, it is one thing to state a law of nature and another to ask the conceptual question of what exactly a law of nature is.

There are two different senses of *law* that philosophers talk about: civil laws and natural laws. Civil laws are laws in the sense of ways that we regulate people's behavior, such as laws against murder or traffic laws. Natural laws are laws in the sense of ways that things in nature behave, such as the law of gravity or Boyle's Law of gases in chemistry.

Although there are various accounts of exactly what civil law is, they all share the notion that civil law is not merely a description of how

Portrait of Sir Isaac Newton from Sarah K. Bolton's *Famous Men of Science*

people actually behave, but civil law is a prescription for how people should behave. That is, civil law is a means for prescribing or suggesting or forcing people to behave in certain ways. This is different than the concept of natural law. Natural law (or law of nature), such as the law of gravity, is a description (and not a prescription) of the behavior of things in nature. Just as philosophers have investigated the nature of civil law—that is, they have asked not about some particular, specific civil law but, rather, about the very nature of civil law—so, too, philosophers have investigated the nature of natural law; what is a law of nature?

One claim is that natural laws are universal. That is, if something is a law of nature, it describes the behavior of all things that are relevant to it. For example, the law of gravity applies to all things with mass, not just to some things with mass. Because laws are said to be universal, they also are nonspecific. This means that they describe behavior of natural things without regard to specific features of those things. For example, the law of gravity applies to things with mass regardless of what color they are or what shape they are. Because laws are said to be universal and nonspecific, some philosophers have claimed that genuine natural laws can be expressed as mathematical formulas or equations. This distinguishes them from mere lawlike generalizations. For instance, some philosophers claim that the law of gravity is a genuine law, but there is no law of evolution, even if there are broad, general features of evolutionary change. Some philosophers, then, claim that natural law describes necessary forms of behavior. Other philosophers, however, say that natural law describes only observed regularities. These philosophers argue that there are always what are called ceteris parabus factors with regard to laws of nature. Ceteris parabus is a Latin phrase meaning "other things being equal." Natural laws, they say, describe the behavior of things, given certain contexts or constraints. For instance, the speed of light will vary depending upon the medium it is moving through (so, it moves slower through water than through air or through a vacuum). Because natural laws are said only to be descriptions of the behavior of things in nature, an important issue for understanding the nature of natural law is how they relate to theories, which are said to explain (not merely describe) those behaviors. Another important issue is whether there can be genuine natural laws outside of physics. Again, there is a question about whether there can ever be a law of evolution.

If there cannot be natural laws outside of physics, this raises questions about the relation between different sciences.

Models

A primary concern of the philosophy of science is to understand how science functions. One component of how science functions are the construction and use of models. Outside of philosophy and of science, the common notion of a model is either of a person who poses for the selling of merchandise (such as a fashion model) or a small replica of some object (such as a plastic model car) or of an excellent example of something (such as a model student). Although none of these common notions are what philosophers and scientists mean by a model, they do all point to features of scientific models.

First, scientific models represent something beyond themselves. Just as a fashion model is intended to represent (perhaps falsely) how someone else would look wearing certain clothes, a scientific model is intended to represent how some aspect of the world is structured or functions. For example, scientists speak of the billiard ball model of the interactions of molecules; like billiard balls bouncing off one another, molecules interact in certain ways of attraction and repulsion. In addition, like small plastic car models, scientific models display certain features of the world by resembling them in ways that matter to scientists. Although molecules might not look like billiard balls, they act like them in particular ways, so the resemblance is with their interactions, not their appearance. Also, like model students, scientific models are not intended simply to describe things in the world but to be idealized, or ideal examples. Again, the movement of billiard balls as a model for the movement of molecules is idealized movement, since scientists disregard certain features of the billiard balls, such as their color, and they idealize their context, such as disregarding the friction of the surfaces they rest upon.

Models in science are used both for the purposes of exploration and of explanation. That is, sometimes models are used in order to explore and find out facts about the world. So, scientists might construct a model to see what happens when billiard balls collide in certain ways and at certain velocities. On the other hand, sometimes scientists use models to explain facts about the world; they argue that we can understand how and why molecules behave in certain ways because of what we know about how and why billiard balls behave. In both senses—exploration and explanation—models lead scientists from what is known to what is unknown and provide a basis for understanding new facts. As a means of acquiring and accounting for knowledge about the world, models are related to other scientific components, such as observation and theory. As such, philosophers analyze and evaluate models in terms of epistemology, the study of knowledge. In large part, models work as analogies, telling us that one kind of thing is like another kind of thing, and philosophers have long studied the ins and outs of analogies.

Age of Enlightenment

The Age of Enlightenment, also sometimes called the Age of Reason, corresponds basically with the 17th and 18th centuries. It is used to speak of the general intellectual and cultural climate, primarily in Europe, during those two centuries. Historians often speak of the Scientific Revolution and the rise of modern political philosophy as major aspects of the Age of Enlightenment. Many enduring names of Western culture lived during this era: Isaac Newton (in science), John Milton (in literature), Adam Smith (in economics), Jean-Jacques Rousseau (in social commentary), Jonathan Edwards (in theology), Thomas Jefferson (in American politics), René Descartes, Immanuel Kant, and a group of French philosophers known as Les Philosophes (in philosophy).

Major philosophical changes that took place during this time were very much connected to the emergence of modern science. At the time, those people who today would be called scientists were usually called natural philosophers. The term *natural philosophy* had been used since early Greek philosophy for the study of the basic principles of nature, and those who studied and practiced it were called natural philosophers (as opposed to, moral philosophers, who studied the basic principles of moral action). During the Age of Enlightenment intellectual and conceptual changes that were connected with science were partly the result of new information and what was discovered about the world, and also partly the result of new assumptions and methods for investigating the world. One of those new assumptions, or at least different assumptions than previous scientists and philosophers had held, was the rejection of what was called final cause. Final cause was the notion that things and events have a purpose, and to fully understand something required knowing not only how something came to be but also why it came to be (that is, what function or purpose or end it had). Since the time of early Greek science, then, natural philosophers had included this notion of final cause as part of any explanation for some thing or event in nature. Although this notion was not completely abandoned during the Age of Enlightenment, to a large extent it was, or at least it was marginalized. Scientists focused on what could be observed and measured and described, without necessarily bringing in any sense of purpose. For example, Newton spoke of the planets in their orbits as being the result of a balance of forces of nature (those forces being gravity, which would, say, pull the Moon into the Earth, and inertia, which would have the Moon move away from the Earth in a straight line). Describing orbits as a balance of natural forces did not require speaking of those orbits being the result of some divine purpose or arrangement (even though Newton himself did not reject God's role in the orderliness of the world). Broadly speaking, previous to the Age of Enlightenment the general view of things and events in nature was teleological (from the Greek word *telos*, meaning "goal" or "end"). This was replaced by a view that was mechanistic and materialistic, meaning that the world was seen as a vast, complex mechanism made of physical, material things, and it could be explained in terms of the movements of those things. The new view was that the world was "matter in motion." This view extended even to explaining human action. The most famous examples of this were in the writings of the English philosopher Thomas Hobbes (1588–1679) and the French philosopher Julien Offray de La Mettrie (1709–51), who wrote a famous work entitled *Man a Machine*.

Nineteenth-Century Science

The assumption and attitude of progress that was so prominent in the Age of Enlightenment continued into the 1800s. The 18th century saw tremendous advances and changes in our understanding of the natural world and in science. The study of electricity emerged in this century, as did a greater understanding of the development of life forms. Modern chemistry came into its own toward the end of the 1700s, as scientists finally dismissed the long-held notion of the four elements (earth, water, air, and fire) that went back nearly 2,000 years to classical Greek science. With the work of chemists such as Joseph Priestley (1733–1804) and Antoine Lavoisier (1743–94), chemists reconceptualized the basic physical and chemical nature of things. These advances and changes expanded even more in the 1800s. Physicists such as Thomas Young (1773–1829) began to unravel the nature of light and were able to use this knowledge (Joseph von Fraunhofer [1787–1826]) to identify the chemical composition of stars (an area of science called spectroscopy). They also came to understand the nature of heat as molecules in motion (Rudolf Clausius [1822–88]), an area of science called thermodynamics. By the end of the 1800s, physicists had shown the interconnections between electricity and magnetism (Michael Faraday [1791–1867]) and showed that light was a form of electromagnetic radiation (James Clerk Maxwell [1831–79]), an area of science called field theory. At the same time, chemists made great strides in describing the nature of fundamental elements by identifying their structures and ways of bonding with each other. By the end of the 1800s, they had established the notion of the periodic table of elements (Dmitri Mendeleev [1834–1907]), showing how they have certain basic properties and that those properties are patterned, not random. In biology, scientists gained a much greater understanding of the nature of the formation of organisms, with the emergence of cell theory (Matthias Schleiden [1804–81] and Theodor Schwann [1810–82]), as well as the transformation of species of organisms, with the development of evolutionary theory (Charles Darwin [1809–82]). At the same time, in medicine, the germ theory of disease came forth, from the work of people such as Louis Pasteur (1822–95) and Joseph Lister (1827–1912). With these advances and changes in the understanding of the natural world came a reflective reconsideration of basic notions of science itself, including in particular the concept of cause.

Cause

The concept of cause is fundamental not only to philosophy and to science but also to everyday life. We take it for granted that when something happens, there is a cause (or set of causes) for it happening, even if we do not know what the cause(s) might be. We even take it for granted that when something does *not* happen, there must be some cause for that. Aristotle provided the first sustained philosophical analysis of cause. In his writings on physics and metaphysics, he analyzed the concept of cause. He argued that a full account of cause involved four components or, as some commentators on Aristotle say, four types of causes. They are: (1) material cause, (2) formal cause, (3) efficient cause, and (4) final cause. All four, for Aristotle, were necessary to fully understand cause, that is, how something (or some event or state of affairs) comes to be. For example, we see a tree (as a natural creation) or a statue (as a human creation) and wonder how it came to exist. The four causes were Aristotle's way of explaining how something comes to be. In effect, the four causes are answers to four separate but related questions. A material cause answers the question: *from* what does something come to be? A formal cause answers the question: *into* what does something come to be? An efficient cause answers the question: *by* what does something come to be? A final cause answers the question: *for* what does something come to be?

Starting with the example of a statue, the point of these four causes can be seen. First, a statue is made out of some material (for instance, bronze or stone). So, part of the explanation for how this statue came to be is the material from which it is made. If it had been made out of other material, it would be a different statue, much like a given person is made out of a particular grouping of DNA. What caused this statue, then, is explained in part by its material cause.

However, that very same material might have been shaped into a different statue. Any material thing, said Aristotle, always has some particular form or structure. That particular form or structure is part of the explanation for what that thing is. So, to explain this particular statue, it is not enough to only speak of the material cause; one must also speak of the formal cause, that is, the form into which those materials are.

An efficient cause is the notion that most people today think of as the (or a) cause of something. For Aristotle, an efficient cause is that by which something comes to be. In the case of a statue, it is by the work of the sculptor, who takes material and manipulates it into a particular form. The actions of the sculptor are the efficient cause of a given statue.

For Aristotle, there is also the final cause. The final cause is the purpose or end or goal that is met by the coming to be of something. In the case of a particular statue, the purpose might be to honor someone or some event. In the case of a tree or any natural thing (including any natural event or process), the purpose might be to promote the survival of some organism or the overall ecological balance of some natural system. The view that things are to be explained in terms of purposes or goals is called teleology (from the Greek word *telos,* meaning "end" or "purpose"). Much of the apparent controversy between science and religion is over the issue of whether teleological explanations, or final causes, of natural things are meaningful. While many philosophers and scientists accepted Aristotle's views about cause, others rejected it, especially with the onset of the Scientific Revolution.

The basic concept of cause is still unclear. When we say that A causes B, one conception is that A is a necessary condition for B. In other words, in order for B to happen, A *must* happen; if A did not happen, then B could not happen. However, we commonly speak of one thing causing another, even if it is not a necessary condition. For example, we might say that smoking causes lung cancer. But some people contract lung cancer even though they do not smoke (or even inhale secondhand smoke). Another suggestion for cause is that, if A causes B, then A is a sufficient condition for B. In other words, if A happens, that is all it takes for B to happen; perhaps some other things might bring about B, but it is enough that A does. However, once again, this notion of sufficient condition does not match common claims about cause. Again, we say that smoking causes lung cancer, but it does not always cause lung cancer. Some people who smoke do not get lung cancer, so apparently, smoking is not a sufficient condition for lung cancer.

Another philosophical view about cause comes from the Scottish philospher David Hume, who argued that cause—or, at least our understanding of cause—is simply "constant conjunction." That is, we simply always, or most of the time, notice that two things happen together; whenever A happens, B seems to follow. This constant pairing of two events is all we can say that cause is, according to Hume. Of course, if that is all that cause is, then there is no difference between cause and very strong correlations between things. However, cause and strong correlations are not the same thing; in fact, we think that cause can explain why there are strong correlations, so cause cannot simply be strong correlations.

The German philosopher Immanuel Kant claimed that cause is not something "out there" in the world but is one of the categories of our minds. That is, he said it is one of the ways in which we necessarily are able to experience and make sense of things, but cause is not itself some thing or event in the world, like trees and cats. For Kant, we experience things and events as being caused, but that is, at least in part, a result of how our minds function.

Some philosophical issues that relate to cause are part of the broad study of metaphysics (or study of reality). For example, there is the question of mental causation. We normally think of cause as being a physical interaction between things. Can there be such a thing as mental causation? If the mind is just the brain, then what we call mental causation is really just physical causation (because the brain is a physical organ). We speak of people acting from reasons (for example, I go to the store to buy chocolate because I like it), but what we call reasons seem to be explainable in terms of actions, which are physical.

There are also issues that relate cause to the broad study of epistemology (or study of knowledge). These are issues about how we know cause or what would justify our claims and beliefs about cause. For example, one issue would be relating cause to explanation. Is explaining some thing or event just a matter of identifying the cause of it? Some philosophers claim that identifying a cause is all that there is to explaining something. In fact, the very word *because* is a shortened form of the phrase *by the cause of.* Other philosophers claim that cause is only a physical interaction (or, if Kant is correct, a mental category) and physical interactions are not themselves explanations but things that need to be explained.

Finally, there are also important issues that relate cause to the broad study of axiology (or study of values). For example, there is the issue of free will and determinism. If people's actions are (all) caused, then it seems that they are determined. That is, if something is caused, then it must happen and cannot not happen. It is puzzling to say that people's actions are not caused. We might not know the cause(s) of some choice that a person makes, but it is assumed that something caused whatever the choice was. On the other hand, how could someone be held to have any responsibility for one's actions if they are caused (and determined)? Yet, the practice of rewards and punishment only make sense if we think that they (that is, the rewards or punishment) cause future behavior. If punishment did not cause people to behave in certain way (or stop behaving in certain ways), then what would be the point of it? At very commonsense levels, then, we assume that people's actions are caused, although it is not clear exactly what that means.

Mill's Methods

One of the most famous attempts to give a philosophical account of cause came from the 19th-century British philosopher John Stuart Mill (1806–73) and is usually referred to as Mill's methods. They are called this because he argued that there are various ways, or methods, that we commonly use to identify a cause. Mill spoke of five methods: (1) the method of agreement, (2) the method of difference, (3) the method of agreement and difference, (4) the method of concomitant variation, and (5) the method of residue.

Illustration of John Stuart Mill from the late 19th century

The method of agreement captures the notion that when we find a pattern in which every time that one thing happens (call it A), another thing follows (call it B). That is, there is an agreement between A happening and B happening. With such a pattern, said Mill, we identify A as the cause of B. For example, every time Bob eats hamburgers he gets indigestion; so he concludes that hamburgers are the cause of his indigestion.

The method of difference focuses on the notion that there is a pattern of one thing (call it B) following another (call it A) such that there is a case in which the first thing, A, is missing and that is followed by the second thing, B, being missing. In this case, there is an established pattern, which is followed by a difference (namely, A not occurring and then B not occurring). As an example, day after day Mary takes her dog, Fido, for a long walk, and when they get home Fido takes a nap; on the one day that she does not take Fido for a walk, he does not take a nap. So, she concludes that taking a walk is the (or a) cause of Fido taking a nap.

The method of agreement and difference is a combination of the previous two methods. It is the case of having a pattern in which whenever A is present, B follows and also when A is absent, B is absent.

The method of concomitant variation simply means that two things vary relative to each other. For example, as a little boy, Bob discovers that whenever he turns the knob of his parents' old radio in one direction, the volume of the sound goes up, and when he turns the knob in the other direction, the sound volume goes down; that is, the knob-turning and the sound volume vary together (there is concomitant variation). So, he concludes that turning the knob causes the change in sound volume.

The method of residues is finding a pattern and, after ruling out other possible causes, having one factor left over—that is, having a residue among all the factors—that is identified as the cause. For example, Mary has two identical houseplants, but one of them is doing well, and the other is doing poorly. They both get the same amount of water, and they are planted in the same kind of soil, etc. The only factor that seems relevant and is different is the amount of sunlight they get. So, she concludes that the amount of sunlight is the cause of the plant's doing well or poorly.

While Mill claimed that these methods describe how, in fact, we often identify causes, others argued that, at best, these methods show correlations between things, not necessarily causes.

Logical Positivism

Logical Positivism

Logical positivism, also called logical empiricism, was a philosophical movement that originated in the 1920s. It was born out of the Vienna Circle, a group of intellectuals (mathematicians, scientists, philosophers, and others) who met regularly in Vienna to share and discuss ideas. The philosophers Moritz Schlick (1882–1936), Rudolf Carnap (1891–1970), Friedrich Waismann (1896–1959), Otto Neurath (1882–1945), Carl Hempel (1905–97), and A. J. Ayer (1910–89) are all considered positivists. W. V. O. Quine (1908–2000) met with the Vienna Circle and is also associated with logical positivism; however, some of his ideas later helped undermine the movement.

According to the classical logical positivist program, science is the only source of knowledge about the world, and most of the claims of religion, metaphysics, ethics, and aesthetics are neither true nor false but simply meaningless. Logic and science, the positivists observed, had advanced even as philosophers continued to discuss the same metaphysical questions without ever arriving at answers. The problem was that these metaphysical questions were nonsense, and philosophy ought to dispense with them. Instead, positivists viewed the purpose of philosophy as using logic to analyze the concepts and the claims of science. Science, in this view, tells us about the world, and philosophy makes it clear precisely what science tells us.

Fundamental to logical positivism was the principle of verifiability. Positivists formulated this principle in different ways, but in each case the idea was that, according to the principle of verifiability, metaphysical claims were meaningless. On one version of the principle, sentences are meaningful only if they are either analytically true or if they are in principle verifiable through sensory experience. That is, meaningful sentences are true either because they are true in virtue of the meaning of the words (or the grammar of the sentence) or because it is, in principle, possible to verify the truth of the sentence through experience based on the five senses. For instance, the sentence "Babies are young" is analytically true because part of the definition of *babies* is that babies are young. So, the sentence is meaningful. The sentence "The cat Happy Jack has black fur" is verifiable through sense experience because in principle it is possible to see Happy Jack and his black fur. So, that sentence is meaningful, too. However, according to positivists, a metaphysical sentence such as "Everything that exists is One" is neither analytic nor verifiable through sense experience. So, the sentence has no meaning: It is not false, it is just literally nonsense. On the basis of this reasoning, most ethical, aesthetic, and religious claims are also nonsense; it is not possible to verify, for example, the claim "The Mona Lisa is a good painting." Also associated with positivism is the view that ethical claims express a speaker's attitude but do not express anything true or false. For instance, on this view, to say that "Cruelty is bad" is just to express one's own negative attitude about cruelty; it is not to say anything true (or false).

Positivists thought that any true, meaningful, nonanalytic sentence similarly mirrors a state of affairs in the world. In addition, according to positivism, any meaningful, nonanalytic sentence can be reduced to a more basic statement about sensory experience. Some positivists argued that basic statements should be about sense data—that is, information about individual sensory experiences. Other positivists rejected this view on the grounds that it made scientific claims too subjective. The concern was that scientific claims are more objective than the sense data view suggests; scientific claims should not be understood as being about individual sensations.

Popper and Falsifiability

Karl Popper

Karl Popper (1902–94) is considered one of the most influential philosophers of science of the 20th century. He was born in Vienna, Austria, and spent his early life there. Being of Jewish background, with the rise of Nazism during the 1930s, he left Austria in 1937 to teach in New Zealand. After World War II, he moved to Britain and taught philosophy at the London School of Economics from 1946 until his retirement in 1969. Because of his influence on philosophers and scientists, as well as his political writings in defense of democracy, he was knighted by Queen Elizabeth II in 1965.

In his political writings he argued for the importance of what he called an open society, and he included strong criticisms of historical philosophers—especially Plato, Hegel, and Marx—whom he saw as supporting, or at least tolerating, totalitarianism. However, among philosophers he was known much more for his work in the philosophy of science and, in particular, his concept of falsifiability.

Prior to Popper, the prevailing view about how science changes and progresses was that scientists observe the world by careful observation and experimentation, and they discover objective facts. Eventually, they notice some patterns that emerge from their collections of these facts. They formulate hypotheses to explain these facts and patterns and look for future observations to confirm these hypotheses. If future observations do confirm these hypotheses well enough, scientists might then propose laws of nature to account for the patterns and finally offer some theory to explain these facts and patterns and laws.

Popper claimed that this prevailing view was both unhelpful and mistaken. It is unhelpful, he said, because it did not explain what makes science different than nonscience. His phrase was that this view did not demarcate science. After all, he remarked, even astrologers and practitioners of voodoo claim that they discover facts and find patterns and have theories. So, this prevailing view did not give us any real understanding of science or how it progresses. In addition, this view is mistaken, he argued, because genuine science does not simply look for evidence that confirms hypotheses, but it looks for ways of testing hypotheses to see if they possibly can be shown to be false. Genuine science, for Popper, takes risks; it gives us useful information about the world by proposing hypotheses that are not obvious and safe. For instance, if someone hypothesized that tomorrow it will either rain or not rain at some location, then no matter what happens, that hypothesis would turn out to be true (it would either rain or not). So, the hypothesis would be confirmed, and it could be confirmed over and over. But we would not learn anything useful or important from the well-confirmed hypothesis that tomorrow it will rain or not rain at some location.

Simply having confirmations for a hypothesis, then, is not useful or informative and is not the hallmark of science, for Popper. Instead, a good scientific hypothesis is one that could turn out to be false. His term is that it is *falsifiable*. If it is a good hypothesis—that is, if it really matches the way the world is—then future observations will not show it to be false, but true. In other words, a good scientific hypothesis is falsifi*able*, but not falsifi*ed*. However, if it is a good scientific hypothesis, we should not be content just because the hypothesis has passed some of our tests in the past. Perhaps we simply have not yet come up with a relevant test that might show it to be false. So, the evidence that we have that supports a given hypothesis, says Popper, is not confirming evidence—that is, it is not evidence that settles the question—but is corroborating evidence.

Corroboration is similar to confirmation, but slightly different. Like confirmation, corroboration is a concept about evidence for some hypothesis. However, corroboration is a softer notion than confirmation. This means that corroboration is merely supporting evidence, but not conclusive evidence. The concept of corroboration is used in legal contexts as giving support for some hypothesis, but a somewhat low level of support. For instance, if a crime was committed last night, someone's testimony that you were at home watching television might be corroborating evidence that you did not commit the crime, but it is not confirming evidence (since you might have slipped away undetected and committed the crime). In the context of science, corroborating evidence, likewise, is supporting evidence for some hypothesis, but not conclusive.

The defining feature of science, then, is falsifiability and this, for Popper, is what distinguishes science from nonscience. Genuine science proposes risky hypotheses and tries to test them to see if they can be shown to be false. If they are shown to be false, this is still scientific progress, because scientists would have learned something about the world. If they are not shown to be false—that is, if they pass the tests we put them to—then these hypotheses are said to be corroborated and informative. Since we can never know for sure whether or not there is some future test that might show a given hypothesis to be false, we cannot ever really say that any hypothesis is true, says Popper. The best that we can say is that it is well-corroborated and, perhaps, better-corroborated than any alternate hypothesis. The term he uses for this is *verisimilitude,* which means truthlike (from the Latin words *veritas,* meaning "truth," and *similitudo,* meaning "likeness"). Science might be getting closer and closer to a true account of the world, but we would never know that for sure, says Popper, since it is always possible in the future that our best hypotheses might become falsified. What we can say is that we have greater verisimilitude.

Popper's account of science, especially his insistence that a defining feature of science is that it rigorously and seriously attempts to test and falsify its claims, has been embraced by many scientists and philosophers. However, other philosophers of science have criticized his views. One criticism is that it is not always clear or obvious when a hypothesis has been falsified. Sometimes evidence turns up that only seems to falsify a given hypothesis, but it turns out not to (perhaps simply because some equipment malfunctioned). A second criticism is that when scientists test a hypothesis, they never test just that one given hypothesis, but many background assumptions at the same time. It could turn out that what is falsified is not really the hypothesis in question but one (or more) of the background assumptions.

Confirmation and Evidence: Goodman and Bayes

Goodman and the New Riddle of Induction

The word *grue* was made up by the American philosopher Nelson Goodman (1906–98), in order to raise a concern about induction as a reliable form of reasoning. Goodman's concern is often called the new riddle of induction. The original riddle of induction was raised by the 18th-century Scottish philosopher David Hume. Hume's riddle, or problem, was how can induction, or inductive inferences, be justified? The very nature of induction is that the conclusion of an argument is not guaranteed, given its premises. For example, based on past experience, we might notice a pattern of events, and as a result, we might infer that this event will happen again tomorrow. However, it is not guaranteed that it will happen tomorrow, even if it is highly probable that it will. For instance, every day for millions of years the Sun has risen in the east each morning, so we infer that tomorrow the same thing will happen. While it is highly likely that it will, there is always the (extremely remote) possibility that tonight the Earth will explode, so tomorrow the Sun will not rise in the east. Hume's question, again, was how can induction, or inductive inferences, be justified?

In the mid-1900s, Goodman introduced the term *grue*. *Grue* is a blend of the words *green* and *blue*. *Grue* is defined this way: Something is *grue* just in case it is green prior to, say, January 1, 3000, and also just in case it is blue after January 1, 3000. So, for instance, someone who speaks English would say that grass is green. Someone who speaks a Gruesome language would say that grass is grue, but after January 1, 3000, that person would say that grass is not grue but that the sky is grue. Goodman also coined the word *bleen,* as: Something is *bleen* just in case it is blue prior to, say, January 1, 3000, and also just in case it is green after January 1, 3000. (So, to the Gruesome speaker, prior to January 1, 3000, grass is grue and after that date grass is bleen.)

Goodman suggested that we might make this example of an inductive inference: Since every emerald that has been observed in the past was green, the next emerald we observe will be green. However, one could also say that since every emerald that has been observed in the past was grue, the next emerald that we observe will be grue. Of course, as we expect that the green inductive inference will be correct (because we expect that after January 1, 3000), the next emerald will, indeed, be green, but as we expect the grue inductive inference will be incorrect (because we do not expect that after January 1, 3000), the next emerald will be blue.

The riddle here is that, while it appears that *grue* is a strange concept because it is defined by some point in time, Goodman claimed that actually *green* could be defined in terms of *grue* and *bleen.* So, *green* means: Something is green just in case it is grue prior to January 1, 3000, and also just in case it is bleen after that date. Goodman's point is that there is no reason to assume that *green* and *blue* are more natural than *grue* and *bleen,* since each pair of words can be defined in terms of the other pair. So, again, there is a riddle about justifying inductive inferences, since two different inferences result in this case depending upon which pair of words is taken as better. But, even if we say that one pair (green and blue) give us a better inference, the only justification seems to be that it works in this case (which lands us right back to the original riddle of induction).

Counterfactuals

Philosophers call some sentences categoricals. This means that they purport to state a fact. For example, the sentence "Cats are mammals" is a categorical sentence. Categorical sentences might be false, however, as in the sentence "Cats can fly." The point is that categorical sentences (even if they turn out to be false) are of the form: S is P. Philosophers call some other sentences conditionals. These are sentences that contain some condition, or hypothetical component. For instance, the sentence "If I sleep in too late, I will miss class" is a conditional sentence. The sentence does not state that I will sleep in too late, but, rather, states a hypothetical situation, or a condition: *if* I sleep in too late, *then* I will miss class. Conditional sentences are of the form: If S, then P.

One kind of conditional sentence is called a material conditional. This kind of conditional sentence involves a straightforward if-then structure, as in the sentence "If cats are mammals, then they are warm-blooded." Another kind of conditional sentence is called a subjunctive conditional. Often in subjunctive conditionals we use words like *could* and *were,* as in the sentence "If I could flap my arms and fly, then I would be happy" or "If I were to break this window, then I would be in trouble." These are often called contrary-to-fact, or counterfactuals, by philosophers. This is because they are not factual claims. In particular, the "if" part of the sentence is contrary to the facts of the world.

Philosophers have wrestled with conceptual problems about counterfactuals. One concern for philosophers is how counterfactuals relate to the notion of dispositions. Some features of things are said to be dispositions, meaning that things have a likelihood to behave in certain ways, even if they do not actually behave that way. For example, if one said that glass is fragile, than that means that glass is likely to break (or has the disposition to break) if it is struck, and it has that disposition even if it is never struck. Counterfactuals are also related to the notion of natural laws. For instance, if one said that it is a law that metals conduct electricity, then that means that if one *were* to give an electric current to a metal, then it would conduct that current. Counterfactuals also relate to the issue of cause. For example, if one said that smoking causes lung cancer, then that means that if one *were* to smoke, then one would get lung cancer.

The reason that philosophers are concerned with counterfactuals is that they are difficult to analyze in terms of what makes them true and also in terms of how to distinguish them from other conditionals. Because by their very nature they are contrary to facts, they are false; yet we have very good reasons for taking them to be true. So, the sentence "If cats were birds, then they could fly" states a truth, even though it is not obvious why. For instance, if that sentence were true, would the following sentence thereby be false: "If cats were birds, then not all birds could fly"? This difficulty of knowing how to analyze counterfactuals is important to philosophers, because as noted above they are so basic to issues about how to understand dispositions and laws and cause. In addition, as Goodman pointed out, they make the distinction blurry at best between sentences that express genuine laws (of nature) and mere lawlike sentences that express accidental generalizations.

Evidence and Bayes

A basic issue in epistemology (the study of knowledge) concerns the justification of our beliefs. That is, what justifies the beliefs that we have? Occasionally, we say that a belief is self-justified (or needs no justification). For example, I might claim that I like chocolate ice cream more than I like vanilla ice cream. If asked to justify this belief (that is, if someone asked me how I know that I prefer chocolate ice cream to vanilla), I would not know what to say; it is just obvious! Also, occasionally, we say that a belief is justified simply by our intuition or gut feeling. For instance, I might claim that people should get what is due to them. If asked why (that is, if asked to justify my claim), I would simply appeal to my sense that it just seems right; I would not know what else to say to justify my belief.

Most of the time, however, justifying a claim involves providing some evidence for it. Philosophically, however, the concept of evidence is not straightforward. First, there is the question of what exactly evidence is. That is, what does the word *evidence* mean? In terms of metaphysics (the study of reality), nothing is inherently evidence. In other words, the world contains lots of things (such as cats and trees), events (such as sneezes and hurricanes), processes (such as physical interactions and ceremonies), even abstract relations between things (such as being older than or being married to), but nothing just *is* evidence. For example, a pencil is just a pencil. Things or events or processes, etc., might come to be taken as evidence of something or evidence for some hypothesis; a pencil might come to be taken as evidence that someone had the means to write a letter. By itself, however, the pencil is just a pencil. So, one philosophical question is how does something come to be evidence?

In addressing this question, philosophers have noted that if anything is evidence, it is always evidence *of* something or evidence *for* something (and never simply evidence in itself). That is, there is some fact that something else is evidence of, or there is some hypothesis that something else is evidence for. For example, the presence of certain noises might be evidence of a small animal running across someone's roof, or the absence of fingerprints on a murder weapon might be evidence that the killer wore gloves and even evidence for the hypothesis that the murder was premeditated.

However, what makes the presence of these noises or fingerprints evidence of something or for something? One answer is that these noises or fingerprints are consistent with other facts or hypotheses. This simply means that the truth of beliefs about these noises or fingerprints does not contradict the truth of these other facts or hypotheses. (If the truth of beliefs about the noises and fingerprints did contradict those other facts or hypotheses, then they would not be evidence for them!) A problem with this notion of evidence—namely, something, call it A, is evidence of or for something else, call it B, if A is consistent with B—is that something could be consistent with something else but be completely irrelevant to it or, at least, not clearly relevant. For instance, certain noises on the roof of my house are consistent with the theory of evolution (that is, those noises do not contradict the theory), but we certainly do not think that those noises are evidence for the theory of evolution (or evidence against the theory).

A second answer to the question of what makes one thing evidence for something else is that the first thing makes the second thing more likely or more probably true. The philosophical phrase for this view is called Bayesianism, named for the work of an 18th-century British theorist Thomas Bayes (1702–61). Bayes constructed a mathematical formula to measure how some thing or event would affect the probability of another thing or event being the case. For example, suppose that the probability of Joe being at some party is one out of two (that is, it is just as likely that he went to the party as it is that he did not). Also, suppose that the probability of his car being parked outside the house of the party is three out of four, if he went to the party, but only one out of four, if he did not. Bayes's formula showed that the hypothesis of Joe being at the party is increased, given that his car is parked outside the house. Therefore, Bayes said, Joe's car being parked there is evidence for the hypothesis that Joe went to the party; it is evidence because it increased the probability of the hypothesis being true (the probability is now stronger than one out of two that Joe went to the party).

Not all philosophers think that Bayes's formula explains the concept of evidence. They claim that it gives a *measure* of evidence, but it still ignores the prior question of what makes something evidence at all. In this case, what makes Joe's car being parked in a particular place evidence at all? Is Joe's car being parked there evidence for the theory of evolution? Once again, there is the assumption that this fact (where Joe's car is parked) is relevant to the given hypothesis, but whether or not it is relevant is not determined by the simple fact that it is parked there.

An additional complication is that of negative evidence, that is, when there is the absence of consistent data. For instance, is the lack of fingerprints at a crime scene evidence that some person is guilty? A common saying is that the absence of evidence is not the evidence of absence; in other words, not having data that is consistent with some hypothesis does not in itself mean that the hypothesis is false. In spite of these conceptual, philosophical concerns, scientists, lawyers, and people in everyday situations continue to speak of things and events as evidence of other facts or for hypotheses.

Thomas Kuhn and Paradigms

Thomas Kuhn

Thomas Kuhn (1922–96) is considered one of the most influential philosophers of science of the 20th century. Kuhn attended Harvard University throughout his student career. While earning a doctoral degree in physics, his attention shifted to the history of science and ultimately to the philosophy of science. During his professional career he taught at Harvard, Berkeley, Princeton, and MIT.

The publication of his book *The Structure of Scientific Revolutions* in 1962 dramatically changed the focus of the philosophy of science ever since. Prior to Kuhn's book, most philosophers and scientists saw change and progress in science as a matter of the accumulation of objective facts about the world. One prevailing view (usually called inductivism) was that scientists carefully observed aspects of the world and rigorously performed experiments to learn new facts. Patterns among those facts would emerge, and then scientists would propose hypotheses to explain those patterns. By testing those hypotheses, new observations and facts would result that would either confirm or disconfirm the hypotheses. Eventually, scientists could formulate laws and theories to explain the observations and facts and patterns that they discovered.

A second influential view prior to Kuhn was the view proposed by Karl Popper. Popper claimed that the defining feature of science is falsifiability, or the attempt to test hypotheses, not by looking for confirmation of them, but by trying to show that they might be false. By rigorously testing hypotheses to see if they could be shown to be false, and then having those hypotheses pass those tests, this would show that the hypothesis was a good one. In either case—that is, either looking for confirming data or looking for possible falsifying data—the prevailing views of how science changes and makes progress was that it is a rational, logical process. Kuhn did not deny that science proceeds rationally, but he claimed that the process was not a straightforward, accumulation of facts or the ongoing attempts to falsify hypotheses. By looking more closely at the actual history of science, he said, a different picture of scientific change and progress emerges.

The most important concept of Kuhn's view is the concept of paradigm. The word *paradigm* comes from the ancient Greek word for "pattern." Kuhn claimed that science—or, more correctly, different sciences—work within paradigms. What he meant by this was that sciences work with shared assumptions about what methods to use and what facts have already been established and what kinds of questions are appropriate to ask within science, etc. A paradigm is basically a shared view and understanding of things, including what has been settled and how to proceed into the future. Kuhn claimed that science, as most people think of it, is normal science, that is, science that functions within a given paradigm. For example, the Darwinian paradigm takes evolutionary change as a given; modern geology's paradigm takes plate tectonics (or the movement of large portions of the Earth's surface) as a given; modern astronomy's paradigm takes an expanding universe as a given. Normal science is a matter of working within these assumptions and not questioning them.

Kuhn used the term *paradigm* in two basic ways. First, he used it to refer to particular, ideal examples or cases (what he called *exemplars*). For example, biologists might point to the Galápagos Islands as a paradigm case, or perfect example, of a self-contained evolutionary system, or historians might point to the rise of Nazi Germany as a paradigm, or perfect example, of how a totalitarian state could emerge from harsh conditions following a war. Second, Kuhn used the word *paradigm* as an overall set of assumptions (what he called a *disciplinary matrix*). This is more like the sense of paradigm that most people mean. Each paradigm has a set of assumptions about what is real and what methods are appropriate for studying the world and even what sorts of values are relevant. For instance, in the Newtonian paradigm space and time are said to be absolute, but in the Einsteinian paradigm they are said to be relative. Likewise, a method such as voodoo is not acceptable within a scientific paradigm, or the value of making information quantitative (as opposed to qualitative) is part of the scientific paradigm. These basic paradigmatic assumptions, said Kuhn, are not questioned or tested. Scientific revolutions occur when there is a change in paradigms. The phrase Kuhn used is *paradigm shift,* a phrase that has become culturally widespread, for instance, in speaking of a paradigm shift from consumerism to sustainability.

For Kuhn, as scientists engage in normal science, eventually and inevitably surprising data appear. These are called *anomalies* (meaning "against the law" or "against the norm"). Usually anomalies can be explained within the prevailing paradigm, and science goes on its way. However, if enough anomalies arise, or some very significant ones arise, and they cannot be explained by the prevailing paradigm, then science enters into a crisis. For example, prior to Copernicus there were mounting problems (anomalies) for the view that the Earth was stationary and at the center of the universe. A crisis can lead to a scientific revolution, which, for Kuhn, meant that the prevailing paradigm is questioned and ultimately overturned in favor of some new paradigm. With the success of a new paradigm in explaining those anomalies, as well as explaining the facts from the old paradigm, scientists enter into a new normal science.

What made Kuhn's view of scientific change and progress different from earlier views was that he said that the change of paradigms is not entirely rational. Besides facts and data, there are many social factors that influence scientists and their willingness to adopt a new paradigm or not, said Kuhn. In addition, he claimed that from one paradigm to another, important concepts and terms do not necessarily mean the same thing. His term for this was *incommensurability.* This term comes from mathematics, and it simply means that between two things that are being compared, there is no obvious, straightforward matching between them. For example, in mathematics, one could say that the whole numbers are commensurable with their squares. In other words, for every whole number (1, 2, 3, etc.) each one of them could be matched up with its square (1, 4, 9, etc.). This is sometimes called a one-to-one correspondence, meaning, again, that for each particular number, it matches up exactly with its square and vice versa. To say that something is *in*commensurable, then, means that two (or more) things cannot be directly paired up; they are *not* commensurable. For Kuhn, between two different paradigms, some basic, important concepts change their meaning, or at least do not necessarily mean the same thing. For example, prior to Copernicus the Sun and the Moon were considered planets because throughout the year they changed their positions in the heavens relative to the Earth (while the stars were said to be fixed). After Copernicus, however, the Sun and the Moon were not considered planets, even though they changed their positions in the heavens relative to the Earth. For Kuhn, the concept and term *planet* changed its meaning from one paradigm to another. As a result, it is difficult and perhaps even mistaken, said Kuhn, to say that one paradigm has made progress over another, since they might be saying very different things. If they are incommensurable, it might be like comparing apples and oranges.

Kuhn's work had tremendous impact on philosophers generally and especially on philosophers of science. He brought social and historical aspects of science to the forefront for philosophers. Because of him, the notion of paradigm has become commonplace both inside and outside of philosophy. Nonetheless, some philosophers have been critical of his view. Some have said that the history of science does not reveal a series of paradigms. Instead, beyond some basic agreement about some features of the world, there are always competing scientific overviews or paradigms to explain the world. It is almost never the case that science, or any single science, is dominated by a single paradigm. Others have argued that he makes science too irrational, that he saw too important of a role in science for social values and issues. Yet others have been very critical of his claim that there is incommensurability between paradigms and, as a result, that we cannot say directly that one paradigm is better than or more correct than another.

The Twentieth Century: Relativity and Quantum Mechanics

Albert Einstein (1879–1955) is a household name, and for good reason. Almost single-handedly he revolutionized fundamental concepts of the universe, in particular the very basic notions of space and time. Because of this radical change in our understanding of these basic notions, philosophers sometimes speak—drawing on the work of the philosopher Thomas Kuhn—of an Einsteinian paradigm, as opposed to a Newtonian paradigm. This is meant to convey the view that how the world is understood from the theories of Einstein is, at least in part, very different than how it is understood from the theories of Newton (in particular how the basic concepts of space, time, matter, and energy are understood).

People often think that Einstein proposed the theory of relativity, meaning that everything is relative; there is no truth about the basic aspects of the world. This, however, is incorrect. In fact, Einstein was trying to show (in part) just what aspects of the universe are constant and *not* relative. Specifically, he wanted to show that the laws of physics are the same for all inertial systems, or frameworks. Indeed, one of the truths about the universe, he said, is that because the laws are the same for all inertial systems, there are no preferred, or privileged, systems. It is this last part (no privileged systems) that is what is relative. In addition, Einstein claimed that in free space the speed of light is the same

Photograph of Albert Einstein receiving his certificate of U.S. citizenship from Judge Phillip Forman on October 1, 1940 *(Photograph by Al Aumuller)*

for all inertial systems; that is not relative. So, by pointing out that one's perspective (or inertial system) was not special or privileged, he was also pointing out that there are objective, absolute (nonrelative) aspects of the universe.

Einstein's theory of relativity is actually composed of two parts, the special theory and the general theory. The special theory of relativity assumes that things are at rest or in relative uniform motion. By relative motion, Einstein recognized what many physicists and people recognized before him: When two things (or inertial systems) are moving relative to one another, each one sees the other as moving relative to it. For example, suppose you are sitting on a bus looking out the window and there is another bus next to you. At the moment when one of the buses begins to slowly move, it appears from your perspective that it is the other bus that is moving, but from the perspective of someone on that other bus who is looking out her window, it appears that your bus is starting to move. After just a moment, you can tell which one is "actually" moving because you have other information (for instance, you can feel your bus moving or you can see other things out your window that you could not before). But, if the two buses were not buses on a street, but, say, two small spaceships out in space with nothing else around them, then you could not tell if you were "really" moving or if the other spaceship were. More important, if there was nothing other than the two spaceships, then there would be no sense in saying that one "really" is moving, while the other one is not. Each one is moving only relative to the other one; neither spaceship has a privileged perspective. So, in this sense, said Einstein, all motion is relative. Given this relativity of perspectives (or inertial systems), he showed that the concepts of space and time are also relative to one's inertial system. Space and time, it turns out, are not absolute, but in showing this, Einstein showed that this is because the velocity of light is absolute (in a vacuum); it is constant for all observers or inertial systems. Another surprising result of this theory is that matter and energy can be defined relative to one another; this is his famous $E=mc^2$.

With respect to the philosophy of science, the special theory of relativity challenged very basic notions of space, time, matter, and energy. It also forced a reexamination of basic claims about metaphysics (or what is real) and epistemology (or what is known and knowable). Are these fundamental philosophical concepts also relative? Is there a sharp distinction between them?

The second part of the theory of relativity is the general theory of relativity. Here all motion, including the motion of accelerated systems (not just systems at rest or moving uniformly) is considered. What Einstein claimed was that there is no important difference—at least, no difference that we can know—between a system that is accelerating and a system that is at rest in a gravitational field. Using his famous "thought experiments" he showed that our experience of the world would be the same if we were at rest in a gravitational field as it would be if we were in motion in an accelerated system. This led to his claim that the path of light in space can be curved in a gravitational field (for example, as it travels past a star). This famous prediction by Einstein was supported in 1919 when an expedition took careful measurements of light as it passed the Sun; the results supported Einstein's claims. Not only was this another surprising result of his theory, but it led to his further claim that what we call gravity is actually the very geometry of space (and time) itself! It is space (and time) that is curved in the vicinity of a massive body, such as a star, and it is this curvature that causes the light's path to bend. (From the light's perspective, it is simply following a straight line, but a straight line on a curved surface.) This curvature of space (and time) led Einstein to predict the possibility of black holes, in which the curvature of space (and time) is so severe that even something moving as fast as light could not escape its gravitational pull. As with the special theory of relativity, the general theory led philosophers to rethink some very basic and fundamental concepts.

Another significant development in physics in the early 20th century that led philosophers to rethink basic concepts was the emergence of quantum theory. At the end of the 1800s, physicists were discovering surprising aspects about atoms. For one thing, they were discovering that in fact atoms were composite, that is, that they were composed of parts. At the very end of the century, J. J. Thomson (1856–1940) identified the electron, and Ernest Rutherford (1871–1937) discovered that atoms had a nucleus. This led to what was called the solar system model of the atom, in which the atom was pictured as having a nucleus with electrons orbiting around it, much like the planets in the solar system orbit around the Sun. A major problem with this model, however, was that, given the understanding of light and the release of energy, it seemed that as electrons orbited a nucleus, energy would be given off, and eventually the electrons would fall into the nucleus, and the atom would, in effect, self-destruct. This obviously didn't happen, so something was wrong with the model.

At the same time, the physicist Max Planck (1858–1947) made one of the most astounding discoveries in the history of physics. What he found was that, in a given experimental setup, energy was released not continuously—as he and everyone else expected—but in discrete packets, or quanta. This led to a monumental rethinking of not only the structure of the atom, but also of energy and mass as well. The physicist Niels Bohr (1885–1962) claimed that the solar system model of the atom was mistaken and that electrons were contained in "shells" around the nucleus. As energy came into the atom, enough energy would cause certain electrons to jump, or make a *quantum leap*, with respect to these shells (and, having made such a jump, fall back to their original shell, releasing energy in the process). As other physicists pursued their research, they came to claim that the behavior of subatomic particles

Niels Bohr and Albert Einstein in Paul Ehrenfest's home on December 11, 1925 *(Photograph by Paul Ehrenfest)*

(such as electrons) revealed a microscopic world in which things were indeterminant and uncertain, where the velocity and the position of an electron were only probable. Physicists began to speak about electrons not as tiny particles but as probability waves, in which they are not like tiny balls but like a wave with certain probabilities of being in a place relative to the nucleus.

In the 19th century, the French physicist Pierre Simon, Marquis de Laplace (1749–1827) had famously said that he could completely and accurately predict the future of the universe if he had complete knowledge of it at any given point in time, because, he thought, the world is deterministic; laws of nature determine what and how things are. With the results of quantum theory, physicists in the 20th century declared that—at the atomic level, at least—things were indeterministic. With respect to philosophy, the results of quantum theory led to even more reconsideration than did the results of Einstein's relativity theory. Quantum theory seemed to indicate that the very act of observing or measuring certain events "created" those events. Prior to such observation or measurement, things were said to be in a state of "superposition" (that is, above having a specific position). When things were observed or measured, this resulted in "the collapse of the wave packet." It was the very act of observing or measuring that resulted in, say, an electron being where it was. Even further, other experimental results (of a situation called "entanglement") seemed to show that by observing or measuring one event or object, this determined the result of another measurement of a related event or object at a distance. The philosophical puzzle that resulted was the question of whether and how the act of observation or measurement could actually cause things to be. Does observation create reality? This would violate not only the distinction between metaphysics and epistemology but also common sense. Nonetheless, as science has advanced through the centuries, we have often had to abandon principles that were previously considered unassailable matters of common sense. While quantum theory has led to many confirmed predictions, many philosophers (and scientists) asked whether or not there must be some deeper underlying aspects of the world—and so, a more complete physical theory—that could account for these very strange results. Quantum theory was and is clearly successful and useful, but, they asked, is it "real?" That is, does it actually capture the way the world is?

Concluding Discussion Questions

1. Is the notion of final cause (that is, things acting purposefully or having their features to fulfill some purpose) needed for biology to explain living organisms? Why or why not?
2. How were Newton's rules of scientific reasoning like and also different from Aristotle's and Bacon's?
3. What did the logical positivists mean by saying that value claims (for instance, the moral claim that murder is wrong) were not verifiable and, hence, meaningless? Were they right?
4. Was Popper right to say that genuine science attempts to falsify its claims? Was he right to say that this is the difference between science and nonscience?
5. What did Kuhn mean by saying that different scientific paradigms are incommensurable? Was he right?
6. What aspects of Einstein's relativity theory and of quantum theory challenge traditional views of science?

Further Reading

Achinstein, Peter, ed. *Science Rules: A Historical Introduction to Scientific Methods.* Baltimore, Md.: Johns Hopkins University Press, 2004.

Ayer, Alfred Jules, ed. *Logical Positivism.* New York: The Free Press, 1959.

Boersema, David. *Philosophy of Science (Text with Readings).* New York: Pearson Prentice Hall, 2009.

Godfrey-Smith, Peter. *Theory and Reality: An Introduction to the Philosophy of Science.* Chicago: University of Chicago Press, 2003.

Grant, Edward. *A History of Natural Philosophy: From the Ancient World to the Nineteenth Century.* Cambridge: Cambridge University Press, 2007.

Kuhn, Thomas. *The Structure of Scientific Revolutions.* Rev. ed. Chicago: University of Chicago Press, 1970.

Losee, John. *A Historical Introduction to the Philosophy of Science.* 2nd ed. Oxford: Oxford University Press, 1980.

Manly, Steven, and Steven Fournier. *Relativity and Quantum Physics for Beginners.* Danbury, Conn.: For Beginners, 2009.

McGrew, Timothy, Marc Alspector-Kelly, and Fritz Allhoff, eds. *Philosophy of Science: An Historical Anthology.* Hoboken, N.J.: Wiley-Blackwell, 2009.

Okasha, Samir. *Philosophy of Science: A Very Short Introduction.* Oxford: Oxford University Press, 2002.

Popper, Karl, and David W. Miller. *Popper Selections.* Princeton: Princeton University Press, 1985.

Rosenberg, Alex. *Philosophy of Science: A Contemporary Introduction.* New York: Routledge, 2005.

Glossary

anomaly   a phenomenon that is contrary to expectation and is not explainable within the prevailing theory.

categories (of the mind)   aspects of the mind, proposed by the philosopher Immanuel Kant, that structure our experiences of the world; for example, time (for Kant) is not "in the world" but a condition for how we experience things in the world.

confirmation   the relation between phenomena and a hypothesis or theory in which the phenomena support the hypothesis to a significant, though vague, level.

corroboration   the relationship between evidence and hypotheses such that there is an attempt to falsify a hypothesis and the evidence in fact supports the hypothesis; usually associated with Popper's falsificationist model of scientific change.

deductivism   the notion that science can and should be conducted by relying on principles and criteria of deductive reasoning.

falsifiability   the possibility of a sentence being shown to be false; usually associated with the writings of Karl Popper, to show that what makes something scientific is that it can be tested and possibly be shown to be false.

final cause   the notion that things and events happen purposefully; there is some nonrandom final end or goal toward which things and events happen.

incommensurability   a relationship between two sets of phenomena such that they are not directly translatable into the other or capable of being put into a one-to-one relationship with each other; usually associated with Kuhn's model of scientific change.

induction, problem of   the problem of justifying an inference about the future on the basis of past and present phenomena; often associated with the inductivist model of scientific change as well as concerns about evidence and confirmation; associated with the writings of David Hume and Nelson Goodman.

inductivism   the model of scientific change based primarily on inductive principles of inference, often associated with a cumulative amassing of empirical knowledge and a bottom-up, observationally based view of scientific method.

laws (of nature)   general principles that describe and structure things and events in the world.

logical positivism   philosophical model of science, often associated with inductivism, emphasizing the criterion of empirical observation as the basis for meaningfulness and embracing a dichotomy between facts and values.

natural philosophy   the term for the investigation of the nature of the natural world; usually considered an older term for what is now called science.

Ockham's razor   a methodological principle associated with the writings of the medieval philosopher William of Ockham; generally understood to mean that explanations for things should be as simple as possible (but no simpler).

paradigm   a framework, including ontological, epistemological, and axiological assumptions, of a scientific discipline within which scientific practice and activities (e.g., those relating to theories, models, experiments, etc.) are carried out; usually associated with Thomas Kuhn's model of scientific change.

quantum theory   the theory that energy is released, not continuously, but in discrete amounts (or quanta); led to reconceptualizing basic notions of matter and energy.

reduction/reductionism   the notion that higher-level entities simply are or can be explained (i.e., reduced) in terms of lower-level entities; for example, water simply is H_2O, or mental events (such as having some perception) just are a collection of neuronal events in the brain.

relativity theory   the theory, proposed by Albert Einstein, that the motion of one body can be defined only relative to some other body; led to reconceptualizing basic notions of space and time.

uniformity/unity the notion that the goal, genuine possibility, and underlying assumption of scientific investigation is to formulate an account of the world, which is itself unified.

verification/verificationism the view that for a sentence to be meaningful there must be some way to test or verify its content; only those sentences that are verifiable are considered to be meaningful; usually associated with the view of logical positivism.

Key People

Aristotle (384–322 B.C.E.)   *Greek philosopher who greatly influenced later philosophy and science, arguing that the world must be understood in terms of goal-directed changes. The selections below focus on Aristotle's basic claim that the world is teleological (that is, goal-directed) and must be understood in terms of change going from potentiality to actuality. In addition, the method is to first consider the broadest, most basic matters and later focus on particular things.*

Since Nature is the principle of movement and change, and it is Nature that we are studying, we must understand what "movement" is; for, if we do not know this, neither do we understand what Nature is . . . Further, movement (it is said) cannot occur except in relation to place, void, and time. Evidently, then, for these reasons and because these four things—movement, place, void, and time—are universal conditions common to all natural phenomena, we must consider each of them on the threshold of our inquiry; for the treatment of peculiar properties must come after that of properties common to all natural things.

We must begin, then, as already said, with movements in general or progress from this to that. Now, some potentialities never exist apart, but always reveal themselves as actualized; others, while they are something actually, are capable of becoming something else than they are, that is to say, have potentialities not realized at the moment; and these potentialities may concern their substantive being (what they are) or their quantity or their qualities; and so on with the other categories of existence . . .

Now, motion and change cannot exist in themselves apart from what moves and changes. For, wherever anything changes, it always changes either from one thing to another, or from one magnitude to another, or from one quality to another, or from one place to another . . . motion is the function of a movable thing, all the time that it is bringing its potentiality into act, not *qua* itself, but *qua* movable.

[Aristotle. *Physics.* Book 3 from *The Basic Works of Aristotle.* Edited by Richard McKeon. New York: Random House, 1941.]

Bacon, Francis (1561–1626)   *English statesman and philosopher who argued in favor of a rigorous form of induction (the drawing of general conclusions on the basis of many individual observations) and the social nature of science. The following selection is from his most influential work,* The New Organon.

There are, and can be, only two ways to investigate and discover truth. The one [based on deduction] leaps from sense and particulars to the most general axioms, and from these principles and their settled truth, determines and discovers intermediate axioms; this is the current way. The other [based on induction] elicits axioms from sense and particulars, rising in a gradual and unbroken ascent to arrive at last at the most general axioms; this is the true way, but it has not been tried.

[Bacon, Francis. *The New Organon.* Edited by Lisa Jardine and Michael Silverthorne. Cambridge: Cambridge University Press, 2000.]

Einstein, Albert (1879–1955)   *Twentieth-century physicist who developed the modern theory of relativity, thus altering our understanding of basic notions of time and space. The following passage is from a lecture given in 1933 on Einstein's view of the nature of science.*

A complete system of theoretical physics is made up of concepts, fundamental laws which are supposed to be valid for those concepts and conclusions to be reached by logical deduction. It is these conclusions which must correspond with our separate experiences; in any theoretical treatise their logical deduction occupies almost the whole book . . .

Our experience hitherto justifies us in believing that nature is the realization of the simplest conceivable mathematical ideas. I am convinced that we can discover by means of purely mathematical constructions the concepts and the laws con-

Photograph of Albert Einstein from 1931 *(Photograph by Doris Ulmann)*

necting them with each other, which furnish the key to the understanding of natural phenomena. Experience may suggest the appropriate mathematical concepts, but they most certainly cannot be deduced from it. Experience remains, of course, the sole criterion of the physical utility of a mathematical construction. But the creative principle resides in mathematics. In a certain sense, therefore, I hold it true that pure thought can grasp reality, as the ancients dreamed.

[Einstein, Albert. "On the Method of Theoretical Physics." In *Philosophy of Science* 1, no. 2 (April 1934): 163–169.]

Goodman, Nelson (1906–1998) *American philosopher who formulated the new riddle of induction, in which he claimed that what counts as confirmation for some hypothesis is not simply determined by facts in the world and, indeed, the "same" facts can support different, even contradictory, hypotheses. The passage below is from his book* Fact, Fiction, and Forecast. *In this book he introduces the following problem: If we observe a green emerald that observation seems to (help) confirm* *the hypothesis that all emeralds are green. However, a green emerald also seems to (help) confirm the hypothesis that all emeralds are grue, where grue means that something is green if it is examined before some specified time (say, January 1, 3000) and blue if it is examined after that time.*

The odd cases [such as grue] that we have been considering are clinically pure cases that, though seldom encountered in practice, nevertheless display to the best advantage the symptoms of a widespread and destructive malady.

We have so far neither any answer nor any promising clue to an answer to the question what distinguishes lawlike or confirmable hypotheses from accidental or non-confirmable ones; and what may at first have seemed a minor technical difficulty has taken on the stature of a major obstacle to the development of a satisfactory theory of confirmation. It is this problem that I call the new riddle of induction.

[Goodman, Nelson. *Fact, Fiction, and Forecast.* Cambridge, Mass.: Harvard University Press, 1955.]

Hume, David (1711–1776) *Scottish philosopher who formulated the problem of induction (that is, how inductive reasoning can be justified). Hume claimed that inductive reasoning cannot be justified; at best we can only say that some inductions in the past have satisfied our inquiries. Even the notion of cause and effect cannot be justified beyond the fact that we accept certain events as usually following other events. The passage below presents his problem of induction.*

All reasonings may be divided into two kinds, namely, demonstrative [deductive] reasoning, or that concerning relations of ideas; and moral [inductive] reasoning, or that concerning matter of fact and existence . . . May I not clearly and distinctly conceive, that a body, falling from the clouds, and which in all other respects resembles snow, has yet the taste of salt or feeling of fire? Is there any more intelligible proposition than to affirm, that all the trees will flourish in December and January, and will decay in May and June? Now, whatever is intelligible, and can be distinctly conceived, implies no contradiction, and can never be proved false by any demonstrative argument or abstract reasoning a priori.

If we be, therefore, engaged by arguments to put trust in past experience, and make it the standard of our future judgment, these arguments must be probable only, or such as regard matter of fact and real existence, according to the division above mentioned. But that there is no argument of this kind, must appear, if our explication of that species of reasoning be admitted as solid and satisfactory. We have said that all arguments concerning existence are founded on the relation of cause and effect; that our knowledge of that relation is derived entirely from experience; and that all our experimental conclusions proceed upon the supposition, that the future will be conformable to the past. To endeavor, therefore, the proof of this last supposition by probable arguments, or arguments regarding existence, must be evidently going in a circle, and taking that for granted which is the very point in question.

[*The Philosophical Works of David Hume*. Vol. 4. London: Little, Brown, 1854.]

Kant, Immanuel (1724–1804) *German philosopher who argued that objects conform to our knowledge, rather than knowledge conforming to objects; he believed that the mind structures experience according to certain categories. In the selection below, Kant relates the laws of nature to how the mind categorizes experience. So, for example, because the mind applies the concept of cause to experience, laws regarding causes are among the laws of nature (we cannot experience nature without such laws).*

We shall here . . . be simply concerned with experience, and the universal and *à priori* given conditions of its possibility, and thence determine Nature as the complete object of all possible experience. I think it will be understood, that I do not refer to the rules for the observation of a nature already given, which presuppose experience, or how through experience we can arrive at the laws of Nature, for these would not then be laws *à priori*, and would give no pure science of Nature; but how the conditions *à priori* of the possibility of experience are at the same time the sources from which all the universal laws of Nature must be derived.

We must first of all observe then, that, although all the judgments of experience are empirical, i.e., have their ground in the immediate perception of sense, yet on the other hand all empirical judgments are not judgments of experience, but that beyond the empirical, and beyond the given sensuous intuition generally, special conceptions must be superadded, having their origin entirely *à priori* in the pure understanding, under which every perception is primarily subsumed, and by means of which only it can be transformed into experience.

[Kant, Immanuel. *Kant's Prolegomena and Metaphysical Foundations of Natural Science.* Translated with a biography and introduction by Ernest Belfort Bax. 2nd rev. ed. London: George Bell and Sons, 1891. Available online. URL: http://oll.libertyfund.org/title/361/54872. Accessed July 20, 2011.]

Kuhn, Thomas (1922–1996)   *American philosopher and historian of science whose book The Structure of Scientific Revolutions led philosophers of science to rethink science in terms of the social and historical aspects that are inherent in the nature of science. Kuhn's work made the notion of a paradigm a commonly used concept throughout and beyond academia. The selection below introduces the notion of a paradigm as a set of assumptions and perspectives that govern any particular scientific community at a given time.*

By choosing [the term *paradigm*], I mean to suggest that some accepted examples of actual scientific practice—examples which include law, theory, application, and instrumentation together— provide models from which spring particular coherent traditions of scientific research. These are the traditions which the historian describes under such rubrics as "Ptolemaic astronomy" (or Copernican), "Aristotelian dynamics" (or Newtonian), "corpuscular optics" (or wave optics), and so on . . . Men whose research is based on shared paradigms are committed to the same rules and standards for scientific practice. That commitment and the apparent consensus it produces are prerequisites for normal science, i.e., for the genesis and continuation of a particular research tradition.

[Kuhn, Thomas. *The Structure of Scientific Revolutions.* Chicago: University of Chicago Press, 1962.]

Newton, Isaac (1642–1727) *English mathematician and physicist who revolutionized the field of physics with his theories of motion and gravitation, as well as the field of mathematics with his formulation of calculus as a means of quantifying the study of motion. The following selection is a brief summary of his statements about scientific method.*

Rule 1: No more causes of natural things should be admitted than are both true and sufficient to explain their phenomena . . .

Rule 2: Therefore, the causes assigned to natural effects of the same kind must be, so far as possible, the same . . .

Rule 3: Those qualities of bodies that cannot be intended and remitted [that is, increased and diminished] and that belong to all bodies on which experiments can be made should be taken as qualities of all bodies universally . . .

Rule 4: In experimental philosophy, propositions gathered from phenomena by induction should be considered either exactly or very nearly true notwithstanding any contrary hypotheses,

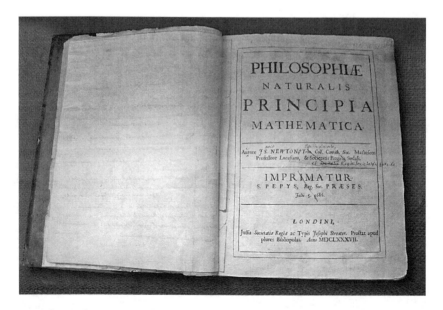

First edition of Isaac Newton's *Philosophiae Naturalis Principia Mathematica*

until yet other phenomena make such propositions either more exact or liable to exceptions.

[*Philosophiae Naturalis Principia Mathematica.*]

For the best and safest method of philosophizing seems to be, first, to inquire diligently into the properties of things and to establish those properties by experiments, and to proceed later to hypotheses for the explanation of things themselves. For hypotheses ought to be applied only in the explanation of the properties of things, and not made use of in determining them; except in so far as they may furnish experiments. And if anyone offers conjectures about the truth of things from mere possibility of hypotheses, I do not see by what stipulation anything certain can be determined in any science; since one or another set of hypotheses may always be devised which will appear to supply new difficulties. Hence I judged that one should abstain from contemplating hypotheses, as from improper argumentation.

[*The Correspondence of Isaac Newton.* Edited by H. W. Turnbull, J. F. Scott, A. Rupert Hall, and Laura Tilling. 7 vol. Cambridge: Cambridge University Press, 1959–1977.]

Ockham, William of (1280–1349) *Medieval philosopher and theologian who is most famous today for Ockham's razor. Ockham's razor is a phrase used to refer to the principle of simplicity, that is, to proceed to explain something with the simplest explanation (but not too simple). Ockham, along with many others, often used the expression "plurality must not be asserted without necessity," so the sense of a razor is to cut away what is not necessary in order to provide a legitimate explanation. In the passage below, Ockham states his view that our explanations of things and events in the world actually hook up with our mental concepts rather than with things and events directly.*

Now the fact is that the propositions known by natural science are composed not of sensible things and substances, but of mental contents or concepts that are common to such things. Hence, properly speaking the science of nature is not about corruptible and generable things nor about natural substances nor about movable things, for none of these things is subject or predicate in any conclusion known by natural science. Properly speaking, the science of nature is about mental contents which are common to such things, and which stand precisely for such things in many propositions . . . This is what the Philosopher [i.e., Aristotle] means when he says that knowledge is not about singular things, but about universals which stand for the individual things themselves. Nevertheless, metaphorically and improperly speaking, the science of nature is said to be about corruptible and movable things, since it is about the terms that stand for these things.

[Ockham. *Philosophical Writings*. Translated and edited by Philotheus Boehner. Indianapolis, Ind.: Hackett, 1990.]

Popper, Karl (1902–1994)   *Austrian philosopher who argued that the difference between science and nonscience is based not on inductive reasoning and the presence of confirming information for a theory or hypothesis but rather on the falsifiability (or possibility of a claim to be shown false) of a given theory or hypothesis. The passage below is taken from his book* Conjectures and Refutations: The Growth of Scientific Knowledge.

1.   It is easy to obtain confirmations, or verifications, for nearly every theory—if we look for confirmations.
2.   Confirmations should count only if they are the result of *risky predictions;* that is to say, if, unenlightened by the theory in question, we should have expected an event which was incompatible with the theory—an event which would have refuted the theory.
3.   Every "good" scientific theory is a prohibition; it forbids certain things to happen. The more a theory forbids, the better it is.
4.   A theory which is not refutable by any conceivable events is nonscientific. Irrefutability is not a virtue of a theory (as people often think) but a vice.
5.   Every genuine *test* of a theory is an attempt to falsify it, or to refute it. Testability is falsifiability; but there are degrees of testability: some theories are more testable, more exposed to refutation, than others; they take, as it were, greater risks.
6.   Confirming evidence should not count *except when it is the result of a genuine test of the theory;* and this means that it can be presented as a serious but unsuccessful attempt to falsify the theory. (I now speak in such cases of "corroborating evidence.")

7. Some genuinely testable theories, when found to be false, are still upheld by their admirers—for example by introducing *ad hoc* some auxiliary assumption, or by reinterpreting the theory *ad hoc* in such a way that it escapes refutation. Such a procedure is always possible, but it rescues the theory from refutation only at the price of destroying, or at least lowering, its scientific status . . .

One can sum up all this by saying that the criterion of the scientific status of a theory is its falsifiability, or refutability, or testability.

[Popper, Karl. *Conjectures and Refutations: The Growth of Scientific Knowledge.* London: Routledge & Kegan Paul, 1963.]

Strawson, Peter (1919–2006) *English philosopher who argued that the problem of induction (that is, how inductive reasoning can be justified) is the result of a misunderstanding by David Hume and other philosophers. Justification of experiences presupposes inductive reasoning and a uniformity of nature, for Strawson. The selection below is taken from his book* Introduction to Logical Theory.

. . . [The] rationality of induction, unlike its "successfulness," is not a fact about the constitution of the world. It is a matter of what we mean by the word 'rational' in its application to any procedure for forming opinions about what lies outside our observations or that of available witnesses. For to have good reasons for any such opinion is to have good inductive support for it . . .

So it is a contingent, factual matter that it is sometimes possible to form rational opinions concerning what specifically happened or will happen in given circumstances (I); it is a non-contingent, *a priori* matter that the only ways of doing this must be inductive ways (II). What people have done is to run together, to conflate, the question to which I is an answer and the quite different question to which II is an answer. . . .

[Strawson, P. F. *Introduction to Logical Theory.* New York: John Wiley & Sons, 1952.]

Vienna Circle   *Name used to refer to a group of philosophers and other academics who met and worked in Vienna at the beginning of the 20th century; they formed the core of the school of thought called logical positivism, advocating the view that philosophy needed to be more scientific and that the only meaningful claims are ones that can be verified. The passage below is from a manifesto authored by three members of the Vienna Circle (Hans Hahn, Rudolf Carnap, and Otto Neurath), in which they state their scientific world conception.*

The scientific world conception is characterized not so much by theses of its own, but rather by its basic attitude, its points of view and direction of research . . . We have characterized the scientific world conception essentially by two features. First it is empiricist and positivist: there is knowledge only from experience, which rests on what is immediately given. This sets the limits for the content of legitimate science. Second, the scientific world conception is marked by application of a certain method, namely logical analysis. The aim of the scientific effort is to reach the goal, unified science, by applying logical analysis to the empirical material. Since the meaning of every statement of science must be statable by a reduction to a statement about the given, likewise the meaning of any concept, whatever branch of science it may belong to, must be statable by step-wise reduction to other concepts, down to the concepts of the lowest level which refer directly to the given.

[Neurath, Otto. *Empiricism and Sociology*. Dordrecht, Netherlands: Kluwer Academic, 1973.]

INDEX